Explore Other Worlds

Take off through the solar system with 10 professional astrologers as they bring their insights to the symbolism and influences of the planets.

After a brief, factual background on each of the planets by well-known astrologer Joan McEvers, tune in to a planet of primary focus—the Sun. The creator and life force in mythology, the Sun is our ego in the natal chart. Next, examine the Moon, our emotional signal to imminent change, along with its nodes.

Mercury is introduced as a mythological god of tricks, wisdom and communication, followed by an in-depth explanation of its retrogradation.

Venus—your inner value system and relationships. Discover your natural archetypal expression of Venus and possible karmic conflicts presented by aspects with the outer planets. Use Mars to your advantage by tapping your cooperative, energizing inner warrior.

Understand Jupiter's expansive and preservative traits and its rulership of both Sagittarius and Pisces. Unfold your identity with Saturn, a source of freedom through self-discipline. Be original and open to change for growth where Uranus is posited.

Elevate to the realm of selfless giving and compassionate love with Neptune. Finally, uncover Pluto's power as a personal force, urging you to analyze, change, transform and eliminate.

These respected authors' viewpoints and writing styles create a book of planetary interpretation that is enjoyable and informative in its variety and scope. Expand your knowledge of the planets, and transform your life as you see and understand these archetypes operating in yourself and the world around you.

Joan McEvers

Author of *12 Times 12*, and co-author with Marion D. March of the highly acclaimed teaching series *The Only Way to . . . Learn Astrology*, as well as *Astrology: Old Theme, New Thoughts*, Joan McEvers is a practicing astrologer in Coeur d'Alene, Idaho.

Born and raised in Chicago where she majored in art and worked as a model and illustrator for an art studio, she moved to the Los Angeles area in 1948 and continued her professional career in the sales field. This is where she met her husband Dean and raised her four children.

Joan started her serious study of astrology in 1965, studying on her own until 1969, when she took classes with Ruth Hale Oliver. Joan has achieved an international reputation as a teacher and lecturer, speaking for many groups in the U.S. and Canada. A professional member of AFA and an AFAN coordinator, she has had articles published in several national astrological magazines.

In 1975, Joan and Marion founded Aquarius Workshops, Inc., with Joan as President. She also helped establish its quarterly publication *Aspects*, which is widely recognized for the wealth of astrological information in each issue.

Her latest individual effort is *12 Times 12*, which came out in a revised and updated version in 1984. In this book, each of the 144 possible Sun/Ascendant combinations is discussed in detail. Every description includes information about personality, appearance, health, likely vocational areas, interests and attitudes. Also in 1984, the latest March/McEvers book *Astrology: Old Theme, New Thoughts* was published. This is a collection of concepts, ideas and lectures on various avenues of astrology and is being well received by the public.

In July 1989, Joan and Marion were the recipients of the esteemed Regulus Award for Education at the United Astrology Congress. This honor is given to those who continually strive to clearly and accurately educate the public on the principles and uses of astrology.

Volume IV of *The Only Way* series is now in bookstores. It is titled *The Only Way to ... Learn About Tomorrow*, and it deals with all kinds of progressions and forecasting. Joan also has a two-hour video, *Simplified Horary Astrology*. When she isn't busy teaching, lecturing, writing or counseling clients, Joan keeps occupied with quilting and playing bridge.

"The concept of having a different astrologer give his or her interpretation of a particular planet in one book is an interesting and innovative way of dealing with the subject. Each style is different and holds the reader's attention.

"Students will particularly like the fuller, in-depth analysis of each planet, and I would think professional astrologers will find it great for review.

"The section on the Moon which includes the nodes will be helpful for many, and the handling of Pluto is clear and well written.

"Overall, I think this book will be well received. It is unique in its concept, and there is plenty of good information included."

—**Edith Custer**
Editor of *Mercury Hour*

"This book gives us a unique opportunity to grasp the subtle as well as the practical nature of the planets. Instead of one or two people tackling the job of writing about all the planets, this book offers a different approach. Each writer, as a professional with years of experience, concentrates on just one planet. That planet has a special meaning for the writer. Because of this fact, the depth of understanding and the insightful points of view are developed to their fullest potential. In a world of generalities, here's a specialized and clear look at each planet."

—**Steve Cozzi**
Planets in Locality

THE NEW WORLD ASTROLOGY SERIES

This series is designed to give all people who are interested and involved in astrology the latest information on a variety of subjects. Llewellyn has given much thought to the prevailing trends and to the topics that would be most important to our readers.

Future books will include such topics as financial astrology, locational astrology, electional and mundane astrology, astrology and past lives, and many other subjects of interest to a wide range of people. This project has evolved because of the lack of information on these subjects and because we wanted to offer our readers the viewpoints of the best experts in each field in one volume.

We anticipate publishing approximately six books per year on varying topics and updating previous editions when new material becomes available. We know this series will fill a gap in your astrological library. We look only for the best writers and article topics when planning the new books and appreciate any feedback from our readers on subjects you would like to see covered.

Llewellyn's New World Astrology Series will be a welcome addition to the novice, student and professional alike. It will provide introductory as well as advanced information on all of the topics listed above—and more.

Enjoy, and feel free to write to Llewellyn with your suggestions or comments.

Llewellyn's New World Astrology Series

PLANETS:

THE ASTROLOGICAL TOOLS

Edited by
Joan McEvers

1989
Llewellyn Publications
St. Paul, Minnesota 55164-0383, U.S.A.

International Standard Book Number: 0-87542-381-7
Library of Congress Catalog Number: 88-38614

First Edition, 1989
First Printing, 1989
Second Printing, 1989

Library of Congress Cataloging-in-Publication Data

Planets: the astrological tools/edited by Joan McEvers.
    p. cm.—(Llewellyn's new world astrology series)
   ISBN 0-87542-381-7
   1. Planets—Miscellanea.   2. Astrology.   3. Horoscopes.
I. McEvers, Joan.   II. Series.
BF1724.P57   1989
133.5'3—dc19   88-38614
                                               CIP

Cover Painting: David Egge

Produced by Llewellyn Publications
Typography and Art property of Chester-Kent, Inc.

Published by
LLEWELLYN PUBLICATIONS
A Division of Chester-Kent, Inc.
P.O. Box 64383
St. Paul, MN 55164-0383, U.S.A.

Printed in the United States of America

Contents

INTRODUCTION

Without the planets, the astrological tools, astrologers could not plot horoscopes. Granted it is necessary to use the signs, houses and aspects, but without the planets none of the rest would be valid. The planets are the actors on the astrological stage and without them there would be no play.

The word *planet* comes from the Greek *planesthai* "to wander." The ancients distinguished the seven planets . . . Sun, Moon, Mercury, Venus, Mars, Jupiter and Saturn . . . because they seemingly moved in the heavens while the rest of the visible stars appeared stationary. To early astronomers who charted the stars, these seven planets visible to the naked eye were extremely powerful forces. How the planets seemed to move at great speeds, to slow down, and to pass each other, coupled with various angles they made in relationship to the Earth's position, convinced ancient astrologers, astronomers and priests that they were watching the gods in action.

More modern astronomers have, of course, discovered that all of the universe is in constant motion. It is just that the planets seem to move much faster than the other stars in our galaxy.

The Sun, the center of our universe, is properly known as the great luminary. . . the Moon, Earth's satellite, is also correctly referred to as a luminary. "And God made two great lights; the greater light to rule the day, and the lesser light to rule the night; he made the stars also. And God set them in the firmament of the heaven to give light upon the earth, and to rule over the day and over the night, and to divide the light from the darkness . . . ." (Genesis 1: 16-19) Luminary is another word for the biblical "light." For the sake of simplicity, both the Sun and the Moon are referred to as planets by astrologers.

Our Sun is moving through our stellar neighborhood in the direction of the bright star Vega at about 12 miles per second and is pulling the Earth and the other planets with it. At this speed, we cross a distance equal to the width of our solar system in just 20 years.

Though it seems that we are sitting still in the vast universe of the heavens, we on planet Earth are revolving, rotating and whirling through the heavens in at least seven different directions and at speeds of more than a million miles per hour! We are being carried along around our globe's circumference once every 24 hours, yet as remarkable as this motion seems, it is relatively insignificant when we consider the annual orbit of our planet around the Sun.

We are zipping along our orbit at the staggering speed of 66,527 miles per hour, or 18.5 miles per second, traveling over a million and a half miles per day. During the course of a human lifetime, we will have journeyed 45 billion miles, five times the size of our solar system. Some of the amazing discoveries about Earth proven by modern astronomers reveal that we are:

- rotating on our axis at about 820 mph in mid-northern latitudes
- speeding through the nearby stars at 12 miles per second
- orbiting our Milky Way galaxy at 490,000 mph
- rushing toward the fixed star Andromeda at 50 miles per second
- falling into the Local Supercluster at 150 miles per second
- flying outward from the Big Bang at 322 miles per second

A few more comments about the Earth are necessary if we are to understand our place in the cosmic system.

Planet Earth

In any book about the planets it is necessary to consider the Earth in relationship to the heavens. We live, move and breathe on this planet and theoretically know more about it than any of the others. Yet, astrologically we rarely use the Earth in the horoscope. With the growth of space exploration in the last decades, it is presumably possible for the day to come when life as we know it may begin on a space station or neighboring planet . . . the Moon, Mars or Venus. Fifty years ago this concept could not have been conceived, but today we must be aware that it is possible.

In doing a horoscope for a person born at one of these locations, the Earth would be visible in the heavens and thereby placed in the natal horscope of that person. In consequence, astrologers should place the Earth in all horoscopes and seek to understand its meaning. Heliocentrically, the Earth is always exactly opposite the Sun by sign, degree and house; thus if the Sun is at 12 degrees Aries in the 10th House, the Earth would be at 12 degrees Libra in the 4th House. We on Earth view the Sun against the backdrop of the constellations, so when the Earth is in Libra, the Sun appears to be in Aries.

Even though most astrologers do not put the Earth in the chart, they perceive it to be the center of the horoscope as well as the center of our astrological universe.

There is a school of thought that considers the Earth as a possible ruler of Taurus, giving Libra solely to Venus. If astrologers would place the Earth in their charts and study this, it may prove correct. Other observers have given the sign Cancer to the Earth, feeling that the Earth and its satellite, the Moon, co-rule this sign. As always in astrology, only time and a good deal of study will tell. As a starting point in Earth studies in astrology, we should consider it as our mission in life as represented in the horoscope.

The Sun—Lifegiver

The Sun is the center of our solar system ... about 93,000,000 miles distant from the Earth, its diameter of 864,000 miles is 109 times that of the Earth. It is an immense globe of matter whose chemical make-up is doubtless identical with ours here on Earth but so hot that it remains completely gaseous. It appears larger than the other stars because of its nearness to our planet. Vast and continuous production of energy has been attributed to the release of energy in a "carbon cycle" involving atomic disintegrations and transmutations and, more recently, to a reaction of proton upon proton.

Since the Sun exerts so much energy in our solar system, it is easy to understand its strength in the astrological chart. It is the heart of the chart and describes our vitality and inner being. The day of the week associated with the Sun is Sunday, biblically the day on which God rested. California astrologer **Toni Glover Sedgwick** explains the Sun's position in the signs and houses beautifully, discussing its mythology and metaphysical individuality as well as its relationship to ego needs.

The Moon—Shadow of the Sun

Luna is the Earth's only satellite and revolves around the Earth in an elliptical orbit. Because the Moon's periods of rotation on its axis and revolution about the Earth are equal, the same side of the Moon is always toward Earth, but about 59% of its surface comes into view in a month because of its librations (Moon wobble). The New Moon phase occurs when the Moon is between the Earth and the Sun and is the only time we may experience a Solar Eclipse. The Full Moon, when Earth is between the Sun and the Moon, is the only time that a Lunar Eclipse can be observed.

The Moon played a prominent role in the mythology of many ancient civilizations as a feminine deity, a queen consort to the king Sun. With the advent of the telescope, astronomers first turned to this most easily observable body in the night sky. Shining only by light reflected from the Sun, it is the fastest moving body in our system, taking approximately 28 days to pass through each sign of the zodiac. Because of its proximity to Earth and its speed through the zodiac, it appears to have an effect upon the emotions of the Earth's inhabitants. Monday is the day of the week affiliated with the Moon.

Joanne Wickenburg from Seattle, Washington explains the Moon and its functions to us. She also presents her concept of how she feels the Moon's nodes work in the chart. The nodes of the Moon are points in space where the orbit of the Moon intersects the path of the Sun. The point passed as the Moon goes north is the ascending or North Node; the point passed as the Moon moves south is the descending or South Node.

Mercury—The Messenger

Mercury, a very small light in the sky moving in a quick little loop, is barely visible here on Earth because of its close proximity to the Sun. It is the smallest planet in our solar system, orbiting about 36,000,000 miles from the Sun, and can be seen by the naked eye for about two weeks at a time, three times a year, either at dawn or twilight, as an evening or morning star shining with a clear white light.

It is surprising that a planet so bright has been seen only by a rather small fraction of the world's population. Mercury, because of its minute size and nearness to the Sun, offers little to space explorers . . . it appears to have almost no atmosphere. It rotates slowly on its axis, completing one rotation while it revolves around the Sun. Were we to travel to Mercury, it would be necessary to protect ourselves from the radiation of the Sun on the daylight side and from the extreme cold on the night side.

Astrologically, Mercury is the planet representative of reason, communication and transportation. Canadian astrologer **Erin Sullivan-Seale** entrances us with Mercury's mythology and her observations on how to cope when this fast-moving planet retrogrades in the heavens. Wednesday is the day of the week identified with Mercury. In Norse mythology the Latin god Mercury translates to Woden, hence Woden's day or Wednesday in English.

Venus—Jewel of the Heavens

Venus moves in an orbit between that of Mercury and the Earth at a mean distance from the Sun of about 67,000, 000 miles. It passes through phases similar to those of the Moon and at its brightest is far more brilliant than any fixed star, often visible in daylight. About every year and a half, Venus becomes so bright that people have mistaken her for the crescent Moon. Venus is ideally situated to be the brightest of all the planets. It is close enough to the Sun to receive a lot of sunlight and is covered with brilliant pink-white clouds to reflect much light back into space.

Venus, being such a beautiful planet, is quite properly associated with all beautiful things . . . peace, love, harmony, art and music as well as money and partnership. **Robert Glasscock** from Los Angeles has written a fascinating and enlightening chapter on this enchanting planet. Friday, the sixth day of the week, is known as Venus' day, which probably relates to Friday night as date night. Again referring to Norse mythology, the Roman goddess Venus translates to Fria or Freya, the wife of Woden.

Mars—The Red Planet

Mars, named for the Roman god of war, was also regarded as the protector of the fields . . . the god of agriculture. Conspicuous for its red color, Mars is the fourth planet in order from the Sun and has a 22-month cycle. It is the first planet beyond Earth at 141,000,000 miles from the Sun and has two small satellites, Deimos and Phobos. The inclination of the planet's axis to the plane of its orbit indicates seasons twice as long as on Earth, and its average temperature is much below Earth's.

For centuries many people believed that the "canals" on Mars were evidence of an ancient civilization. The *Pioneer* spacecraft (aptly named) determined through scientific analysis that no life forms are now, or ever have been, present on this planet. The canals are now believed to have been caused by volcanic activity long ago. Mars' red color ties in with its astrological reputation for assertiveness, temper and competition.

The month of March was named for Mars, and its sign Aries starts at the Vernal Equinox each March 21. Tuesday is the day of the week associated with Mars. Tuesday is a derivation of Tiu, the Teutonic god of war. Eugene, Oregon astrologer **Johanna Mitchell** explores three facets of this "warrior" planet in conversations with her clients.

Jupiter—The Giant

Jupiter, the largest of the planets with a mean diameter of 87,000 miles, is the middle planet between the Sun and Pluto at the (current) farthest reaches of our solar system. The planets, starting with Mercury, become gradually larger until Jupiter; those following become smaller and smaller. Jupiter shines with a clear, bright light; only Venus is brighter in the sky. It revolves around the Sun in 11.86 years and four of its large satellites which were discovered by Galileo in 1610 were the first celestial objects ever discovered by means of a telescope.

According to scientists, because of Jupiter's large mass

and extreme cold due to the low intensity of radiation received from the Sun, its atmosphere seems to be very dense. Conditions on this planet in no way resemble those on Earth. Its atmosphere composed of gases of lower atomic weight than oxygen fits in with the low density of the planet. By whatever means the solar system was formed, the outer planets seem to have a very different chemical constitution from the inner ones. Jupiter is similar to the Earth in one facet . . . the extreme flattening of its poles. It revolves around the Sun at a mean distance of 483,310,000 miles in an orbit between Mars and Saturn. It is totally enveloped by atmosphere and has 12 satellites.

Due to its girth, Jupiter has become associated in astrology with magnitude and expansion. Its action is considered to be most beneficial and enlightening. **Don Borkowski** from Salem, Oregon illuminates Jupiter for us as he explains its connection to both Sagittarius and Pisces. Traditionally Jupiter's day of the week is Thursday. Thor, the Norse god of thunder, relates to the Roman deity Jupiter.

Saturn—Watcher of the Threshold

In olden times Saturn was known as the planet farthest from the Earth and as an ancient wanderer, a dim, slow-moving light that passed through the sky every 29.5 years. Its movement was the least erratic of the planets. Galileo observed that there was something very unusual in Saturn's appearance. It seemed to him that appendages existed on each side. Approximately 50 years later, Huyghens, equipped with a better telescope, discovered that these were the projecting parts of a ring that surrounded but did not touch the equator of the planet. Twenty years later Cassini found a dark line dividing the ring in two. As time went on and telescopes became more powerful, more rings were discovered.

In more modern times spectroscopic observations and space satellites have established that the rings are composed of a dense swarm of small bodies. The ten best known satellites of Saturn are Mimas, Enceladus, Tethys, Dione, Rhea, Titan, Hyperion, Phoebe, Themis and Japetus. Saturn revolves around the Sun at a mean distance of 886, 120,000 miles and has an equatorial diameter of about 75,000 miles. It shines with a yellowish light, and its density is only about one-eighth that of Earth. Its day of the week is Saturday.

Since Saturn was the outermost of the visible planets, it came to represent physical limitation and form. California astrologer **Gina Ceaglio** tells about Saturn's influence in the horoscope and the significance of its cycles.

Uranus—The Awakener

On March 13, 1781, astronomer William Herschel, using his seven-inch telescope, was examining some stars in the constellation of Gemini. Seeing one which appeared larger than the rest, he suspected it was a comet. On March 19, he found that the object was moving eastward among the stars at about 2.25 of seconds of arc per hour. On April 6, he reported that the object appeared perfectly sharp around the edges without any appearance of a tail. After months of observation and calculation, the orbit was found to be almost circular, very different from the long, narrow ellipse of the typical comet. At last it was realized that a new planet had been found . . . the first discovery of its kind. Originally named for its discoverer, Herschel, it is now known as Uranus. Herschel himself named it "Georgium Sidus" in honor of his patron King George the Third of England.

Uranus is barely visible to the trained eye and has a sea green color. It revolves around the Sun at a distance of 1,782,700,000 miles in a period of 84 of our years. Its diameter is about 30,878 miles and its rotation period is approximately 10 hours and 45 minutes. It rotates on its equator instead of its axis and is known as the "oddball" of the zodiac, much like those born in the sign it rules, Aquarius.

Astrologically, Uranus is the first of the outer or transcendental planets, meaning the first to be discovered in "modern" times. Astrologer **Bil Tierney** from Atlanta, Georgia enlightens us as to the qualities of this unique planet.

Neptune—The Illusionist

More than a century after the death of Isaac Newton, his discovery of the law of gravitation led to one of the most remarkable discoveries in the history of astronomy—the finding of Neptune in 1846. After observing Uranus, scientists found that it did not travel exactly in its calculated orbit. By 1840 it was out of place by nearly two minutes of arc. This gap was too large to be explained by errors of observation, but it was still a very small amount. Jupiter and Saturn's perturbations could not be influencing Uranus' orbit that much.

On July 3, 1841, British astronomer John Couch Adams, in examining the irregularities in the orbit of Uranus, decided that it must be influenced by yet another body. His calculations were totally mathematical since no body was visible in the sky. Adams attacked this mathematical problem in 1843 and communicated his findings in October 1845 to Sir George Airy, the Astronomer Royal. If Airy had looked to the spot indicated by Adams, he would have seen Neptune, but Adams was young and inexperienced and Airy was too busy.

In the meantime, Leverrier, a French mathematician, attacked the same problem without knowledge of Adams' work. Adams had not published because Airy was not responsive to his discovery. Leverrier published a paper in June 1846 announcing his theoretical position for the planet.

At last the existence of the planet Neptune was officially acknowledged.

After the first approximate orbit of Neptune was computed, it was found that, like Uranus, it had been observed as a star many years before. Uranus and Neptune are practically identical twins. Their diameters are about four times that of Earth. The period of Neptune's revolution around the Sun is 164 years, almost twice that of Uranus. Neptune's distance from the Sun is about 30 times that of the Earth, while Uranus is only 19 times as far.

Both Uranus and Neptune have diameters less than half those of Jupiter and Saturn but are considerably larger than the other planets. These four giants are really very much alike. They all rotate rapidly, have extensive atmospheres of methane and ammonia, and are made up of light materials highly concentrated toward their centers. Their densities range from 0.7 to 1.3 times that of water. The four inner planets—Mercury, Venus, Earth and Mars—are comparatively small and have higher densities.

In primitive Roman religion, Neptune represented a god who was involved with the perpetuity of springs and streams. Later, he was completely identified with the Greek Poseidon as chief god of the sea. Astrologically, Neptune is equated with illusion, dreams and anything misty or nebulous, quite in keeping with a planet that was discovered mathematically long before it was sighted astronomically. Neptune is explored in this book by **Karma Welch**, a well-known California astrologer.

Pluto—Planet of Power

The success in predicting the existence and position of Neptune led to efforts to find a still more distant planet. Even after the gravitational effect of Neptune was taken into account, the observed positions of Uranus did not exactly agree with the predicted ones. Several scientific investigators attacked the problem around the beginning of the 20th century. Percival Lowell was the most persistent. He had founded an observatory at Flagstaff, Arizona for the purpose of observing the planets. He decided there were two solutions to the mathematical problem, the most probable being the possibility of a planet beyond the orbit of Neptune. He felt this planet to be most likely in Gemini. His search was carried on until his death in 1916 after which his brother, A. Lawrence Lowell, provided the funds for a 13-inch telescope put in operation in 1929.

Finally on February 18, 1930, after nearly a year of work, Clyde W. Tombaugh, a young assistant at the Lowell Observatory, found a faint object of the 15th magnitude whose shift in position was about right for an object a billion miles beyond Neptune's orbit. Subsequent observations proved that this was a trans-Neptunian planet, later named Pluto. Pluto appears by telescope as a point of light, and its estimated diameter is judged to be approximately 4,000 miles. Its mean distance from the Sun is about 3,680,000,000 miles, and its period of revolution is 248 years. Its mass is much smaller than expected, and some astronomers believe it to be too small to have any appreciable part in the deviations of Uranus and Neptune. It is considered a binary planet because its Moon Charon is nearly as large as Pluto itself.

Pluto's discovery is linked to the rise of dictatorship, crime syndicates and the underworld. Mythologically, Pluto was the god of the lower regions and wielded much power. Though small, Pluto's influence on Earth is mighty as New Jersey astrologer **Joan Negus** points out.

The discoveries of *Voyager II* have added to our knowledge of the planets from Mars to Neptune. We suggest publications such as *National Geographic* for further enlightenment as to the physical make-up of the planets.

Bibliography

Alter & Clemenshaw. *Pictorial Astronomy.* Thomas Y. Crowell, New York. 1952.

Columbia Viking Desk Encyclopedia. Viking Press, New York. 1953.

The Old Farmers Almanac. 1989.

Rey, H.A. *The Stars.* Houghton Mifflin Company, Boston. 1954.

Snyder, George Sargeant. *Maps of the Heavens.* Abbeville Press, New York. 1984.

Webster's New International Dictionary. G. & C. Merriam Company, Springfield, MA. 1942.

Toni Glover Sedgwick

Toni Glover Sedgwick has been involved in astrology and other metaphysical fields since 1972. Her specialties also include the Tarot and Qabalah where she has combined her B.A. in Art with symbolic wisdom from worldwide sources in order to form courses rich in both ancient mysticism and modern practical adaptation.

Toni has served in leadership capacities in a number of astrological/metaphysical organizations, including Philosopher's Stone, a research interest group dedicated to the exploration and verification of metaphysical and occult studies. She has lectured and taught throughout the country and appeared on numerous TV and radio shows. Currently, Toni writes articles for various publications in the United States.

Known for her vivacious and thought-provoking presentations, Toni is welcomed as a lecturer and teacher wherever she goes. A Capricorn Sun, Libra Moon and Sagittarius Ascendant, she presently resides in the Los Angeles area where she continues teaching and consulting.

THE SUN

"And God said, 'Let there be light'; and there was light. And God saw the light, that it was good. . . ." So begins the story of creation as quoted in the first chapter of Genesis . . . and so begins our discovery (or perhaps *rediscovery* is a better term) of the Sun as the first and most important planet in the astrological map. In Scripture we learn that the light of the Sun is a most necessary ingredient with which to begin creation, and if we follow the natural order of things, it would make sense to begin our study of the planets of astrology with the brightest "light," the "giver of life," the Sun.

In astrology, the Sun through its sign placement is what we are "becoming" within a specified incarnation. It is what we are learning how to be with the idea that once we have learned the lesson of the Sun in a given sign, we may progress to other signs, ultimately moving to a higher energy than our solar system provides.

In recent years, specialization has become a key idea in many areas including science, technology, the arts, even astrology. If we are born under Sun signs that have less-than-charming material written about them, we tend to emphasize areas of our charts other than the Sun's position. Yet the Sun represents approximately 99.8% of our solar system. It would stand to reason that the Sun's position in our charts takes on more significance simply by virtue of its size . . . indeed, its "presence."

15

From the beginning of time, the Sun has been a representation of power, authority, enlightenment and deity in cultures and religions throughout the world. It symbolizes the boundless power of creativity and life in all forms in addition to the formless, or spirit side of life. Ancient civilizations worshipped the Sun and recognized its tremendous importance in the yearly renewal of life. Great calendrical monuments were constructed all over the world tying the movement of the Sun, the Moon and other planets into the cycles of solstices, equinoxes, eclipses, and in a more earthly sense, life, death, rebirth, and especially fertility.

Religion was naturally woven into the fabric of ancient cultures, and the Sun most often represented the principle deity with the physical Sun itself symbolizing the body of the god. In cultures throughout the world, both ancient and modern, the solar symbol is that of a circle (eternity) with a face (embodiment of the god energy) in the center. This is noted today in the advertising of suntan lotions, airlines, travel brochures, etc. Without realizing it, mankind has perpetuated the idea of the life-giving force of God in the symbol of the face in the Sun.

Mythology (which always tells more than just a good story) also places the Sun in a principle position, no matter which culture the myths embody. In the Western tradition, there is a bit of confusion as to the "proper" god to which we ascribe the Sun. In reality, Helios was the Sun god of the Greeks and Romans who drove his fiery chariot across the skies on a daily basis. Apollo, however, is the Greco-Roman deity most people think of when asked to identify the Sun god.

Apollo, whose epithet was "Phoebus" (meaning "light" or "shining"), was the god of enlightenment, based upon his association with music and the arts. He was a patron especially of music, symbolized by his lyre, a gift from his little brother Mercury/Hermes. The binding friendship between Apollo and Mercury symbolizes the tie between enlightenment and the mind.

Medicine was another specialty of Apollo suggesting the association between a balanced and enlightened mind and physical well-being.

Lastly, Apollo was considered to be the most handsome and perfect representation of manly beauty. The paradox here was that Apollo was more famed for his unhappy love affairs than for his satisfying ones. (Leo, ruled by the Sun, is the sign of love.)

Thus Apollo came to be associated with the Sun and all the astrological things we have learned about the sign Leo. Apollo is the only god of major significance whose name was not changed in the transition from Greek to Roman mythology, which suggests the universality of the Sun's influence.

Scientifically speaking, the Sun directly or indirectly furnishes all the energy which supports life on Earth. This is because all foods and fuels are ultimately derived from plants which use the energy of the sunlight through photosynthesis. The Sun is a star about 4.5 billion years old with a temperature range of about eight thousand to 29 million degrees Fahrenheit. In addition to eclipses (perhaps the most studied astrological event of the Sun), the Sun also has peculiar revolutions, sunspots, solar flares and winds, etc., which greatly influence our weather patterns on Earth. Weather patterns, of course, influence food production and economic conditions, and thus every society living on Earth.

The Sun is composed largely of hydrogen (71%) and helium (27%), with the remaining 2% other elements. In the astrological study of fixed stars, these two elements comprise those most beneficial to us on Earth.

A special phenomenon of the Sun is its sunspot cycles.

The sunspots occur in pairs, one on each of the northern and southern hemispheres of the Sun. Following an 11-year cycle, the magnetic fields of the Sun reverse poles, and they recur for another 11 years. The total sunspot cycle is 22 years . . . 11 and 22 both are considered to be master numbers in the study of numerology.

From a metaphysical viewpoint, the Sun is considered to be the physical body of a spiritual being. While this may seem to be an outrageous statement to some people, when we consider the necessity of the light and heat manifested by the Sun in order to develop and sustain life on Earth, the concept does not seem so far-fetched.

Mankind has developed the idea that human beings are the only form of life to have responsible consciousness. In fact, the *one* thing we can be certain of is that humans are the supreme form of consciousness only on the physical plane of Earth. If we are to truly understand the concept of ego (a Sun-related term), then we must mentally allow other, more advanced forms of consciousness to take any form they wish, be it mineral, chemical, flesh or energy.

In the world's great religions, the parallel is drawn between the physical Sun in the sky giving life to creatures and plants on Earth and the Son of God giving everlasting life (spiritually through eternal Truths) to the souls who inhabit the bodies on the earth plane. The parallels are remarkable indeed when one considers that the words *Sun* and *Son* are even pronounced the same.

When we eat plants or animals who have eaten plants, we are literally taking sunlight into our bodies. We are essentially using the Sun's light and energy to sustain our physical beings. We are taking into our bodies the "spark" of Divine Life represented by the Sun. And what we do physically is simply a representation of the spiritual process.

If we take the essence of these philosophical Truths and attempt to translate them into our mundane reality, then we can understand just how important the Sun is in the astrological chart in discovering the core of our specific incarnations into each of the Sun signs.

Having thus established the supreme importance of the Sun in related areas, let us proceed to the Sun as a primary tool in the work of astrology. The symbol for the Sun consists of a circle with a dot in the center. The circle, with no beginning and no end, represents eternity (as in the eternity of the soul), and the dot in the center suggests the "spark" of Divine Life, essentially creative in nature. Like the nucleus of an atom or a cell, it is the center around which everything else revolves . . . it is the point of light at the beginning of life.

The Sun represents *the main ingredient of the blueprint of a given incarnation.* It describes the nature of the individual, his or her vitality, leadership capabilities, instinctive creativity (the ability to "give life" to his or her environment), and shows how the individual may develop success in life. The Sun, by its sign and house placement, suggests physical characteristics and shows how we reason out specific situations in our lives. In addition, the Sun shows how we develop our egos . . . our beingness . . . with respect to all the surrounding conditions of life. From the spiritual perspective, it is the development of this ego or character within a specific sign that is the main reason for being in the "classroom" of planet Earth. Behind our mundane reality, it is the drive toward the goal of spiritual perfection—reunion with the Higher Self—that keeps us returning to classroom Earth until we have learned *all* the lessons of the signs.

The Sun in our charts shows where and how we may make a significant contribution both personally and globally, how we may maximize our creative potential—how we may be inspirational to those around us. Though the Sun is primarily thought of in terms of what it gives out, we should also examine its position in our charts to tell us how we may receive the generosity that life returns to us. For among other things, the Sun represents love . . . love of such great splendor and magnitude that it completely dispels pettiness in any form. Love seeks not for personal gain but freely gives of its radiance. So while we are on Earth, we must also learn how to receive the good gifts of physical life in compensation for our contributions.

The Sun represents the will or will power, whether it be the personal, ego-centered desire or the refined will, which is open to and receives the Divine Will. When personal will is at one with Divine Will, then what we think of as problems or mistakes cease to exist in our mundane existence. Perhaps this is the lesson of the Sun . . . to blend personal will with Divine Will. When this is accomplished, the knowledge of the Sun in a specific sign is complete.

Ego is a concept associated particularly with the Sun and its sign Leo. *Ego* is the Latin word for "I," suggesting beingness or existence. In psychological terms, the ego is the filter which experiences external conditions, mediating between those conditions and the primitive urges of the id (subconscious). When we say that someone is egocentric or self-centered, it is a rather derogatory term, suggesting that all the individual is concerned about is him- or herself. If we take our solar system as a model, however, we can see that proper balance of things consists of a *Sun-centered* personality with all the other elements moving about it. It is, therefore, necessary to develop the potential of the Sun, but it does not have to be done at the exclusion of other energies. We must fully realize the potential of our Sun sign personalities, but we need not alienate others in the process. Our solar system is proof of the proper development of the Sun (the self) and all the other elements in our existence.

In an astrological chart, the Sun represents:

The basic character/nature	Vital energy—life force
Drive for power, significance	Physical strength
The will/will power	Courage, faith
Men; male relationships	Responsibility (the ability to respond)
Creativity	Generosity
Ability to give *and* receive	Leadership
Love—pure, unadulterated and all-encompassing	Loyalty

In the physical body, the Sun rules the heart, the spine and the upper back. (In older teachings, the Sun is said to rule one eye and one hemisphere of the brain, while the Moon rules the other. This would certainly make sense in terms of left-brain/right-brain development and helps to split rulerships in case of injury . . . one side/eye may be injured, but not both.) The Sun is specifically related to the health or vitality of an individual. It is the life force or prana which sustains the soul in its sojourn on the earth plane.

In a given lifetime, the Sun symbolizes the soul's development and it is, in fact, that center around which all the other planetary energies move. Used positively and given the respect it is due, the Sun opens the way for perfect development and evolution; used negatively or in less-than-optimum conditions, we experience the difficult side of the self-centered personality, and we most certainly set up a future opportunity to learn the same lessons.

Most people know their Sun sign, the zodiacal sign the Sun was in during the month they were born. As we are learning, that particular sign is extremely important in the personal evolutionary process. We will examine what the Sun represents in each of the 12 astrological signs and each of the 12 houses of the astrological chart. For the purpose of houses, we will use the "natural" chart in which Aries is associated with the 1st House, Taurus the 2nd, Gemini the 3rd, Cancer the 4th, Leo the 5th, Virgo the 6th, Libra the 7th, Scorpio the 8th, Sagittarius the 9th, Capricorn the 10th, Aquarius the 11th, and Pisces the 12th.

Sun in Aries

Aries rules beginnings, whether it is the beginning of the descent of spirit into physical form or the beginning of a project or phase of life. Like the spark needed to start an engine, Aries is of a fiery nature and a welcome place for the Sun. The symbol for Aries is a Ram, and its glyph is a stylized set of ram's horns. The planetary and mythological ruler for Aries is Mars, the Greco-Roman god of war. The part of the body ruled by Aries is the head.

The Sun's entrance into Aries each year marks the Spring Equinox, the beginning of life renewal upon Earth. Plants, animals, and even ideas begin their process of re-creation. The individual born with the Sun in Aries symbolizes the highest hope for this re-creative process since s/he is the human who will lead all the subhuman processes in their new beginnings.

In Aries, the Sun bestows light and heat upon the development of the personality and upon the sense of sight, both physical and spiritual. Because the nature of the Sun and the sign Aries is fiery and inspirational, Arians are natural leaders. They have great courage and can think and act quickly. This comes in handy in pioneering and adventurous situations, such as space travel, sports and war. Arians possess great initiative and are inspiring, especially when it comes to getting projects started. Don't expect them to wait around till the projects are completed, however ... they'd much rather be off starting something new!

If the Sun in Aries is not used positively, the individual can become self-centered, arrogant and domineering. The admired courage and daring can turn into foolhardiness and recklessness. The seemingly boundless energy of the Arian must be constructively channeled or it can lead to boisterous and destructive characteristics. An example of the positive use of Arian energy is the ancient Roman army that built aqueducts, walls and other engineering structures to fortify the nation when not in battle.

The task of the Sun in Aries is to develop the self or personality in accordance with the highest ideals possible. The gift of the Sun in Aries is all the resources available for this task ... for the asking, *not* for the taking. The responsibility of the Sun in Aries is to recognize that development of the self is intimately entwined with the development and progress of others so that what is good for others carries just as much weight as what is good for the self. The reward for the Sun in Aries is the recognition and appreciation of its initial place in the cosmic scheme of development, not only by others but by its own self.

Sun in the First House (Personality)

When the Sun tenants the 1st House in the astrological chart, it is similar to having the Sun in Aries with some important and subtle differences. The drive for recognition and significance is paramount. Leadership, energy, enthusiasm, generosity, courage and a "sunny" disposition characterize these people. As with the Sun in Aries, they sometimes resent authority, feeling their own instincts to be superior to anyone else's. Energy and attention is naturally focused on the self and individual development. The personality may be magnetic, attracting favors from others; conversely, if self-gratification is a strong focus, the individual may be overbearing, repelling others. The Sun in the 1st House favors health; moderation is recommended in all activities. In this house, the Sun may give a Leonine appearance—often a glowing face and a distinctive "mane." Radiant smiles characterize those with the Sun here, and others seem to feel good basking in the warmth and energy of this creative Sun-child.

Sun in Taurus

Taurus rules possessions or things that bring us security. In the astrology of the past, possessions encompassed money and personal goods. Now, however, we have come to recognize other things which bring security such as relationships, recognition, development of talents, or spiritual unfoldment. This enlightened view is what the Sun in Taurus represents. The idea that possessions/money block the way to a spiritual life has evolved into the concept that we must fully integrate with the things of a material nature (earth plane) if we are to get enough karmic momentum to escape the necessity of coming into matter in the first place.

Taurus is symbolized by the Bull, a most significant animal during the period of history when agriculture began to take the place of nomadic living. The bull represented fertility for crops and human development. Though world overpopulation is now a threat, having enough people to carry on the race was a big concern three to four thousand years ago. The Age of Taurus witnessed the development of the alphabet, suggesting that the "I Am" (key words of Aries) became the "I Have" of Taurus in terms of knowledge, rather than just physical possessions.

Currently we say that Venus, Greco-Roman goddess of love and beauty embodied in physical form, rules the sign Taurus. This sign's glyph is a circle with an open semi-circle attached to it on the top, suggesting the bull with its horns. In Egyptian mythology, the goddess of Nature is Hathor, represented with a cow's head. Taurus rules the throat, and Sun in Taurus people often have beautiful singing voices since the Sun highlights the area of the body where it appears.

In Taurus, the Sun (which is the essence of creativity in its own right) focuses on creativity on the earth plane. It seems to want to take the natural raw materials of Earth (human beings included) and make something beautiful out of them. One may be born with a lovely voice, but practice and training can maximize the potential. This creative potential is brought to fruition in human beings when they gain the capacity to create new life of themselves. (Note the change in male voices as they complete the cycle of puberty. This signifies the connection between Taurus and Scorpio, its opposite sign, which rules the sexual organs and the ability to create new physical life.)

When the Sun shines in Taurus, it seems to create from any available resource. Taurus rules money, the medium of exchange, which itself has been created out of raw materials (though paper money is only representative of carefully guarded raw materials in vaults).

Because Taurus rules the sense of touch, negative influences can make these people very possessive. Taurus is the most fixed of all the signs, indicating immovability. While this quality may serve well in some situations ("... steady as the Rock of Gibralter"), it can also cause great consternation when change is indicated—in fact, demanded—and that change is resisted by the Sun in Taurus.

The Sun in this sign must develop to maximum potential the physical resources of planet Earth and must integrate fully and harmoniously with the world of matter, thus releasing the necessity to do so. Inherently, the Sun in Taurus has the ability to be creative with the least of resources, "making something out of nothing," so that it owns or possesses that which it creates and takes pleasure in the beauty of it.

Its gift then is its instinctive way of creating, seemingly without effort. Its responsibility comes in recognizing that the *knowledge* gained from developing the personality (Sun in Aries) is behind the development and possession of resources. The reward for the Sun in Taurus comes in the sharing of possessions, talents, gifts, etc., not for the "owning" of friendships and affection but for the awareness that connectedness on the physical plane is simply a representation of the love on a higher spiritual plane. The idea from a metaphysical standpoint is that no separation exists between physical and spiritual energies—when something is given away or shared, it is replaced both in form and in spiritual energy. It's rather like making a deposit in the "Karmic First National Bank." (The Sun in Taurus rules banking.) This reward can be summed up in Washington Irving's words, "If you always give, you will always have."

Sun in the Second House (Possessions, Money)

When the Sun is in the 2nd House, there is an emphasis on possessions and security; more important than the idea of "owning" is the idea of "exchange." People with this placement have an ability to attract money, gifts and things of value in direct proportion with their willingness to share what comes to them. They also have a knack for growing things, whether plants, families, businesses or good will.

Any difficulties encountered by this Sun position stem from the small-minded view that there are only so many resources available, and if one doesn't grab greedily there won't be any left. Remembering that the Sun represents pure love, enlightenment and creativity, the goal for the Sun in the 2nd House should be "spiritual security." For where there is faith, there is always abundance.

Sun in Gemini

Communication is emphasized when the Sun shines in Gemini. This can be through communication with the world around us . . . people, situations, Nature (animals, plants, etc.), the environment (neighborhood and working place) . . . and more significantly the communication which flows between our individual self- and subconsciousnesses. Gemini is an Air sign, symbolized by the Twins of self- and subconsciousness awareness. Its glyph consists of two vertical parallel lines connected by two horizontal parallel lines at bottom and top (much like the Roman numeral two). The glyph illustrates the proper communication between these two forms of consciousness— close together, in balance and harmony, but *equal* in stature and function. Mercury, the mythological ruler of Gemini, was the messenger of the gods, transferring information from higher consciousness to lower (human) consciousness, and back again. This is, in fact, the function of the Sun in Gemini—to perfect this mode of transference of thought. Mercury figured in more myths than any other god, usually helpful (sometimes the trickster) to both gods and men alike. Parts of the body focused by the Sun in Gemini are the lungs, arms, hands . . . anything that occurs in pairs . . . and especially the thinking process.

Truly the word "enlightenment" is a focus of the Sun in Gemini. It represents what we must do with respect to understanding the mental process on the earth plane. Because physical manifestation requires a step-by-step growth process, we must come to terms with understanding how the thinking apparatus works. Gemini Sun people are considered to be very charming, intelligent, and noncommittal (even heartless). This is because they are busy "thinking" about every event in life, considering several things at the same time, which only Geminis can do with ease. But thinking in its balanced form includes the emotional, nonrational part of the process (remember the Gemini glyph).

When negatively influenced, the "trickster" aspect of the Sun in Gemini takes over so that these people can seem to be dishonest, even with themselves. They may be overly dramatic and irresponsible with their words. Since actual speech and the tacit speech of thought are both ruled by Gemini, what is created is often less than what is desired.

The task for the Sun in Gemini is to integrate with harmony the process of thinking and communicating (the flow between self-conscious to subconscious to super-conscious and back again) so that it harmonizes with all of life. This picture of perfect communication is shown in the Lovers card of the Tarot where the man is Adam/self-consciousness, the woman is Eve/subconsciousness, and the angel is Raphael/God or super-consciousness. The angel's name, *Raphael*, means "God the Healer"—a powerful message of the mind's importance in the healing and harmonizing process. The Sun shining in Gemini has the gift, more than any other sign, of being able to tap the Omniscient . . . for knowledge, problem solving, healing, or creating harmony in its environment. Gemini's responsibility is to teach and to share what it learns through the process of communication, verbally, visually, even emotionally. In the teaching process, Gemini lengthens its attention span enough to heal itself and bring harmony to the environment . . . and this is its reward.

Sun in the Third House (Mind, Environment, Siblings)

Aries (I Am) and Taurus (I Have the necessities for life sustenance) are succeeded by Gemini (I Think). At this point, mankind is separated from the other creatures of Earth in terms of responsibility (or response-ability). The Sun in the 3rd House focuses the theme of communication in terms of the environment more than any other position. Sharing information, whether within the trinity of the self, the immediate family, the neighborhood, or the world at large, is what powers evolution (and sometimes destruction). Like the great oak tree which grows from a tiny acorn, seeds of thought are the beginnings of future realities.

Often those with the Sun in the 3rd become the center of family relationships. They counsel, mediate and plan or influence activities of those around them. Difficulties arise when the Sun in this house does not take the time to get to know itself in terms of spiritual and psychological self-discovery. If one is in harmony with him- or herself, then all else flows positively outward in the vibrational energy that heals the environment. To paraphrase the song "If Everyone Lit Just One Little Candle," "If everyone thought one positive thought, what a bright world this would be."

Sun in Cancer

Summer officially begins when the Sun enters zero degrees of Cancer around June 21. As has been demonstrated throughout the centuries in music, literature and theater, summer is a carefree time when abundance flows and the Earth creates food to nourish all her creatures. The key word here is *nourish*, for Cancer not only cares for young innocent things but also provides care during the critical time prior to entrance into "light," or birth. This nourishment is highly emotional as suggested by the key phrase for Cancer, "I Feel," and by the fact that Cancer is a Water sign. Parts of the body ruled by Cancer include the breasts, the stomach and the uterus.

The Moon is the planetary ruler of Cancer and is represented, oddly enough, by the virgin huntress goddess Diana (twin sister of Apollo, the god of light). Diana was protectress of innocent things, thus the association with Cancer. As we begin to incorporate mythology and psychology more fully, other goddesses take on more significance. Ceres/Demeter, goddess of the grain and mother-supreme, is often suggested as a Moon-mother since her central myth concerns mourning the loss of her daughter and using the entire Earth as leverage in her return.

Cancer's glyph consists of two small circles with curved lines extending from each to the other representing the voiceless Crab. In many ways, the Sun shining in Cancer is a focus on the powerful forces necessary to bring us into full light or recognition of our total creativity. This is described in the nurturing process which gets all of life ready to be born into the physical and in the way that mothers prepare their young to cope in their respective societies. Cancer is the sign which precedes Leo (the Sun's "own" sign).

As the Sun warms the Earth, so it highlights the Cancer personality. It seems to give supreme respect to the nurturing qualities of Cancer since this is the place wherein the Sun deposits its creativity in physical form. Cancer Sun people are quite subject to mood swings because their planetary ruler, the Moon, changes signs every 2.5 days. The paradox of Cancer is that while it is the most sensitive of signs, it is least able to communicate its feelings. This moodiness without explanation is often difficult for those living in intimate situations with the Cancer Sun. These people should take a hint from the preceding sign Gemini and work at communicating more of their feelings. This can be done through talking, writing, art, drama, music, etc. Writing poetry is a particularly good form for letting out the emotions.

The task for the Sun in Cancer is to nurture without being possessive, for when the child, project, etc., is ready to begin its work/function in the world, it cannot fulfill its potential with mother hanging on. Cancer's gift is its natural instinct to care for everything in a loving, nonbinding way. The responsibility of the Sun in Cancer is to learn to nurture the self so that emotional dependence is not placed on those in one's care. The reward for Cancer is its own satisfaction and the respect it receives for its perfect contribution to the sustenance and development of life on Earth. For the Sun in Cancer rules memory, and without cosmic memory (Akasha), there would be no benchmark for evolution.

Sun in the Fourth House (Home, Parent/s)

When the Sun is in the 4th House of the astrological chart, home, surroundings and family ties are emphasized. Many activities take place in the home, sometimes even employment. This house signifies a place of rest, relaxation and unity so that everyone who enters the home of one with the Sun here feels like a member of the family. Attention and creative energy are lavished on this most basic of environments. Usually respect and great love are factors which influence relationships with one or both parents.

The Sun in the 4th is very "foundational" in nature, and those with this placement must learn to interact in other areas, rather than tending to "stay in the womb." The exercise of rebirthing is often quite helpful in assisting them to understand their function outside the confines of the home.

Sun in Leo

In Leo the Sun shines in all its radiant glory, for Leo is the sign ruled by the Sun. Leo is fiery and fixed in nature, suggesting the constancy of the spark of Divine Force in the continual creative process. Leo is symbolized by the Lion whose shaggy gold mane looks rather like the spurts of fire leaping off the golden Sun. The lion is the "King of Beasts" presiding over the animal kingdom, and the study of lions in their natural habitat can reveal much about the nature of the Leo Sun. One marked characteristic of lions is that they live in packs or "prides," unlike other great cats who remain solitary. This life style is suggestive of the fact that the creator, in this case the male lion, needs its creation to adore it. Raised to a metaphysical level, this idea is the stimulus behind spiritual evolution.

Leo's glyph is a loop with one end in a small circle and the other end hanging free. It symbolizes the serpent power, or nerve current, which is the basis of the Creative Life Power. This nerve current travels the spine in animals, and the spine and heart are the parts of the body ruled by Leo.

Although Helios is the mythological Sun god, Apollo, "the shining one," is the god most closely associated with the Sun. Apollo in many ways represents the ideal of creation as does the development of the Sun in its home sign of Leo. This ideal, in astrological terms, represents the development of the conscious self into the God-self. Leo Sun people are warm, magnetic and extremely creative. Leo's key phrase, "I Will," represents not the personal will over the will of others (as is often suggested), but the will to dominate the baser animal nature. This takes great courage, love and purity of the subconscious to tackle what is often the greatest enemy of all ... the personality self.

Leos are loyal and loving and seem to need but one thing to keep their sunny disposition—adoration! They have tremendous energy but are often slow to start. Leos are especially inspirational to others but need to recognize that while they do for others, they can also provide for themselves.

When negatively influenced, Leos can be egotistical and overbearing. Their pomposity can be too much for others to take. Leos seem to take charge of most situations and would rather give than take orders. They often resent authority and should really seek to place themselves in leadership positions indicated by the house their Sun is in. Such positions must be earned, however, and cannot be taken by "divine right."

The task of the Sun in Leo is mastery of the personality self so that the Higher Self shines through. This is the essence of true leadership. Leo's gift is that all of Nature, including human consciousness, provides response to Leo's creative force. Leo's responsibility is to be aware that no act of personality is self-generated but comes from a higher Source. This understanding dispels the negatively egocentric characteristics of Leo. In addition, Leo is the sign of love in its purest form, and Leos must recognize the connection of all life in order to radiate abundance. The reward is to bask in the glow of that Supreme Love of which Leos are the most direct messengers.

Sun in the Fifth House (Creativity, Romance, Children)

When the Sun tenants the 5th House, there is a tendency to focus on the pleasurable aspects of life. (Current trends in society suggest that most of us should place more emphasis on enjoyment!) Being creative in one way or another is essential to these individuals. They may be artistically creative or creative in more mundane ways, such as learning auto mechanics or coaching Little League. If there is no focus on development of creativity, the person withers.

The results of 5th House Sun creativity are evident within the lifetime of the individuals, children being the most obvious form of creative expression. This Sun has, more than any other position, the ability to bring "romance" (divine love) into everyday situations. With difficult aspects to the 5th House Sun, there can be challenging issues with children, romantic liaisons and personal attachments. Karma is strong in the 5th House, for it is emotions which bind us to the wheel of rebirth. If 5th House Suns would let go of personal control in such situations, then love would shine abundantly, and any sense of impending loss would be replaced with mastery and leadership regarding the true nature of love.

Sun in Virgo

When the Sun is shining in Virgo, it represents the process of perfection in physical form/reality. As an extension of the Sun in Leo (integration of spiritual consciousness with self-consciousness), Virgo seeks to carry that sublime realization into the plane of matter. Virgo is symbolized by a woman, sometimes with wings, carrying a shaft of grain. The Virgin, from which *Virgo* is taken, does *not* signify that the woman has never had sexual intercourse but really means "purity of essence," indicating that the evolution suggested is one of purification. The wheat represents a harvest of the five preceding steps (Sun in Aries, Taurus, Gemini, Cancer and Leo) in which the individual becomes fully developed before the soul begins to integrate with the world at large.

Virgo's glyph looks like the letter *M* with a third loop closed down over the third vertical line of the *M*. The Sun in Virgo is the last sign in zodiacal succession where concentration is focused on the self. Traditionally, Virgo's ruling planet/god is Mercury. From the evolutionary standpoint, other mythological deities are being considered . . . Ceres (goddess of grain/cereal/harvest); Vulcan (a "working" god of the forge whose festival was celebrated upon the advent of the Sun into the constellation Virgo and who is the only physically imperfect deity); Chiron (a centaur, wise in the healing arts and wisdom but not one of the twelve Olympians); and Athena (goddess of wisdom, war/ peace, protectress of weavers). All have something to contribute to the Sun in Virgo, but speculation is still awaiting the planetary discoveries to correspond with theory.

The Sun in Virgo emphasizes physical well-being, stemming from the Virgo key phrase, "I Analyze." Analysis in scientific terms suggests regulation of substances which power the physical vehicle. In ancient times, people ate what was available . . . now, in most sophisticated civilizations, taste buds are given complete reign over the diet so that what we fuel our bodies with is not as important as how it tastes! Movements have begun to reacquaint ourselves with the importance of taking care of our bodies (the "vehicles" our souls drive during a given incarnation), but this often seems to be at the occlusion of all the lessons the preceding five Sun signs have taught us. Moderation is a key word for Virgo. The intestines, organs of assimilation, are ruled by Virgo.

When difficult aspects occur for a Sun in Virgo, criticism of the self or others can get out of hand. The Sun is always meant to enlighten the sign it transits, not worry or confuse it. Since Virgo is an Earth sign, it is inherently creative. In addition to analyzing, this Sun sign should be building on the earth plane. In so doing, it perfects and doesn't have time to worry.

The Sun in Virgo's task is to strive toward perfection on the physical plane. Its gift is that all the kingdoms of Nature offer their wisdom to this end—mineral, plant and animal are all tuned in to the healing forces inherent in the Virgo Sun. The responsibility of the Sun in Virgo is to share the wisdom it gains during its journey toward perfection— teaching, healing, digesting and assimilating physical attrib- utes, which make the body healthy, and spiritual knowl- edge, which perfects the soul. The Sun in Virgo brings home the lesson that all four aspects of ourselves (physical, mental, emotional and spiritual) must be elevated if we are to reach perfection. The reward of the Sun in Virgo is the satisfaction of being of service to others and the attainment of perfection, reached not by being the "best," but by hon- estly committing oneself toward the goal.

Sun in the Sixth House (Health, Service)

When the Sun is placed in the 6th House of the astro- logical chart, healing ability is focused. This can be for the self or for others and should, ideally, be both. These people are often chosen as leaders among coworkers or those beneath them in the corporate structure. Their presence seems to lighten the load of repetitive tasks represented by 6th House jobs. The Sun here also assists in breaking habits. While some habits are not life threatening, others are. It is easiest for a Sun in the 6th to break negative patterns or to be of assistance to others who are trying to do so.

Being of service to others often endows a 6th House Sun with excellent health. The more they help (heal) on the emotional and physical level, the more healing they receive. One of the lessons of the Sun is to learn how to receive gracefully. If the energy is only self-directed, however, chronic health conditions can result. Vitamin therapy is always helpful for 6th House Suns. Cooperation and humility along with patience are lessons for this Sun position.

Sun in Libra

When the Sun shines in Libra, it focuses the beginning of communal development as opposed to the preceding six signs which developed the individual. Libra is an Air sign, suggesting the mental process, and its glyph is a horizontal line with a parallel line above it containing a hump in the center. It is said to represent the Sun going down in the evening. This corresponds with the time of day represented by the Sun in Libra in the natural chart. Balances or Scales of measurement/weight are the symbol of Libra; the word *libra* is Latin for "weight." It is the only zodiac sign which is not represented by a living creature.

Venus serves as the planetary/mythological ruler of Libra, although some speculate that a planet known as Persephone (the mythological mate of Pluto, ruler of Scorpio) is waiting to be discovered and assume rulership of Libra. (Venus did not rule over marriage (Libra) but simply over romance and attraction.) The kidneys are the body part associated with Libra, for it is the kidney function which removes waste from the system, continually working to maintain balance within the body.

The Sun in Libra wants to create balance and the harmonious flow of "give and take." Individuals with this position are often giving when it comes to emotional relationships, especially to their partners, but they need to recognize that their giving is frequently self-motivated so that they will receive back just what they are giving. When the ebb-and-flow of sharing is not reciprocated, the Libran often becomes disenchanted, thinking that the partner is not living up to his or her expectations.

Libra Sun people enjoy social events of all kinds and make excellent negotiators and diplomats. Sometimes they can become "fad-conscious," taking up every new idea, clothing design, etc., that comes along simply because they seek approval and popularity. What the Sun in Libra really needs to know is that balanced relationships should not be sought but developed from harmonious interaction between the self- and subconscious within. Rather than seeking happiness externally, internal nurturing makes all outside relationships blossom.

The task of the Sun in Libra is to balance the self, intimate and personal relationships, and the environment. Librans may do this easily with the gift of the ability to view *equally* all conditions in any situation in order to make a decisive, rational judgment. However, they often get into dilemmas in the decision-making process. The solution is simple . . . if you believe in what you are doing, do it. If you are unsure, defer the decision. Libra's responsibility is to recognize that *all* interactions are karmic in nature and that only through balancing or equalizing the karma in relationships are we truly freed of cycles of manifestation. The Libra Sun finds its reward in the creation of truly balanced relationships encompassing the body, mind, heart and soul.

This takes place only when there are no selfish motives, no "sweet" manipulation of the results. When Libra replaces selfishness with self*less*ness, there's a good chance that sainthood is in order!

Sun in the Seventh House (Partnership, Marriage, Divorce)

Creating the ideal partnership, whether business or personal, is the goal of the Sun in the 7th House. These individuals tend to attract solar types of personalities, those who shine in their own right. This all seems lovely to other Sun positions who struggle to maintain relationships, but if the 7th House Sun puts too much energy into relationships, s/he can lose his or her identity in the bargain. Thus it is necessary for 7th House Suns to develop and maintain their own identities, regardless of whether they are in relationships or not. This can be done by following up on interests that bring satisfaction and that don't necessarily require participation with others.

This Sun placement is very good at representing others; they make very good lawyers and mediators. They must remember, however, to balance love (the "light" principle) and justice (the "dark" principle) so that they may unite the two into the gray (principle of the union of opposites) of harmony.

Sun in Scorpio

Scorpio is the sign of the hidden. When the Sun shines in that part of the zodiac, the mysterious is brought to light. Fittingly, Scorpio is ruled by Pluto, god of the underworld. It is a Water sign whose glyph resembles the letter *M*, with the third vertical line extending down and coming up with a little arrow on the end—the Scorpio barb or "sting." The animal representative of Scorpio is, of course, the Scorpion, with the lowest form of the triple sign being the snake or lizard and the highest the eagle.

"I Desire" (sometimes "I Create") are the watchwords of the Sun in Scorpio. It is the sex sign of the zodiac, but the idea of sex in the context of Scorpio represents the mechanism by which the Infinite Power regenerates itself, providing new vehicles for souls to inhabit during their spiritual evolution. (The romantic, "sexy" part of intercourse really relates more to Leo.) Since all energy in the universe remains constant (no new energy is created or destroyed), the Sun here focuses on the cycle of life/death/regeneration. It is what we call transformation or going beyond form. When we go beyond the need for form, we have earned our degree in spiritual evolution.

Though Scorpio is an emotional Water sign, it is one of the most difficult to read, for it keeps its true feelings hidden below the water line. The Sun is refracted when it shines into water. In the deepest oceans the water is black, for the Sun's light cannot penetrate the depths. Yet the oceans teem with life, an indication that the Sun's energy is there even though it is unseen.

Scorpio rules the generative organs in the physical body. In general, it represents resources in some way connected with others. More than any other Sun sign, Scorpio wants to experience every side of life . . . the good, the bad, the ugly, and the transformative. People with this Sun will subconsciously put themselves into situations to do just that. Scorpios have great energy and personal magnetism which they often use for their own secret purposes. Scorpio placements are among the most prominent in the fields of both astrology and psychology.

Extremes are the norm for the Sun in Scorpio, and, unlike the preceding sign Libra ("peace at any price"), Scorpio will destroy itself (like its symbolic figure) if it thinks it can keep control by doing so. This is the legendary vindictiveness of Scorpio. Scorpios can also be extremely loyal.

The task for the Sun in Scorpio is to purify the baser

nature so that higher wisdom may be incorporated into the evolutionary process. The difficulty here is that Scorpio often manifests a false sense of control. Like its opposite sign Taurus, Scorpio has as its gift abundant resources, but it must learn to use wisdom (knowledge combined with love) in the purification process, not just power, or the results can be destructive. The enlightenment of the Sun wants Scorpio to take the responsibility of working this transformative magic on itself and not push it off onto others to avoid personal exposure. The reward for Scorpio is that in giving up power, it gains it all back. Scorpio, in its eagle form, can be the most spiritual of Sun signs, but cooperation, not control, is required to wield the power!

Sun in the Eighth House (Resources of Others, Transformation)

There is something magnetic and mysterious about people whose Sun is in the 8th House. They attract people, resources, sexual innuendos, psychic energy, and possibly a whole lot of other things most of the other 11 Sun signs don't know about! If integrity is not present in their lives, they can associate with criminal types for fun and profit. At the other extreme, they can completely share the higher gifts of spirit with everyone they contact. Somewhere along the line, most 8th House Sun people have probably been exposed to both.

Death, whether emotional or physical, will be an experience in the lives of Suns in the 8th House, regardless of sign. In having such an experience as the death of a loved one or of a relationship, the 8th House Sun will be able to demonstrate strength for others who go through similar traumas but don't possess as much endurance as this placement. Death is essentially a change in energy, and 8th House Suns have the ability to comprehend and master such energy.

Sun in Sagittarius

Departing from the extreme intensity of Scorpio, the Sun finds itself once more in a sign of a fiery nature ... Sagittarius. Jupiter, father of the gods, is the planetary/ mythological ruler of Sagittarius, and its glyph is an arrow pointing toward infinity. The animal representing Sagittarius is the Centaur, half man and half horse. Chiron is the centaur in question since he traded his immortality to relieve an endlessly painful wound. Jupiter placed him in the sky as a constellation in compensation.

When the Sun shines in Sagittarius, it brings higher knowledge to the forefront. A generally good attitude and playful nature characterize these people. But like Scorpio, the Sun in Sagittarius has something more going on just below the surface of its cheery "Hello." The Sun in Sagittarius represents the knowledge acquired in the search for the truth ... the real TRUTH. This spiritual knowledge becomes the foundation for philosophy and prophecy, both ruled by the Sagittarian Sun as expressed in the Sagittarian key phrase, "I Perceive." The hips, suggesting movement, are the part of the body ruled by Sagittarius.

Sun in Sagittarius people love to travel to other countries or to other states of mind and expand their horizons. Their vast expanse of knowledge makes them good ministers, teachers and counselors. When they are not too busy giving out their own opinions, a higher wisdom seems to flow through their words. Profound and inspiring, they have enterprising minds and adventurous spirits and are always seeking the ideal (which resides just beyond the tip of their Sagittarian arrows).

When the Sun shines in Sagittarius, it suggests that these people will be instrumental in pointing the way to knowledge of a spiritual nature—knowledge that expands mundane concepts into perpetuity of the soul. The purpose of the Sun here is to create the concept, the belief, and ultimately the psychic/experiential conviction that there is life after physical life!

The task of the Sun in Sagittarius is to create the "rainbow bridge" between physical reality and spiritual existence. (The life/death/regeneration experience of the Sun in Scorpio presents strong evidence of the unseen world; the Sun in Sagittarius must develop the philosophies to explain this experience). Their gift is that everything in Nature, both seen and unseen, is willing to share information with them, providing they open up these subtle perceptions. Responsibility for the Sun in Sagittarius lies in the fact that the knowledge available to them is for everyone; they are simply the ones chosen to diffuse the message. When this responsibility is not considered, Sagittarians often use their perceptions for their own gain, making personal relationships and business commitments a game which they must win, no matter what the cost to others. Fourth dimensional experiences (and beyond!) are available as the reward for Sagittarius Suns and confirm the knowledge they have obtained. While other Sun signs may have such experiences, the Sun in Sagittarius is the most capable of understanding and explaining them. Their concepts are the ones which propel all mankind into the future toward his spiritual destiny.

Sun in the Ninth House (Travel, Foreign Affairs, Philosophy)

Adventure is a central idea of 9th House Suns, whether a physical journey or a mind trip. Like their symbol the arrow, they want to fly into the future and bring back a better world. Quite often, these people not only talk about their "adventures" but write and publish them. They are interested in cultures other than their own and often form relationships with people in foreign countries. As humanity is perched on the brink of interstellar travel, Sun in the 9th

House folks are looking at a whole new world (worlds!) of exploration.

When the quest for knowledge is ignored or pursued but not incorporated into the fabric of life, feelings of discontent can plague 9th House Sun people. Restlessness pervades their environment, and if they do not realize that all they need do is pursue this quest (by taking a trip or taking a course of learning), relationships, businesses and lives can be interrupted in their search for peace of mind. The Sun shines on knowledge in the 9th House; "get it and share it" is the message.

Sun in Capricorn

Capricorn is at the top of the chart of the natural wheel, suggesting a culmination of all the personal and companion development that has gone before. Saturn is the planetary/mythological ruler of Capricorn, an Earth sign. Our modern celebration of Christmas takes its traditions from the ancient Roman Saturnalia, a festival in honor of the agricultural god Saturn. The glyph for Capricorn is like the letter *v* with the letter *s* attached to its right side. This is to represent the Sea-goat, the animal for Capricorn. The sea-goat rises from the depths of the ocean floor to the top of the highest mountain, suggesting the perseverance that is typical of the Sun in Capricorn. Actually, Capricorn is a triple sign with the lowest form being the alligator, the evolving form the sea-goat, and the highest form the unicorn with its magical horn.

The Sun in Capricorn highlights the creative use of all the knowledge gained so far in the soul's journey. It wants to make the information practical or useful not only for itself but for humanity at large. This is the meaning of the Capricorn key phrase, "I Use." This is the ultimate good that the Sun in Capricorn can do as expressed in the Tibetan Wheel of Transmigratory Existence where Capricorn is the final dwelling place of the soul in physical form. Spiritually, the soul is said to leave the body by way of the knees, the body part ruled by Capricorn.

The Sun in Capricorn gives wisdom during youth and playfulness in old age and is said to portend a serious disposition. Capricorns are willing to work hard—very hard—to attain their goals, for reputation is very important to them. While they are busy building recognition for what they are achieving (usually in business since Capricorn rules corporate structure as well as career), they should remember that karmic credit is the most important of all. To some Capricorns material things are important here on Earth because they represent achievement and power, but to others they signify the complete integration of the soul with the plane of matter (the process which began with the Sun in Taurus).

The Sun in Capricorn represents structure (large buildings in big cities where corporate business is transacted as the ultimate example), but it also calls upon its children to spend time in natural settings. Earth signs need this because they are the ones most closely connected with the Earth. Capricorns have a tendency to overcommit themselves, so they usually need an extra push to "get back to Nature." Capricorns, along with Virgos, can be the biggest worriers in the zodiac, and the serenity of Nature can help greatly in reducing stress.

The Capricorn Sun has the task of using to the fullest advantage all the experience, knowledge, energy, etc., available to it in order to improve the quality of life not only for itself but for the good of the planet at large. Its gift is its natural capacity for leadership in such areas. It instinctively knows what to do and how to go about doing it, but sometimes Capricorns try to do everything themselves rather than delegate authority. Then they often get miffed because no one appreciates all the work they've done! The responsibility for this placement is to recognize that what one does for or against oneself is done for or against humanity and that personal recognition is not a selfish ego event but an award for the soul's progress in evolution. Capricorn needs to *share* . . . the work as well as the achievement. The reward for Capricorn is grace, serenity and peace of mind, whether the achievement be known or unrecognized, for "what you are born with is God's gift to you . . . what you do with it is your gift to God."

Sun in the Tenth House (Career, Reputation, Achievement)

When the Sun is in the 10th House, there is tremendous drive toward the career potential. Natural leadership, charisma and favor are bestowed on this person. Government, corporate structure, positions of prestige and power could well be foci for these people. Material acquisition is also important to Suns in the 10th House as a way of showing the world what they have achieved.

When the basic drives for significance and security become more important than anything else to 10th House Suns, they often become stressed out and sometimes neurotic. Though the Sun is meant to highlight the house it tenants, it is not the only planet or house in the chart. 10th House Suns need to allow time for relaxation and open other areas of the horoscope for development so they can balance out the powerful energy of the Sun. People who are not involved in a career but have this placement are often married to or otherwise involved with the individual just described.

Sun in Aquarius

Aquarius' symbol is the Water-bearer, pouring out cosmic dust on all the universe. Its glyph is two wavy parallel lines like stylized waves, but the lines are angular rather than curved, indicating that Aquarius is an Air not a Water sign. Its planetary/mythological ruler is Uranus, the original sky father. Aquarius rules the ankles in the physical body.

The Sun in Aquarius focuses on ideas; this is the most mentally creative sign in the zodiac. Many geniuses and those with great mental acuity have the Sun here. The creativity of the Aquarius Sun relates to humanity at large; Aquarians are very friendly people, rarely meeting a stranger. In fact, they are so interested in whatever is new that they sometimes neglect those closest to them. Aquarius, the opposite sign of Leo (where the Sun shines the brightest), can often seem detached where emotional intimacy is concerned. Perhaps too much has been written about personal detachment; the Sun in Aquarius really means to create detachment from emotional bondage in relationships, thus experiencing those relationships in pure, unconditional, perfect love. This is the way of evolution for humanity. Emotional bonds, positive or negative, have the little "self" involved, and they are what keep us tied to the wheel of karma. Loving in its unconditional form releases us from that wheel and allows our *soul*-ar evolution.

Aquarius Sun people are one step into the future— usually unconventional, sometimes revolutionary. They champion underdogs and unpopular ideas, for their vision of the future sees that their ideas will be the framework of tomorrow. This is what their key phrase, "I Know," means.

The task of the Sun in Aquarius is to prepare the way for the present to meet the future. This can be done in positive ways, such as scientific discoveries, or by writers such as Aquarian visionary Jules Verne. Other conditions, such as civil unrest and revolution, represent more destructive ways in which change is achieved. Nevertheless, change is the only constant in the universe, and one way or another, things will change. The gift of Aquarius is its uniqueness, drawing in energy, charisma and sometimes stimulating controversy in the interest of moving mankind forward in its evolution. When Aquarius Suns subjugate their personal desires in the interest of humanity's needs, great deeds are accomplished and lasting contributions are made. It is the responsibility of the Sun in Aquarius to understand the real meaning of love in both the personal and humanitarian sense. Compassion is a part of the unconditional love hoped for in the Age of Aquarius, and Aquarius Suns should be the ones to lead the way. Commitment to this goal is part of the responsibility. The reward for Aquarians is the realization of the vision of a brighter tomorrow where the world learns to live in peace and harmony. If Aquarians remain true to what the Sun wants to create in their sign, they will certainly realize this on a personal level.

Sun in the Eleventh House (Goals, Hopes, Friends)

When the Sun is in the 11th House, it gives more than enough energy to make dreams come true. Many times this is unrecognized by those who have this placement, and they can seem restless and unfulfilled. Once this Sun placement is stimulated by a cause or belief, however, the power gets turned on and dreams can become reality.

Friends are important and influential in the lives of 11th House Suns. They certainly sparkle and shine in groups, whether humanitarian, local interest, political or financial groups. Social gatherings provide opportunities to meet people who can be of assistance in many other areas of life. Since the Sun rules the male principle, many friends of the 11th House Sun are often male.

Sun in Pisces

The Sun in Pisces shines on the emotional nature and the psychic mind. Its symbolic animal is two Fishes swimming in opposite directions. The glyph for Pisces illustrates this with two vertical parallel lines curving outward but tied in the middle by a horizontal bar. Pisces rules the feet in the physical body. On the physical level, the feet represent what the soul does mentally and emotionally on the path of spiritual evolution. Pisces is a Water sign ruled by the planetary/mythological god Neptune. Neptune was lord of the seas, rivers, physical land between heaven and hell and the weather. Placid and serene or stormy and rocky . . . these terms can describe weather and terrain—or personalities. That is why Pisceans are considered to be so emotional. They have very sympathetic natures, thus their key phrase, "I Understand."

When the Sun is in Pisces, it is almost as if it is shining underwater, giving off an eerie, spellbinding glow. Pisces people seem to have a strange indefinable enchantment about them. They often do not seem to be in touch with the cold hard facts, but that is because they have something of the spiritual plane in their auras. It is rather like being in a cloud . . . it's beautiful, but you have to navigate by faith.

Sacrifice is a word often associated with Pisces and the Piscean Age. We have had the mistaken notion that to sacrifice something we have to give it up so that there will be good for others and only detriment for ourselves; the only redemption comes when our souls are saved and we leave the earth plane. If we examine the true derivation of the word "sacrifice," we see that it means "to make holy, or worthy of reverence." There is nothing in the meaning about personal loss for the saving of the soul. Spiritually, the Sun in Pisces is the last place where the soul makes itself worthy to return to Spirit. In light of this, it is disturbing and somewhat mystifying to reflect on how much negativity has been associated with this sign.

In Pisces, the Sun focuses on the psychic mind and on the creative side of one's nature. It is important for Pisces people to have creative, constructive energy manifesting somewhere in their lives. The house where the Sun resides would be a good place to focus this creative energy. When they don't pursue their creativity, they can be drawn into the spheres of others, lose their own identity, or become addicted to alcohol, drugs, or even medicine due to psychosomatic illness. These chemical substances are ruled by Pisces.

Spiritual orientation along with creativity are solutions for the Pisces Sun. Often very romantic, they seem to need to fall in love with whatever they are doing or whomever they are with. They "know" that separateness does not exist on our originating plane to which they are preparing to go; they are simply trying to bring that sense of unity into their experiences while they are dwelling on Earth.

Pisces Sun people want to be helpful and are often found in service professions and health care. They are the ones, more than any other sign, who can show the connection between the physical world and the mystic, spiritual realm. As the New Age of awareness begins, Pisces Sun people will become the leaders more and more, rather than the followers they have been in the past. For in the Age of Pisces we all were learning the meaning of love so powerful that it was willing to accept not only its own karma but the karmas of all who truly believed in such perfect love. The Sun in Pisces instinctively understands this process and will show the way to unconditional love in the Age of Aquarius.

The Piscean task is to bring understanding and acceptability of the spiritual side of life. The gifts with which it may do this are sensitivity, receptivity, creativity and understanding. The Sun in Pisces has the responsibility to fight against becoming morose or bogged down in the process—to keep its own identity through creativity. Its reward is the vision/experience of that spiritual reunion that it so longs for in its heart.

Sun in the Twelfth House (Psychic Mind, "Confinement")

The Sun in the 12th House highlights the subconscious mind, psychic phenomena, other lifetimes, and the dream state. It is a place of exploration of many things which lie just below the surface of the everyday rational mind. Time to be alone and time spent in meditation and relaxation is important for this position. This is necessary to regenerate the self, for these people are constantly soaking up the subconscious vibrations of those around them. The 12th is a house of confinement in a spiritual sense, for when an ethereal thing like the soul is made to dwell in a confined space like the body, there is a sense of being trapped, if only for a while. This trapped feeling can be released through meditation or in the dream state where astral traveling often occurs. It is important for 12th House Suns to understand this "need to escape" and to work with it creatively (painting pictures, dancing, writing books or poetry, working in film/photography), or they may do themselves bodily harm by attracting even more confining situations like illnesses, even jail terms. Groups for psychic development are good resources for 12th House Suns, for they can share experiences the average person does not understand.

No matter what sign or house your Sun enlightens, remember to let it shine creatively. The proverb says, "You can't bring sunshine into the lives of others without getting it on yourself." Accepting, loving, *being* your Sun, its lessons and rewards—that's your purpose in life!

Joanne Wickenburg

Joanne Wickenburg is a practicing professional astrologer serving a large clientele in the greater Seattle area. She has lectured extensively throughout the U.S. and Canada and markets an internationally recognized correspondence course in astrology. Ms. Wickenburg is one of the first astrologers to develop a straightforward psychological approach to astrology. She has been a faculty member at many conferences, including AFA, UAC and NORWAC, and is past President of the Washington State Astrological Association, where she was instrumental in creating a certification program for astrologers. She was presented the Most Inspirational Astrologer award in 1982. Joanne is also a certified neuro-linguistic practitioner.

She is the author of many popular books on astrology, including *A Journey Through the Birth Chart, In Search of a Fulfilling Career,* and *Intercepted Signs—Environment Vs. Destiny.* She is the co-author of *The Spiral of Life, The Digested Astrologer,* and *When Your Sun Returns.*

THE MOON

The Moon deals with the most intimate aspect of human nature . . . emotion. Why does one person respond emotionally one way with another responding to the same situation on an entirely different level? Why do some people appear emotionally aloof while others gush with sensitivity? Why are some people emotionally defensive while others take the offense when emotionally aroused? Why are some people eager to grow while others fear the process growth entails? Why? Because each person has a different *past,* and the past qualifies emotional response. This past is described by the Moon in the natal chart.

The Moon rules memory. It is the caretaker of the silo where memories of all past experiences are stored. Each new experience accepted into life is processed through this memory bank, integrated with existing knowledge, and then used as a reference when making future choices. Information and experiences that do not go through this processing phase make no impact on life. They are messages never received.

Just as the female egg accepts or rejects the sperm, the Moon encompasses the potential for similar discrimination. The Moon's role is to sustain and to nurture. Its purpose is to protect what it has taken as its own. Its function is to determine whether or not to accept new experiences, new seeds for growth, new concepts for living. It represents the archetypal mother whose sole aim is to embrace, nurture and protect. In the natal chart, the Moon describes your early experience with maternal energy. Its sign, house and aspects depict the emotional impact your mother has had on your life and how her presence, or absence, shaped your concern for safety and protective boundaries.

You have learned from childhood experiences that a certain reaction or emotional response will protect you when you feel vulnerable. This was an important early lesson in emotional survival. "Messages" were delivered early in life that have become the foundation upon which all future emotional responses are based. Emotional fantasies as well as fears were instilled. Their remnants remain intact for life. These fantasies and fears with your responses to them may have, at one time, saved your life. Survival techniques were developed out of your awareness of vulnerability.

While early lessons in survival are important, even potentially life saving, it is imperative that you don't become so psychologically attached to childhood responses to emotional stimuli that growth is inhibited. If you never develop new responses, growth and maturity are squelched. It is easy to become so entrenched in old modes of reacting to challenge that you become trapped in habits of the past; you no longer accept new challenges out of fear of the unknown. If the Moon is not integrated with the other functions of personality (planets), you remain in an immature, childlike state with childlike behaviors and fears. These fears can be broken down into the following categories by sign:

Moon in Aries Fear of being attacked OR fear of losing personal identity.

Moon in Taurus Fear of personal loss OR fear of poverty.

Moon in Gemini Fear of lacking information OR fear of appearing ignorant.

Moon in Cancer Fear of being emotionally stranded OR fear of not belonging.

Moon in Leo Fear of personal embarrassment OR fear of domination.

Moon in Virgo Fear of being criticized OR fear of illness.

Moon in Libra Fear of being alone OR fear of being out of harmony with surroundings.

Moon in Scorpio Fear of involvement OR fear of being out of control.

Moon in Sagittarius Fear of the truth OR fear of all that is foreign or different.

Moon in Capricorn Fear of being used OR fear of losing reputation or status.

Moon in Aquarius Fear of the unexpected OR fear of losing individuality to conformity.

Moon in Pisces Fear of being trapped OR fear of losing your separateness to the collective.

Don't misunderstand the function of the Moon and think of it as only a negative force. The Moon has an important job to perform. Its purpose is to alert you through an *emotional signal* when change or impending threat to security is present. Once the alarm has been triggered, other functions of personality (planets) must be allowed to fulfill their duties.

First, the power of the mind must be used to ascertain whether or not the feelings or fears are appropriate to the situation at hand. The emotion may be based on a memory that might not be applicable to the existing circumstance. Information must be gathered. This is the function of Mercury.

Next, Venus must work to determine the personal value available from the experience at hand. Do you want what is being offered? The Sun brings illumination and confidence regarding what actions are appropriate to take. It provides consciousness or understanding of the process that is unfolding.

Mars is activated. Through Mars' energy, action is initiated. If the information has proven the Moon's fear is justifiable, Mars empowers you to take defensive action. If the Moon's alarm has been determined to represent a simple warning that you stand on the threshold of something new offering potential for positive growth, Mars provides courage to act on the opportunities at hand.

Jupiter encourages you to expand into the larger community. Next, Saturn requires you to define your place within and to learn the rules of the society you have joined. Uranus enters to challenge you to look beyond the limitations of your particular society and to experiment with new possibilities. This leads to new beliefs and new visions (Neptune) regarding what is possible in the future not only for yourself but for the universe. Then Pluto brings an urge to contribute to society's evolution by regenerating social systems and beliefs that prohibit progress.

Planets nearest Earth (Mercury and Venus) represent functions of personality. These inner planets are continually being shaped and challenged by factors outside the self. Social and collective issues are always impacting life, encouraging you to grow and to adapt with social change. Because the Moon is the nearest body to Earth, it is challenged to adapt by all other planets.

It is important to realize that the energies of slower orbiting planets (Mars through Pluto) must be funneled through the functions of all planets that are faster in orbit. This shaping process is sequential, based on the order set up by their orbits. Pluto, having the slowest orbit, must be processed through the functions of all other planets before the Moon accepts or rejects its power.

For example, you cannot truly contribute to society's evolution (Pluto) until you have tuned in to its needs for transformation (Neptune). You cannot tap in to collective values (Neptune) until you have broken free (Uranus) from the limitations of the establishment (Saturn). You cannot free yourself from cultural limitations (Uranus) until you have acknowledged your place within it (Saturn). You cannot become a part of society's structure (Saturn) until you have expanded outside of your protected environment and entered the world as a social participant (Jupiter). You cannot expand into society (Jupiter) without courage and initiative (Mars). You cannot initiate new experiences and act on personal desire (Mars) without the urge for life and personal growth (Sun). You cannot develop consciousness and a sense of personal importance (Sun) if you place no value on your life and want nothing for yourself (Venus). You cannot define what you want (Venus) without first acquiring information regarding what is available (Mercury). You cannot perceive new information (Mercury) with no personal past to rely on or no capacity for recall (Moon).

The Moon rules the brain. Mercury represents the nervous system that brings new information to be stored. Venus gives that information personal value. The Sun brings enlightenment and helps you develop consciousness to find purpose or importance in new information offered. With a strong sense of selfhood, you are ready to use Mars' energy to go out into the world to develop through social and global experiences (Jupiter, Saturn, Uranus, Neptune and Pluto).

Due to its close proximity to Earth, the Moon takes on the role of the protector. Its duties involve protecting you from forces that are not understood. All foreign energies must be funneled through the Moon's security system. The Moon sets off an emotional signal to alert you when something unknown is present or when some memory from the past is being triggered. At the same time, with each new experience encountered the Moon is challenged to adjust its responses. Once a new experience is accepted by the Moon, it becomes part of the ever expanding memory, and the greater consciousness (Sun) is developed.

Each planet has a specific part to play in life's drama. If all planets don't work in harmony as a team, important gaps are experienced which ultimately trigger emotional fear. Memories are stored in the brain, which is considered by some religions to be the soul. When seen from this perspective, abstract as it may be, the Moon takes on a very significant role. The Moon is like a watchdog, the castle guard, the mother . . . always looking out for strangers, always on guard to protect, and always needing to adapt according to the level of the development of the child.

The role of the mother is not to retard a child's growth but to protect without inhibiting development. If you become so concerned with maintaining the status quo to the degree that you fear all new experiences that enter life, emotional breakdown occurs. If the latter becomes the case, you have permitted the Moon to take onto itself a greater responsibility than is rightfully its role. Like an overly protective mother, the Moon can inhibit growth in its attempt to protect. An attitude based on "what worked in the past will work in the future" may feel safe, but if you hold on to that belief, stagnation occurs. The Moon is concerned with instinctive emotional survival. Yet, survival is not growth. A life only built around survival becomes a life of stagnation, a cesspool of inactivity.

How does this apply in an actual chart interpretation? The **house** containing the Moon points to an area of life where emotions are easily aroused. Your internal mother is concerned for your safety here and will send out signals whenever something new is presented or a past memory is triggered. This house describes where you are frequently challenged by outside circumstances to flow, to adapt, and to adjust in order to maintain your emotional equilibrium. The Moon's **sign** describes **how** you respond to emotional stimuli.

The Moon rules the sign Cancer. The house with Cancer on the cusp shows where you need security, where you seek safe boundaries within which to operate. It is the Moon's responsibility to provide the safety required by Cancer. Yet security in the Cancer department of your life cannot be attained until you have learned to adapt and flow with the daily changes occurring in the Moon's house.

Realize that the Moon controls the tides of our oceans. Change is frequently experienced in the Moon's house much like the predictable changes occurring with our oceans' movements. You must learn to adapt to it. Don't permit the Moon to dominate; let it warn you of an impending change of direction.

Look back in your life to determine how strongly your mother has influenced your emotional reactions to experiences encountered in the Moon's house. Are you responding the way you have been taught? Are your responses truly your own? Do you own your feelings, or do you let outside influences keep you off balance? Are you overly protective here? If so, you don't really own what you're so desperately trying to preserve. Do you accept or reject growth in this area of your life?

The following brief descriptions of the houses will give you a basic idea of how these principles operate in the natal chart. You will need to research houses in greater depth to grasp the full significance of the Moon's placement in your chart.

In general, wherever the Moon is posited, you are required to adapt without losing your focus or center; to protect without inhibiting growth; and to flow with daily changes in order to maintain a positive stream of energy when operating in these various areas of life.

Moon in the First House Your overall outlook on life; the way you present yourself to the world; the way you view yourself, which determines how others see you.

Moon in the Second House The way you handle financial responsibilities; the value you place on your life; material security and personal survival; the use of personal resources and talents.

Moon in the Third House The way you acquire information; the way you utilize environmental learning facilities and interact within the community.

Moon in the Fourth House The building of emotional foundations for life in the outer world; the way you deal with security and family matters; the home and family.

Moon in the Fifth House Creative interests; issues involving personal pleasure, love, recreation and self-expression; how you preserve your life through creative procreation; how you relate to children; your legacy.

Moon in the Sixth House The way you handle daily responsibilities regarding health and job maintenance; dealing with the routine requirements of the job; developing a sense of usefulness through productivity.

Moon in the Seventh House Interactions with others; the way you approach and learn from personal relationships; public and private involvements requiring equality or competition.

Moon in the Eighth House: The way you cope with major life changes; life changes resulting from intimacy; the way you maintain relationships and the sacrifices they require; joint financial dealings.

Moon in the Ninth House Your philosophical orientation and desire for extended learning; the way you deal with foreign people or ideas; travel.

Moon in the Tenth House Your experiences with authority; career aspirations and public reputation; the way you experience success and failure.

Moon in the Eleventh House Social or group interaction; personal goals for advancement; humanitarian concerns regarding the future; the quality of your friendships.

Moon in the Twelfth House The way you merge with the collective; services rendered based on social commitment; how you face the results of past thoughts and deeds; karma.

Realize that the energies or functions described by all the other planets in your chart will be accepted or rejected on the basis of the emotional stability established in the area of your life defined by the Moon's house.

Planets in aspect with the Moon describe functions of personality having a significant impact on emotion. The nature of the aspect determines the level of ease or difficulty experienced in the process of integrating the energies. Harsh aspects suggest difficulty accepting the experiences or changes presented by the slower planets due to unpleasant memories from the past or lack of information. These aspects (conjunction, square, quincunx, opposition) challenge you to break out of established habits of responding and accept new challenges introduced by the slower planets. These planets and aspects require you to deal with emotional issues from the past. Learning, adapting and evolving can result from what were once considered "malefic" aspects.

Conjunctions describe issues that must be confronted. The conjuncting planet is merging its energy with the Moon, requiring you to integrate its function and use its energy when making emotional choices. The planet conjunct the Moon influences all emotional issues that impact life.

Squares always involve risk. They provoke change by challenging you to break out of old patterns and avail yourself of experiences thus far untried. When squared, the Moon feels particularly threatened since it is presented with situations it has no comfortable past experience to call upon for support.

Quincunxes to the Moon also are frustrating. The slower planet seems to pull you away from security, challenging you to adapt to change that can never be foreseen.

Oppositions bring stress due to alternatives presented by others. The Moon is challenged to make choices on the basis of objective analysis rather than pure instinct. Oppositions encourage you to think before acting on emotional impulse. Always evaluate all alternatives available when confronting emotional situations.

Keep in mind that the Moon deals with memory—what you already know to be true based on previous life experiences. These preconceived ideas are sometimes incongruent with new knowledge available (Mercury). Old habits may be restricting you from attracting what you really want (Venus). Old emotional patterns may be out of alignment with what you need for personal growth (Sun). On the other hand, your instinctive, primal urge to move into life, to get what you want (Mars), may be in conflict with your security concerns. Conditioned responses and habits may limit your understanding of what is possible for you to attain in the larger community (Jupiter) or what is your social place and social responsibilities (Saturn). Security issues may restrict or attempt to control major life changes that could ultimately free you from habits that inhibit growth (Uranus). When this becomes the case, Uranus brings chaos into the emotional life to get your attention. The part of you that wants to dream about what is possible in the future, to be aware of collective as well as personal needs for spiritual growth, and to unite with higher energies (Neptune) can be inhibited from performing its task by an overly protective Moon. The godlike power inherent within you, the part that wants you to use its power to create change by recycling the past (Pluto), can seem overwhelming to the Moon's concern for safety.

If your natal Moon has primarily harsh aspects, you will experience difficulty accepting change creatively and letting go of old patterns. Fear of change or ignoring valid protective needs creates problems when faced with challenges or confronting obstacles.

When viewed theoretically, planets in harsh aspect with the Moon bring challenges much like those a mother confronts when sending her child, who is fearful of leaving the nest, off to experience the first day of school. A more dramatic analogy can be seen in the anxiety experienced when a mother sees her child off to war. She may know that war is a means to assure freedom in the world, yet the urge to protect is strong. On the other hand, she may disagree with the government's stand regarding war only to find that those in higher places (Saturn through Pluto) will have the final say. The protector (Moon) knows from experience the risk involved in all change. At the same time, an effective parent will weigh the risk against the growth potential available and accept change.

If the Moon is easily aspected (sextiles and trines), life presents few traumatic emotional challenges. The past has been sufficiently helpful in teaching you to accept new experiences with little threat to security. You may have memories that are compatible to the urges these planets represent.

Planets **sextiling** the Moon imply that you have access to tools that help you feel safe in the face of new emotional challenges. While there is effort required to adapt, the tools at your disposal make the adjustment relatively easy.

Trines promise ease of operation. They suggest that you have experience or knowledge from the past that makes transition comfortable. Trines and sextiles made by the Moon, however, do not insure a well-developed emotional life. They can indicate a life of ease built on dependencies. Planets trining the Moon simply indicate ease in maintaining emotional stability, filling emotional needs and insuring emotional safety.

There are two distinct urges involved in the process of nurturing that everyone experiences—the tendency to be overly protective and clinging and the urge to nurture growth that breeds independence and self-sufficiency. On the one hand, there is a part of you that wants to keep all harm and future pain away from your "inner child," no matter what the cost. On the other, a part exists that is capable of nurturing growth that builds confidence. Both are protective instincts. Both are ruled by the Moon.

In your struggle to maintain emotional balance when dealing with the issues described by the Moon's house, do you call on past experiences and make your choices solely on the basis of the level of expertise you have already developed? Or do you seek new input, new information, new guidelines, to help you in this process, even though you know some discomfort could be experienced as a result of what you learn? Where in your life have you established a fixed pattern of responding that promises predictability but doesn't provide new stimuli? What area of life promises you new insights and tools to aid you in creating a progressive future?

Your birth chart can help locate areas of life that provide facilities and opportunities that encourage growth and maturity. It also shows other fields of activity that draw you to the past and encourage you to hold on to old memories, sometimes at the expense of building a new future. You are constantly being pulled between these urges and areas of life until integration through agreement takes place. These conflicting urges and seemingly conflicting fields of life are defined by the relationships existing between the **North** and **South Nodes** of the Moon.

The North Node shows where (house) and how (sign) you are encouraged to use your nurturing skills to cultivate **growth**. Its house describes where new experiences are available that assist this developmental process. Even though activities available in the house containing the North Node are novel, your inner mother (Moon) realizes the value and growth that can be attained by encouraging the pursuit of new interests.

The North Node/Moon relationship can be likened to the illiterate mother who encourages her child to pursue an education, knowing that the knowledge acquired by the child could threaten their relationship and, if nothing else, will change it. Yet, the love she has for the child is stronger than the fear of change. The North Node presents a challenge and sometimes requires emotional risk.

Seen from another point of view, the experiences described by the North Node/Moon relationship can be compared to the excitement of a carnival ride. While fear is present, there is also a promise that when the ride is over the fear will be gone and only personal pleasure remain. In truth, once the anxiety has dissipated, there is no further desire to repeat the same ride. You seek new experiences to move you. If you choose to face the challenges life presents (North Node), you must first consider the danger (Moon). You must use your senses to determine whether the challenge, though scary, is safe. The Moon's response (fear, excitement, etc.) is only a signal. You must acknowledge the signal as only a warning. When evaluating these responses, remember that it won't do you much good if your signal works (Moon) but your car won't run. If the car runs but you ignore all signals, danger is imminent.

Growth is always challenging as it necessitates an openness to new experience. Anything new carries the potential for risk or danger if only in the fact that it challenges the status quo. The North Node shows where a fountain of new experience and knowledge is available. Your challenge in this area of life (house) is to welcome new input and to take from society or the universe what you need to continue your journey into life. A challenge exists simply in the fact that what is available to you through North Node experiences may be foreign to the life style you have been taught and tests what has been comfortable and predictable in the past.

The North Node requires you to reach out to take advantage of the new experiences life offers—to be more today than you were yesterday, more tomorrow than you are today. It invites you to seek relationships that promote growth and maturation in an environment described by its house. This is the point of "taking in." This is the part of the lunar function that wants you to accept new vistas.

At the opposite point of your chart is the Moon's South Node. The house containing the South Node describes an area of life where you have established habits that have become a source of **security**. These patterns have supported you in the past (the past including experiences from yesterday to the beginning of existence beyond) but do not encourage growth in the future. The natural response of the South Node is to reject anything new or challenging to the status quo.

The South Node represents the protective urge to

maintain old patterns in order to assure safety. It is easy to become dependent upon what you have already established in this area of your life. A certain proficiency has been developed that at one level can be used as an anchor for stability. This anchor, however, can easily be dropped so deeply that progressive movement is restricted. This part of you doesn't want to let go of existing security even if progress is denied to other personality urges that want and need new input. You may find yourself taking the "path of least resistance," always choosing the easy way out.

Don't mistake the role of the South Node and consider it only as a negative point. The South Node describes by sign and house skills that are already well developed and must not be wasted! The challenge met by the polarity defined by the Nodal axis is one of **integration** and **cooperation.** Established talents and skills (South Node) become obsolete if new input (North Node) is rejected. At the same time, new experiences available through the North Node are of no value if not assimilated with the knowledge you already possess (South Node).

While the Moon and her nodes represent conflicting urges at one level, they yearn to become a partnership. A common pact must be made between these two opposing poles to work in harmony if life is to function creatively and progressively while still assuring an element of emotional safety. Each node plays a specific role. Once their individual purposes have been defined, the trio they form with the Moon can perform in harmony and with productivity.

If you cannot adapt to the minor changes experienced in the Moon's house, you may develop dependencies that trap you in what is now familiar. When this becomes the case, the South Node begins to dominate life and stagnation occurs. You become dependent on existing talents or knowledge, rather than greeting and embracing fresh challenges and developing new skills that stimulate growth.

Once the nodes have become integrated, you are able to take in new experiences through North Node involvements and release the benefits of those experiences into the area of life described by the house containing the South Node. You no longer must repeat over and over again life experiences that lead to disillusionment, disintegration and repetition, either personally or in relationships with others.

You have natural abilities in the area of life described by the South Node's house. Part of your spiritual responsibility includes sharing those skills with others just as the role of a mother is to nurture her child. It is important, however, that you don't give to the point of becoming emotionally, mentally, physically and spiritually drained. This tendency can be avoided only by cultivating new interests and seeking new sources of stimulation through the experiences available from the North Node and by maintaining emotional flexibility toward your Moon-ruled activities.

You may naturally attract people who need the skills you innately possess. To a certain degree, it is your spiritual responsibility to offer them the value of your expertise. These people need, to enhance their growth, the types of strengths natural to you. Your innate maternal instinct wants to provide for them. The challenge met through these South Node relationships involves giving without becoming a martyr; giving without losing yourself. You must constantly develop new strengths, investigate North Node activities and accept people into your life who have the tools you need to pursue your own growth (North Node). As a result, you will find you have more to give and less to lose. You can be revitalized through the experiences available in the North Node's department of life. With this new sense of vitality you grow personally and find you have more to offer others through South Node activities.

An important point to remember is that the South

Node is a point of *giving,* not receiving. If you expect personal happiness to be gained through South Node activities, you will be left very disappointed. The more you focus on South Node experiences (house), the more you become buried in patterns that inhibit growth. It is equally essential to realize that while the North Node encourages you to take, you can absorb only a limited amount of information before becoming sated. Once you have learned something new through North Node ventures, you must release them into the South Node activities of your life. This "digestive" process creates a positive flow of energy. The North Node feeds and the South Node cleanses. Once this polarity begins to operate creatively in your life, integration takes place, and the two once conflicting parts of your nurturing nature find harmony in working together. You have found the key to nurture the self *and* others in a way that promotes growth while assuring security. Once you have understood the nodal axis and how it functions in your chart, you have found the key to personal integration. The nodal polarity shows how you can pull your life together. When not functioning in harmony, it points to sources of disintegration. An equal level of importance must be placed on both poles.

When you find yourself in situations that trigger your "Moon alarm," you are immediately confronted with choices. Do you move ahead or do you fall back on what is familiar? Where can you find new tools to help you maintain solid emotional foundations? To find the answer, look to the house containing the North Node of the Moon.

Where have you accumulated wisdom in the past that can be useful to you in this growth process? Where have you stored memories that can either assist or inhibit growth? The answer lies in the South Node's domain. Where is the future beckoning you? Look to the North Node's house for the answer. The nodal axis shows where, by pooling what is available in these two areas of life, you can build new strengths that nurture and sustain those you already possess. Realize that you can always call on the accumulated wisdom of the past. You have established strong roots in the department of life described by the South Node's house. Yet, living in the past does not lead to a successful or fruitful future.

The Moon has stored its accumulated wisdom and past memories in the South Node department of your life. You have a swell of experience to call on here. Natural talents and memories of previous accomplishments and failures wait to be used in conjunction with the new. The North Node contains the "brain cells" that have not yet been tenanted. Once these cells have been filled, they automatically are transferred to the South Node for storage and protection. Unless this transference occurs, fragmentation is experienced.

The following "do's and don'ts" may be useful when evaluating the significance of your particular nodal axis.

North Node in 1st House—South Node in 7th *DO* cultivate independence. Be your own person. *DO* develop self-confidence, and demonstrate it to others through personality, presentation and body language. *DON'T* lose yourself to another person. *DON'T* become dependent on others' responses. *DON'T* become a martyr to your mate. Remember, the more powerful and self-assured you become, the more you have to offer to important relationships in your life.

North Node in 2nd House—South Node in 8th *DO* always strive to develop personal resources and strengths. *DO* build confidence in your ability to earn your own way. *DO* learn to maintain your life independently. *DON'T* become reliant on the resources of others for survival. *DON'T* give your power or assets away indiscriminately. Remember, the process of merging skills with those of others is only productive when you have personally developed something of substance to bring to the relationship.

North Node in 3rd House—South Node in 9th *DO* use the power of your own mind. *DO* accumulate and use the information available within your community. *DO* learn the value of concise communication. *DON'T* look for a guru. You are one. *DON'T* look for greener pastures before first investigating your own surroundings. Remember, you will have wisdom to share with others only if you keep yourself informed and develop confidence in your own intellectual abilities.

North Node in 4th House—South Node in 10th *DO* value the importance of home, family and personal security. *DO* build solid emotional foundations upon which to construct your life. *DON'T* become so focused on vocational success and prestige that you lose touch with your emotional needs. *DON'T* strive so diligently for success that you ignore either family responsibilities or your own need to belong.

North Node in 5th house—South Node in 11th *DO* develop personal creative skills. *DO* make your personal mark on all ventures you undertake. *DO* enjoy the pleasures life offers. *DON'T* lose your creative uniqueness to the group. *DON'T* sacrifice your need to be important by losing yourself in group or humanitarian goals. *DON'T* rely on friends to provide creative inspiration. Remember, the more you cultivate your creative potential and charismatic flair, the more you have to offer friends and the better you can function in the social arena.

North Node in 6th House—South Node in 12th *DO* develop good routines and learn to organize your time. *DO* establish a working environment that encourages you to design useful systems to meet daily responsibilities. *DO* pay attention to your daily health care needs. *DON'T* lose yourself in fantasy. *DON'T* allow yourself to be the sacrificial goat. *DON'T* become so involved with causes that fail to take care of your personal health and work requirements. Remember, to contribute to society's growth without being drained in the process, you must have order in your daily life and tend to personal routine responsibilities.

North Node in 7th House—South Node in 1st *DO* reach out to others for feedback and cooperation. *DO* learn to delegate and share. *DO* understand the importance of competition, partnerships and equality. *DON'T* accept others' responsibilities out of fear of confrontation or inability to delegate. *DON'T* withdraw into yourself to the degree you stop interacting with others. *DON'T* expect more from yourself than what you expect from others. Remember, the more you learn to delegate and share, the stronger and more confident you become.

North Node in 8th House—South Node in 2nd—*DO* merge energy and resources with others in order to create more than what you could do alone. *DO* welcome change that breeds growth. *DO* look beyond the world of materialism and investigate life's mysteries. *DON'T* focus so strongly on personal values and material desires that you leave no time to share with others. *DON'T* become so absorbed with protecting your own resources that you avoid intimacy. Remember, power lies in numbers. By detaching from the ego, you can produce results that benefit not only yourself but those around you.

North Node in 9th House—South Node in 3rd *DO* welcome information which extends beyond that available in your community. *DO* develop ethical principles and moral values. *DO* dare to explore the world of philosophy. *DON'T* become trapped in a narrow mental framework that does not encourage abstract thinking. *DON'T* become so entrenched in your environment that you never look beyond it. *DON'T* limit your intellectual investigations to concepts based only on factual data. Remember, there is more to life than meets the eye. Developing interest in ideas and ideals that extend beyond your culture will enhance your life.

North Node in 10th—South Node in 4th *DO* go after success in worldly terms. *DO* fill your need to be important in the world. *DO* strive to develop a solid reputation through social or career involvement. *DON'T* become so concerned with personal security that you fail to accept social challenges or acknowledge career aspirations and ambitions. *DON'T* expect family to support your emotional needs. *DON'T* stay at home waiting for fulfillment to come to you. Remember, security for you can only be maintained through accomplishment in a worldly sense.

North Node in 11th—South Node in 5th *DO* develop group affiliations. *DO* share your talents so others can benefit from them. *DO* realize the importance of goals and the need to work with others to attain them. *DON'T* become so attached to your creative projects that you fear sharing them with the larger community. *DON'T* expect your children to fill your own growth needs. *DON'T* become so involved with personal desires that you ignore collective, humanitarian causes. *DON'T* expect romance to fill all your dreams. Remember, you are creative. Your growth will come by using your skills to achieve humanitarian goals.

North Node in 12th—South Node in 6th *DO* take time out of your daily routine to experience solitude. *DO* learn the value of meditation. *DO* be willing to help others in need. *DO* develop faith in what cannot be proven. *DON'T* become trapped in your daily work routines. *DON'T* become attached to health problems. Remember, work comes naturally to you. You are challenged to use your skills to accomplish something of social significance rather than depending upon work routines to fill your needs.

As you can see, the role of Luna is a complex one. The process of protecting yet nurturing growth is never-ending. Every day you meet new challenges, some great and some barely noticeable (though no less important when considered in the larger picture of life). Will you accept them? Or should you reject them? Ultimately, it is the Moon's function to make the choice.

Moon **transits** describe these daily challenges and show where they impact your life. The Moon moves through the entire chart in less than one month, scurrying through each house or sign in approximately 2.5 days. Daily the transiting Moon shows where the need for adaptability will arise. As it transits from house to house, like a mother going from room to room, its role is to check to see that everything is under control. Changes that have occurred since its last transit (less than one month prior) are noted. An alarm goes off whenever it encounters incongruities. Minor changes are noted and accepted or rejected based upon knowledge currently possessed. If the Moon senses danger or causes you to experience discomfort while it is transiting a particular house or aspecting a natal planet, you must confront the fear and determine what techniques to use to adjust to it. Don't hold on to the fear based only on the signal of change. You must use the input provided by other planetary functions to evaluate whether the discomfort is justified or if it simply represents fear of repetition or lack of sufficient information.

The transiting Moon can be likened to the second hand of a clock. If it stops moving, time stands still—the minutes and hours of the day are paralyzed. A second in time seems insignificant just as the Moon's transits often go unnoticed. Yet, a second of time is what separates one minute of time from the next. It is what unites our whole system of time. It is an important part of synchronicity. The Moon's transits can be viewed in a similar way. If you cannot adapt from one experience to the next, life cannot remain mobile. All other systems cease to function.

Moon transits, while often ignored by astrologers, are extremely important to consider in the larger picture of human development. If you do not learn to accept the minor changes life presents, how can you expect to deal with the major life changes such as those brought into play by the transits of Saturn, Uranus, Neptune or Pluto?

The transiting Moon represents your personal regulator. It shows where and how you must learn to adapt to the changes (great and small) occurring around you and within you each day of your life. Its role is to protect and assist you in your personal development. You need to regulate or synchronize all other aspects of life with your personal "second hand" to keep your life's timing manageable. When emotions run amok, all other systems break down. Logic fails (Mercury), relationships crumble (Venus), consciousness is limited (Sun), and so on.

How can you use the Moon's transits to keep your life running smoothly? Adaptation is the first step. You must learn to adapt to changes of mood and circumstance, both minor (Mercury/Venus/Sun/Mars) and major (Jupiter/Saturn/Uranus/Neptune/Pluto). This adaptation must occur in both attitude (sign) and external behavior (house). New experiences presented by life must be linked with the knowledge already present. You must consider new information based on current understanding. You must evaluate how your existing knowledge can be used as a foundation for the new information or experiences being presented.

As you can see, even though Moon transits are repeated frequently, Luna's job is never done. Often not appreciated or taken for granted for the role she plays in holding the "family" together, the Moon's transiting role deserves respect. It's easy to dismiss minor daily occurrences or to forget the frustrations of a bad day only to repeat similar aggravations approximately 27 days later when the Moon returns to the same house or aspect or one week later when it squares the original problem point. The behavioral and circumstantial loops that can easily entrap you can be transformed into a flowing spiral of growth once you tune in to your fundamental cycles. When you do not adapt to your Moon cycles, you find yourself walking down the path of least resistance. The area of your life described by the South Node's house begins to dominate, and your options and potential for personal growth become limited or altogether cease to exist.

Listen to your Moon's signals. Heed her warnings and appreciate her role. But don't let the South Node/Moon habits inhibit your maturity. Your inner mother knows that you must learn to crawl before you walk. Let her hold your hand when it is appropriate to do so. Let her protect you, and be grateful when she alerts you to periods of danger or impending change. But allow her to let go when it's time to move on to experience growth, and knowing she is always there within you, open your arms to embrace the promises offered by the energies described by the other planets in your chart. Once each function (planet) has had an opportunity to express itself and has been welcomed by the Moon, your entire "family" will be happy in its home.

Throughout the span of your lifetime, you are continually being bombarded by external influences requiring you to adapt. Some of these changes will be welcomed. Some feared. Some will be embraced. Some will simply be ignored. Transits describe these outside influences. The transiting Moon's job as protector is to be on guard constantly, watching and gauging what is occurring at any given moment. At times, the part of you represented by the Moon seems overwhelmed.

Your inner mother also has yearnings regarding change. She wants her child to grow up! She dreams of the day when her responsibilities will be lessened because of the level of maturity you have reached. The secondary **progressed** Moon shows where and how this phenomenon is taking place throughout your life. It describes where an inner urge to do some major housecleaning, to make some changes in strategies, to gradually ease away from old necessities and to encourage greater independence is being experienced.

Deep psychological changes are occurring in the area of life described by the progressed Moon's house. You are being encouraged here to make *internal adjustments in preparation for external change.* Old emotional dependencies and security habits are being reassessed. This is a very personal process of internal unfoldment that is not conditioned, forced, or tampered with by outside factors.

While transits outline outside energies and conditions that are influencing your personal life, the progressed Moon represents the inner mother who wants something for herself! She is patient but persistent. It takes the secondary progressed Moon approximately 27 years to circle the chart, while the transiting Moon completes its cycle in only 27 days. As the progressed Moon moves into a house, you begin to alter or adjust your orientation toward and emotional investment in the area of life that house defines. It denotes a time in your life when it is appropriate to review your nurturing and emotional patterns. Its sign indicates attitudes and personal needs that are associated with this transition. The progressed Moon has an important message—it's time to grow up; it's *time for change.* The changes that occur as a result of secondary progressions affect your outer life only through reflection. The way you feel about life, which changes with the movement of the progressed Moon, is reflected in what you bring to it and what you expect from it.

Remember that the Moon would be literally nonexistent if it were not for the Sun's power to set our solar system in motion. It is always dangerous to isolate any one factor in the astrological chart and attempt to make a thorough diagnosis; a physician cannot look at one physiological factor and form a total evaluation of a patient's condition. The Moon represents only one part of a complex personality. If you do not integrate its importance with that of all other planets, you fail to recognize its full significance. A natal chart must be viewed in its totality before an in-depth conclusion should or can be made. The Moon cannot fulfill its role, astrologically or astronomically, if the Sun and planets are inoperative. The Moon would have nothing to protect, to nurture or to adapt to if the other planets did not exist in the natal chart or in transit and progression. If you totally dissect the person, there is no life. If you totally disassemble the chart, there is no horoscope. If you look at the chart in bits and pieces and never put those pieces together, you are missing the beauty of astrology. You are missing the picture of the person possessing the chart. Synchronicity is the answer. You must assess the Moon with all other astrological factors. While the material here is strictly Lunar-based, you must go several steps beyond what this or any textbook can do. You must learn to use the tools of astrology skillfully and artfully to design a picture of a living person.

Erin Sullivan-Seale

Erin Sullivan-Seale has been a full-time practicing astrologer for 15 years, having taken up the study in 1965. She has lectured all over North America and in Australia during the last ten years. Her articles have appeared in all the astrological trade journals and also in other venues. She has been involved in the founding and activities of many astrological groups and has served two terms on the AFAN Steering Committee. She was on the first UAC Committee establishing the format for the Hospitality Program. She founded the AFAN Media Watch Program and remains an active advisor to AFAN. The FCA (Canada) has awarded her three distinctions in the last six years: The Sun award, The Mars award, and in 1986, the International Venus award for her work on international relations between Canada and the United States in astrology.

Her private practice centers around transpersonal counseling, and she has facilitated workshops on self-development for the Cold Mountain Institute, Cortez Centre for Human Development and presently for P.D. Seminars in B.C. She is a long-time student of Jung's work and is on the board of directors for the Jung Society in Victoria.

Erin is studying Classics at the University of Victoria and has a work in progress titled *The Transit of Saturn: The Heroic Journey.*

HERMES/MERCURY

Trickster, Teacher, Theos
and
The Cycles of Mercury Retrograde

THEOS: The god—his origins and nature

Modern astrological terms, particularly our planetary names, are an English translation of a Latin translation of a Greek rendition of a Babylonian nomenclature. An ancient mythology and religious system, based on origin myths and lineage descended from the Chaldeans and Babylonians and reflected in the Egyptian pantheon, was incorporated wholesale by the mathematical Greeks who amalgamated and translated the mythic characters into their existing cultural religion. By doing so, they wove the celestial beings from the Mediterranean cultures into the fabric of their own myths. Strictly speaking, astrology as we know it today did not exist for the philosophers of Hellas, the Greeks of the sixth and fifth centuries B.C. They did, however, translate the visible planets into their Olympic gods' names from the Babylonian *cum* Egyptian counterparts.[1] For example, Hermes was named by the Greeks to replace the Babylonian sidereal divinity, Nebo, and the Romans in turn rendered him as Mercurius, the Mercury of our current astrology.

There is also some historical evidence that Hermes was linked with fertility in ancient Greece, and indeed his Egyptian antecedent Thoth was distinctly a fertility figure associated with the intercalary days set aside for festivals worshipping the five god-offspring of Nut (sky goddess) and Geb (earth god). Thoth acted as a sort of inseminator/midwife of their children Osiris, Horus, Typhon (Set), Isis and Nephthys. The Egyptian Thoth, later known as Hermes Trismegistus to the Greeks, founder of alchemy and author of the alchemical writings, is featured in the work of Manetho, an Egyptian who wrote about Egyptian religion in Greek in the third century B.C., but has no classical relationship to our astrological Mercury. (The assimilation of Thoth/Hermes/Mercury/Mercurius into the composite figure does fit well with our astrological Mercury as we shall see. He seems to embody all the symbolism collected over time, creating one of the most complex archetypes of the astrological pantheon.) The fertility aspect of Thoth *cum* Hermes, however, was reflected in the Greek statues called *herms* found at crossroads, in front of doorways and in other transitional places. These were square pillars supporting large phalluses and the head of Hermes. In the classical period, a herm was found at the bounds of one's home or property, ostensibly to bring luck, prosperity or perhaps fertility in the most generic sense of the word.

The Greek god Hermes and his attributes, epithets and roles in the classical works offers much to think about when we are dealing with Mercury in the astrological realm. Of the earliest literature on Hermes, we find Homer's *Iliad* and *Odyssey*, Hesiod's *Theogony* and *Works and Days* along with the anonymous *Homeric Hymn to Hermes (Number four)* to be replete in information about the nature of this fascinating god.

In the *Homeric Hymn* we read of the birth of Hermes: "He was born at dawn, by midday he was playing the lyre, and in the evening he stole the cattle of far-shooting Apollo."[2] This shows him to be a trickster *par excellence* as well as having great charm. Making and playing the lyre involved tricking a tortoise out of its own shell. Hermes, restless after his birth, went in search of the cattle of his brother Apollo, and along the way he happened upon a tortoise whom he told would make a good dinner companion. Indeed he did, because Hermes promptly ate him for dinner! He also promised him that he would make beautiful music when he was dead. The helpless tortoise's shell was to become the prototype lyre which Hermes eventually gave to Apollo to appease him for the theft of his cattle.

To continue with the *Hymn*, the most remarkable thing to note about the cattle theft is that in order to confuse any search party Hermes ". . . made their hoofs go backward, the front ones last and the back ones first; he himself walked straight ahead."[3] This is the literary origin of the dualistic path and deceptive brilliance of Hermes the Trickster. For only minutes before, he had been happily playing his new lyre, but ". . . his heart was set on other pursuits."[4] Versatile, wily, double-edged Hermes doing one thing while planning another. In this way the formation of the archetypal Mercury is forged, and today in our horoscopic delineations we employ this description for Mercury.

Too, the *Hymn* celebrates the charming youth, the *puer aeternis* component of Hermes/Mercury, for it is just a babe in swaddling clothes who performs all these fanciful tricks, and he does use his babyhood as a defense when questioned about the cattle heist. He commits a crime which would not be found amusing if done by another and even impresses and amuses Zeus, a normally wrathful god, with his hubris. The trickster is present in humor when proportion is realized. That instant of recognition of perspective that occurs spontaneously and with no forewarning resulting in a gust of pure laughter is precisely what Hermes the Trickster is all about. It was after Hermes gave a long-winded and rather sophistic account of his innocence, winding up with the plea, "Be on the side of a defenseless baby," that Zeus laughed at the child's deviousness.[5]

A strong Mercury with a twist will enhance the horoscope of the humorist as if the archetype of Hermes lives through one who has the ability to bring sudden perspective to a situation that could otherwise be dull or perhaps even terrifying without the charm of Hermes. The comedian is a healer, bringing into sharp relief priorities hitherto unconsidered—a new reality, so to speak—the shock of which spurs laughter.

For all of the attributes of youth, humor, grace and prankishness, there are serious facets to Hermes/Mercury. The rare appearances of Hermes in the *Iliad* is a clear contrast to his strong presence in the *Odyssey*. Perhaps it is more appropriate to his nature that Hermes should appear so frequently and prominently in a tale that deals primarily with a journey rather than with heroic acts in a war or the nature of a wrathful hero in conflict. In the *Iliad*, Hermes is sent to lead Priam to the gates of Achilles, acts as a protective guide, and ". . . mazes the eyes of those mortals whose eyes he would maze. . . " in order to allow the mourning father to pass though the guards at the gates unscathed.[6] It is with the caduceus, his wand, that he performs this magic at will. This act of leading Priam to the body of his slain son Hektor is a foreshadowing of Hermes' function as a soul guide, a *psychopompos*.

It is also in the *Iliad* that Hermes is designated to be the companion of man when Zeus speaks thusly to him: "Hermes, for to you beyond all other gods it is dearest to be man's companion. . . ."[7] In the horoscope, Mercury acts as the important "translator" of all sensory data, assimilating them into the consciousness. In fact, Mercury might be the single most important planet in the horoscope as it is through Mercury that we not only absorb but also disseminate all of our perceptions. In *Hermes: Guide of Souls*, Karl Kerenyi writes:

It is not without good reason that Hermes was supposed to be the inventor of language. It belongs to the Hermetic wisdom of the Greek language itself, to one of its most ingenious chance hits, that the word for the simplest mute stone monument, *herma*, from which the name of the God stems, corresponds phonetically to the Latin *sermo*, "speech" or any verbal "exposition." The word *herma*, which in the Greek does not have this meaning, does however form the basic verbal root for *hermeneia*, "explanation." Hermes is *hermeneus* ("interpreter"), a linguistic mediator, and this is not merely on verbal grounds.[8]

As previously mentioned, one of Hermes' serious facets is his patronage of the journeyman. I emphasize this distinction between journeying and traveling. A traveler has a point of departure and a destination, whereas a journeyer is simply somewhere in between at a liminal place with no given parameters. A traveler has an itinerary, a past, a place from whence he came, and a known future to which he heads with a sense of direction. A journeyer has left from some secure place and heads out, *sans* map, into unknown territory to arrive at an unanticipated place in the unknown future. It is with this attitude in mind that we recognize Hermes/Mercury as the guide of those liminal souls. Essentially, he lives in the threshold of existence, in the limen of experience. Whenever we are not who we used to be or who we are to become, or are somewhere between here and there, in a state of transition, we can expect Hermes to appear at important junctures with messages from the unconscious. These messages can come in the form of external events or internal realizations, but Hermetic they are, regardless of the form. After all, Hermes, as well as Hekate, is a god of the crossroads. These "accidental" discoveries, including luck, that are Mercurial in nature are not necessarily Hermetic but have all the overtones of the trickster god in action. The Greek word for windfall is *hermaion*, again a derivative of *herma*.

There is even an oracular nature to Hermes/Mercury which is not commonly known, and it takes the form of a chance experience. Greek travelers, seeking oracular answers or indications, would stop up their ears and walk behind the marketplace to the temple. Upon unstopping their ears, the first words they heard were attributed to Hermes and interpreted according to the nature of the request— a kind of *sortes Mercurii.*

The viewpoint that Mercury is a planet that rules the mind addresses the creative process that spontaneously occurs when one is trying to evolve an idea or plan, employing both the conscious and the unconscious mind simultaneously. While creating the structure of the idea on a conscious level, the unconscious is processing the information in a nonlinear fashion. It is this phenomenon that results in the apparent spontaneous emergence of the so-called brilliant idea that comes out of "nowhere."

Hermes' connection to Hades/Pluto was powerful and singular. Of all the gods, Hermes was the only one to travel at will to Hades and return. He escorted both the dead and the living to the nether place either to remain or to visit in the world of the Shades. This corresponds to our descent into the unconscious to bring information or material to the conscious mind for processing in a linear fashion. The most hidden, the most recessive and suppressed contents of the psyche can be brought to light.

Conversely, we can send a conscious wish or desire to the realm of the unconscious for processing in a nonlinear fashion in order to be refined and delineated by the greater intelligence of our unconscious, which can then emerge as creative manifestation of will. This is also where Hermes/Mercury acts as a fertility function in animating seminal thought. The popular story of Archimedes of Syracuse (c. 287—212 B.C.), an adviser to King Hiero II, who was purportedly trying to work out the contents of the king's crown—

whether it was pure gold or alloyed with silver—illustrates this phenomenon beautifully. Archimedes spent hours, possibly days, working intellectually on the problem at hand. In exhaustion he drew himself a bath and sank into it, relieving himself of the pressures of analytic, logical thought. As he submerged himself, the truth emerged from out of his unconscious, and he leaped up crying *"Heureka!"* (I've found it!), thus discovering the theory of displacement. The key word here is *discover*. This lateral shift from the left to the right hemisphere of the brain, resulting in the inspirational "flash" of knowledge, is a product of what could be likened to an alchemical transformation. In other words, the preparation for discovery is long and arduous and takes place "aboveground," so to speak, but all the while the "underground" is processing the information in a holistic, nonlinear fashion, which is only transferred across the boundary in a time of disengagement from the intellect. This is frequently the way we discover or create.[9] It is Mercury who assists the artist in his discovery and travels into the unconscious to bring the results of subliminal conclusions to the conscious mind for articulation.

This creative intellectual process is reminiscent of Hermes/Mercury and his trips to Hades and back. The trips to Hades were numerous: he brought Persephone back up to her mother Demeter after her abduction by Hades; he and Athena, a frequent partner in helping, assisted Herakles in his twelfth labor by procuring the hound Cerberus of Hades, bringing him back to Eurystheus, and finally returning him to Hades; he escorted Eurydice back to Hades when Orpheus lost her for the last time to Hades.

However, as previously mentioned, the Hermes of the *Odyssey* is Hermes in all of his facets. The hero Odysseus has many characteristics of Hermes—guile, wit and luck. This "wily Odysseus" is a journeyer, too. Yes, he had left Troy and was heading home to Ithaka, *but* the ostensible three-week return trip took ten years and numerous unexpected turns and adventures. Essentially, Odysseus left the known world of successful heroism and entered a supernatural realm of monsters, witches and enchanted scenarios. Hermes acts as a Trickster, Teacher and Psychopompos (Theos) in the epic, thus fulfilling his nature in its entirety.

Hermes is equally present as a helper; again the surprise factor is an ingredient. As a messenger of the gods, Hermes will often appear as a last resort or a last retort! Hermes tells Odysseus how to counter the sorceress Kirke's charms and gives him the antidote, the moly root, which he drinks and thus escapes being turned into a swine like his crewmen. Zeus sends Hermes to Ogygia where Odysseus is dallying with Kalypso, the beautiful goddess who promises him immortality and eternal youth if he will only stay with her. Hermes warns Kalypso that Zeus wants Odysseus to continue on his way and that she should not detain him any longer. He is called "Hermes the Wayfinder" in this episode. He also appears at the opening of the last book of the *Odyssey* when he leads the slaughtered suitors' ghosts away:

> Meanwhile the suitors' ghosts were called away
> by Hermes of Kyllene, bearing the golden wand
> with which he charms the eyes of men or wakens
> whom he wills.
>   He waved them on, all squeaking
> as bats will in a cavern's underworld,
> all flitting, flitting criss-cross in the dark
> if one falls and the rock-hung chain is broken.
> So with faint cries the shades trailed after Hermes,
> pure Deliverer.[10]

I think the key word in the above quotation is *pure*. This denotes the absolute neutrality of Hermes/Mercury—the clean, nonpartisan mediator, mere messenger of the gods, guileless guide of souls.

TRICKSTER: The nature of the trickster and the astrological Mercury

The nature of Mercury, as we have seen, is essentially not only dualistic but polymorphic as well. One of his epithets is *stropheus*, the "socket" upon which things like doors, joints, etc., revolve or turn in all directions. This implies a particular kind of versatility, a type of protean character that can turn on a dime, that can metamorphose in an instant, that will adapt to any given situation at any particular time. He is not unlike the Roman god Janus who was positioned at the gates of a city to watch for arrivals and departures, guarding both simultaneously.

As a god of accidental happenings, Mercury is underestimated by traditional astrology. His role as the communicator and the educator is not always via conventional means. As mentioned previously, his affinity with Hades of the underworld sheds an interesting light on the function of Mercury in bringing up the contents of the unconscious at surprising times, hence his association with the trickster figure. The trickster figure is not deliberately or necessarily cruel. Carl Jung has pointed out the subtlety and variety within the motifs of trickster figures using ". . . the alchemical figure of Mercurius . . . his fondness for sly jokes and malicious pranks, his powers as a shape-shifter, his dual nature, half animal, half divine, his exposure to all kinds of tortures, and—last but not least—his approximation to the figure of a savior."[11] He then continues on to say that these trickster figures manage to ". . . achieve through their stupidity what others fail to accomplish with their best efforts."[12]

How fitting for the astrological Mercury! It is certain that Carl Jung did not have the transit of Mercury retrograde in mind when he wrote those words, but he did understand how these motifs arise spontaneously from the unconcious of an individual in particular relation to his or her own life or consciousness. As a messenger (*angelos*), he brings to our conscious mind unevolved information stored deep in the wellspring of the unconscious, often delivering his messages in a surprise form.

> One can see this best of all from the fact that the trickster motif does not crop up only in its mythical form but appears just as naively and authentically in the unsuspecting modern man—whenever, in fact, he feels himself at the mercy of annoying "accidents" which thwart his will and his actions with apparently malicious intent. He then speaks of "hoodoos" and "jinxes" or of the "mischievousness of the object." Here the trickster is represented by counter-tendencies in the unconscious, and in certain cases by a sort of second personality of a peurile and inferior character, not unlike the personalities who announce themselves at spiritualistic seances and cause all those ineffably childish phenomena so typical of poltergeists.[13]

This "second personality" suggests that the phenomenon of "channeling entities" is in fact a function of Mercury bringing to consciousness a variety of extant personalities that lie, undeveloped and unknown, in the unconscious of the individual. Mercury's role in the surfacing of this information that is "channeled" is paramount, and the individuals who lay claim to channeled entities are highly susceptible to the trickster function. It must be emphasized that this is not an "evil" source; it is without value attachment. It is their personal access to the collective unconscious as seen through the "eyes" of their personal unconscious. Information that is considered to be channeled may or may not have value, but it must be looked at for potential negative trickster energy. Conversely, it may have the healing function available to it, for as indicated previously, the trickster can appear as a savior.

Also, it must be clarified that sometimes the trickster is serendipitous. The finding of a lost article at an unlikely time, the emergence of a piece of information that completes an inquiry, the synchronistic experience, or the eventual finding of your keys in your bag after a frustrating search throughout the home—these fairly insignificant events are the more playful and harmless pranks of the trickster at work.

More serious is the shaman energy, which is also trickster energy. The wounded healer is a fine example as it is necessary for the shaman to experience in order to heal. The very aspect of healing comes from knowing, and knowing is not always conscious. One must actually incorporate the disease to expel it, and this is not always successfully accomplished while attempting psychological or somatic healing. Hence, the healer, the psychoanalyst, the astrologer and such are particularly susceptible to the dangers of trickster energy. This is not to say that Mercury retrograde is *the* signature of the trickster/healer, but it is to say that Mercury is not to be controlled by the conscious mind. When we think we are smugly in control, we are most likely to experience the trickster in all his magnificent glory.

TEACHER: The transit of Mercury retrograde—bringer of awareness

In his book *Synchronicity*, David Peat introduces a simple, yet undeniably profound, concept regarding the twofold aspect of perception which illustrates the attitudes of Mercury direct and Mercury retrograde. He speaks of a "selfless place" in which there is a kind of "full void," which Jung called the *pleroma*, where the seeds of all origins reside.

He continues by distinguishing **awareness** from **attention**. Basically, he defines *awareness* as a state in which the self is undifferentiated from the environment—there is no separation between the observer and the observed. This state is essentially a divine state of unconsciousness. *Attention* is described as acute separation resulting in definitive focusing on details that give rise to conscious participation and relationship to the environment. He states: "While awareness without attention gives rise to an overall sense of meaning, it cannot provide a differentiated understanding of the details of particular explicate [i.e. external] objects and their behavior. On the other hand, attention without awareness would consist of isolated, explicate forms without any sense of their overall context or meaning."[14]

This is a rather pedantic way of saying that we need both a divine and a profane state of being to wholly appreciate our nature and its relationships. The cycle of Mercury as receiver and disseminator clearly supports this. I perceive the Mercury **direct** phase as the **cycle of attention** and the Mercury **retrograde** phase as the **cycle of awareness**. The natural rhythm of the entire cycle allows for both to be incorporated into our lives and provides us with a graphic outline of the timing for creative use of both immersion and participation in our world.

The most unfortunate aspect of the transit of Mercury retrograde lies not in the nature of the symbol itself but in our facility to accept it as a **teaching device**. It is most common for us to blame it on fate or external circumstance when things apparently go wrong. We usually think that the conscious mind should be in control; this is a fallacious and dangerous idea because it so often ends in disaster. If we are to use the astrological model in all its potential, then we must listen to what it says. If it is saying that Mercury is retrograde, then it is telling us that something important is calling for awareness and that something will emerge from the unconscious through the agency of Mercury. It is in the retrograde phase of Mercury's cycle that we discover that life, like art, is discovery, not design. "The disastrous idea that everything comes to the human psyche from outside and that it is born *a tabula rasa* is responsible for the erroneous belief that under normal circumstances the individual is in perfect order."[15]

So, why do we still invoke Murphy's Law when Mercury is retrograde? Why do we insist that all will fall apart and then be magically righted when Mercury returns to its direct motion? I suspect that we are not consciously conditioned to the cyclic adjustment that is necessary to alternate from an immersed consciousness to a participating one. Otherwise we might not need an excuse for the emergence of spontaneous information that has all the potential for correcting our own willful conscious mind. Quite frankly, I believe that the emergence of this mercurial information is a positive step forward in civilizing certain aspects of our psyche, one of which is the shadow function. The trickster has all the earmarks of the shadow or umbra that stands behind the self and the persona, and if the "presentation" of personality does not ring true or denies fullness of expression of the whole self, then often the shadow disguises itself as an event or an external circumstance which forces the individual to come to terms with the more primitive undeveloped side of him- or herself. All this takes on particularly appropriate shape that is peculiarly recognizable since it conforms perfectly to the person and his or her needs in development. In a sense, Mercury will assist the shadow function in moving to the foreground in order for fuller expression and hopeful development of repressed unconscious material.

To illustrate this, the Greek concept of Hades, where all the souls went after death, was a place where one went exactly as one was at the time of death. Indeed, one took to

Hades the sum and total of one's life, including the latest personal concerns, for all eternity. In this way it would seem that we don't really *improve* anything in the unconscious; we don't really correct any situation until it is brought to consciousness for repair. Once we achieve awareness, we need to give it some attention. Thus Mercury acts as an agent for recollection, for *anamnesis,* and for the curing of the soul through illumination. So as Mercury travels to and from Hades (the unconscious), he brings to light all our primitive undeveloped aspects for correction. This is to say that any information, event, fact or awareness that Mercury brings up during the retrograde cycle is completely within character and totally relevant to the needs of the individual. In the case of the generic view, this awareness is also a collective awareness. In this way, Mercury acts as a civilizing agent.

THE CYCLES OF MERCURY RETROGRADE

The Nature Of the Cycle

When interpreting Mercury in the horoscope, keep in mind that the process being defined is multifaceted. We are analyzing not only the ability to receive information but also the ways that information is processed. Mercury represents the human mind's capacity to symbolize reality and to translate symbols into reality. The Sun is our symbol for the self, and it is our reality as well as our reference for all life force. The regularity of sunrise and sunset, the apparent seasonal changes and the measurement of time and space are all a result of our observation of the Sun. In the same manner, the direct and retrograde phases of Mercury are our geocentric references for the mind as it faces inner questions about outer challenges.

Mercury shows the ability to formulate and articulate

ideas that originate in the abstract. It represents the use of words as symbols of what is seen, touched, smelled, heard or tasted; in other words, it represents the translation of gross sensory perceptions into concepts. As the planet of communication, Mercury functions as the "teller of the tale" and relates the inner perceptions to another individual's Mercury, who then becomes the "hearer of the tale." John Lilly says communication is ". . . the creation of information in one mind by means of signals from another mind. The second mind acknowledges the reception of the signals and the formation of the information by feeding back other signals to the first mind, which then creates new information."[16] Much can be lost in the translation!

The retrogradation of a planet traditionally turns the world upside down. Astrologers are fond of invoking this phenomenon particularly when that planet is Mercury. This natural purgative is one way that we can come to terms with the fascination with our dark side. The lessons that are learned from the transit of Mercury retrograde concern several levels, but for the sake of simplicity and an astrological guideline, let's say that they are dual. On one level, we have the generic trends where the whole world is experiencing Mercury retrograde by *element*; on the second or personal level, the individual is experiencing Mercury retrograde by element in his or her *horoscope*, which affects the series of houses in the chart that are occupied by the signs of the particular element. In the table (Figure 2), you will notice that there are extended periods of time when Mercury will be retrograde in a certain element. It is fascinating to note that this table reveals the peculiar trait of Mercury's *apparent forward motion* through the zodiac while it gradually *slips back through the elements* in a precessional manner. This will be explained more fully later.

When Mercury is direct, as it is most of the time, the mind is in operation on a very functional level. There is little time for retrospection, and energy is directed into productive action. Our contemplative side is on hold. The period when Mercury is retrograde gives rise to issues that have lain dormant for the prior three months. This is the time when much of the unconscious information that has been absorbed and stored will begin to surface in a fashion specific to our needs.

The retrogradation of Mercury is our instinctive "down time" and is associated with *re*doing, *re*thinking, *re*organizing, *re*associating; anything that can be prefaced with *re* will define this rest period. It is as natural as sleep is to waking. Imagine the state our minds would be in if we didn't recognize the need for unconsciousness and dream time. If we ignored the signals for sleep, within a matter of days the unconscious and the conscious would mingle and cause no end of confusion and difficulty in discerning the real from the imagined. Mercury is the guide during the journey we take from "awake" to "asleep," from consciousness to unconsciousness and back again. The Mercury retrograde cycle reflects the natural rhythm of the spaces between here and there, the liminal space of the journeyer on the way to discovery.

Just as we recognize days, years, seasons, time zones, clocks and all regulatory mechanisms, so we should recognize the ordering mechanism of Mercury retrograde. Natural states of rest are to our advantage. To be able to predict and utilize these states is an infinite aid to greater consciousness. The holistic viewpoint in astrology is very sensible . . . if a system is reflected in many other systems, it should be used as a tool for development and not ignored. It is through this approach that an expanded psychology helps us in a greater sense of wholeness and stimulates a more active emergence of latent or suppressed characteristics for conscious development.

Out of the need to eliminate chaos, we have organized

and classified our lives to a minute degree. The prison of culture, the oppression of civilization, has essentially de-sacralized the world, and we are now experiencing the extremes of the separation of Nature from culture. This is an age-old dichotomy, but the disenchantment we are experiencing today has manifested in a sense of extreme alienation. I believe astrology reconnects Nature with culture by including a cosmic paradigm for earthly activity. Recognizing and incorporating astrological cycles allows us to reengage our individual timing apparatus in accordance with a macrocosmic system, reclaiming power that has been subordinate to the organized, external world timing. We now acknowledge both *awareness* and *attention.* The use of Mercury retrograde cycles in the horoscope reconnects us with our natural rhythms. These periods offer an opportunity to align our inner clock with the cosmic rhythm.

Some very revealing indications in the astronomical cycle of Mercury retrograde are shown in Figure 1 (page 98).

Mercury's stations always occur when it is farthest from the Sun in longitude, either in the east or the west. When it appears stationary, it is either traveling toward or directly away from Earth in its orbit.

When Mercury is at its *greatest eastern elongation* (**Epimetheus**), it appears in the sky as the evening star and is at its stationary **retrograde** point. It is heading toward Earth in its orbit, symbolically "bringing home the knowledge of experience." The Epimethean phases demand careful consideration and retrospection.

When Mercury is at its *greatest western elongation* (**Prometheus**), it stations and begins **direct** motion, rising ahead of the Sun and moving away from the Earth in its orbit. The Promethean phases of the cycle (from inferior conjunction to superior conjunction) signal the time when risk and

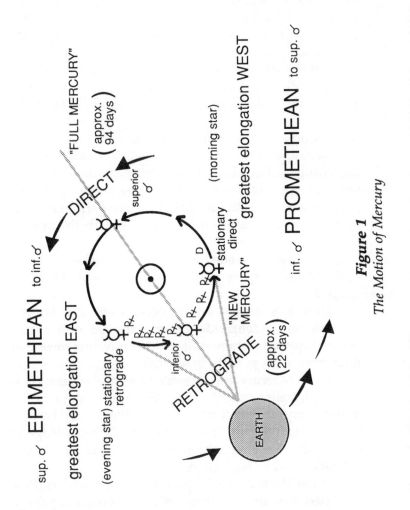

Figure 1
The Motion of Mercury

adventure are the primary motivating forces. The symbol of mind is as far from the symbol of reality as it can be . . . this is especially important in understanding the process of Mercury retrograde. At this time Mercury doesn't remain visible for long and usually reaches its greatest eastern elongation (evening star) a week or so *prior* to its ret-rogradation. In contrast, the greatest western elongation of Mercury (morning star) occurs a week or so *after* its di-rect station.

Both main cycles of Mercury's orbit as seen from Earth have a direct and retrograde period. Mercury phases as seen from Earth are: a new and waxing phase from the inferior (retrograde) conjunction to the station in the west turning direct, and the full or waning phase after superior conjunction (direct) back to the retrograde station in the east. We only see Mercury in crescent phases as it appears to swing behind back and forth across the Sun. Its visibility occurs at these elongation points; we can only comprehend Mercury when it is distant from the Sun. In other words, distance equals perspective.

The Epimethean phase of Mercury is a time of reaping results. In contrast, the Promethean phase of the cycle is symbolized by the urgency to move away from introspec-tion and experiment, often heedlessly, using only inner guidelines.

Cycles of Awareness for Long-Range Planning

Mercury Through the Elements

Approximately every four months, Mercury stations and turns retrograde for about 22 days. The retrograde occurs in consecutive zodiacal order as the calendar year progresses, yet the overall cycle indicates a subtle sub-cycle of a gradual precession of Mercury *backwards through the*

Mercury Retrograde Cycles

Year	Date	Sign	Element
'73	Mar 4	28° ♓	Water
'73	July 6	3° ♌	Fire
'73	Oct. 30	26° ♏	Water
'74	Feb. 15	12° ♓	Water
'74	June 17	13° ♋	Water
'74	Oct. 13	10° ♏	Water
'75	Jan. 30	25° ♒	Air
'75	May 29	23° ♊	Air
'75	Sept. 26	24° ♎	Air
'76	Jan. 14	9° ♒	Air
'76	May 9	4° ♊	Air
'76	Sept. 8	8° ♎	Air
'76	Dec. 28	23° ♑	Earth
'77	April 20	14° ♉	Earth
'77	Aug. 22	21° ♍	Earth
'77	Dec. 12	7° ♑	Earth
'78	April 1	26° ♈	Fire
'78	Aug. 4	3° ♍	Earth
'78	Nov. 26	21° ♐	Fire
'79	March 15	8° ♈	Fire
'79	July 17	14° ♌	Fire
'79	Nov. 8	6° ♐	Fire
'80	Feb. 26	21° ♓	Water
'80	June 28	25° ♋	Water
'80	Oct. 23	20° ♏	Water
'81	Feb. 8	5° ♓	Water
'81	June 9	5° ♋	Water
'81	Oct. 5	4° ♏	Water
'82	Jan. 23	18° ♒	Air
'82	May 21	15° ♊	Air
'82	Sept. 19	17° ♎	Air
'83	Jan. 7	2° ♒	Air
'83	May 1	25° ♉	Earth
'83	Sept. 2	1° ♎	Air
'83	Dec. 22	16° ♑	Earth
'84	April 11	6° ♉	Earth
'84	Aug. 14	13° ♍	Earth
'84	Dec. 5	1° ♑	Earth
'85	March 24	18° ♈	Fire
'85	July 28	25° ♌	Fire
'85	Nov. 18	15° ♐	Fire
'86	March 7	1° ♈	Fire
'86	July 9	6° ♌	Fire

A full cycle of all the elements as seen in precession through the zodiac.

Notice that Mercury goes retrograde three times every 12 months.

Figure 2

Year	Date	Sign	Ele.
'86	Nov. 2	29° ♏	Water
'87	Feb. 18	14° ♓	Water
'87	June 21	17° ♋	Water
'87	Oct. 16	13° ♏	Water
'88	Feb. 2	28° ♒	Air
'88	May 31	27° ♊	Air
'88	Sept. 28	27° ♎	Air
'89	Jan. 16	12° ♒	Air
'89	May 12	7° ♊	Air
'89	Sept. 11	10° ♎	Air
'89	Dec. 30	26° ♑	Earth
'90	April 23	17° ♉	Earth
'90	Aug. 25	23° ♍	Earth
'90	Dec. 14	10° ♑	Earth
'91	April 4	29° ♈	Fire
'91	Aug. 7	6° ♍	Earth
'91	Nov. 28	24° ♐	Fire
'92	March 16	11° ♈	Fire
'92	July 20	17° ♌	Fire
'92	Nov. 11	8° ♐	Fire
'93	Feb. 27	24° ♓	Water
'93	July 1	28° ♋	Water
'93	Oct. 25	22° ♏	Water
'94	Feb. 11	7° ♓	Water
'94	June 12	8° ♋	Water
'94	Oct. 9	6° ♏	Water
'95	Jan. 26	4° ♒	Air
'95	May 24	18° ♊	Air
'95	Sept. 22	20° ♎	Air
'96	Jan. 9	5° ♒	Air
'96	May 3	28° ♉	Earth
'96	Sept. 4	3° ♎	Air
'96	Dec. 23	19° ♑	Earth
'97	April 15	9° ♉	Earth
'97	Aug. 17	16° ♍	Earth
'97	Dec. 7	3° ♑	Earth
'98	March 27	21° ♈	Fire
'98	July 31	28° ♌	Fire
'98	Nov. 21	17° ♐	Fire

Approximately every six years this triangulation cycle returns.

Year	Date	Sign	Ele.
'99	March 10	4° ♈	Fire
'99	July 12	9° ♌	Fire
'99	Nov. 5	2° ♐	Fire
2000 A.D.			
'00	Feb. 21	17° ♓	Water
'00	June 23	20° ♋	Water
'00	Oct. 18	16° ♏	Water
'01	Feb. 4	0° ♓	Water
'01	June 4	29° ♊	Air
'01	Oct. 1	29° ♎	Air
'02	Jan. 18	14° ♒	Air
'02	May 15	10° ♊	Air
'02	Oct. 1	0° ♎	Air
'03	Jan. 2	28° ♑	Earth
'03	April 26	20° ♉	Earth
'03	Aug. 28	26° ♍	Earth
'03	Dec. 17	12° ♑	Earth
'04	April 6	2° ♉	Earth
'04	Aug. 10	9° ♍	Earth
'04	Dec. 1	26° ♐	Fire
'05	March 20	14° ♌	Fire
'05	July 23	20° ♈	Fire
'05	Nov. 14	11° ♐	Fire

elements. See Figure 2. This occurs because Mercury stations in each of the signs at an earlier degree each time and gradually drops back into the prior element. Though the elements progress from Fire to Earth to Air to Water in the natural order of evolution, the successive retrogradation cycles accent those elements in reverse order.

There are discrepancies in that regularity. In 1976-77 the Earth trigon was hit only once. Mercury made a brief return to that element as if something may have been undone and needed consideration. This is due to the perturbations of Mercury's orbit and the eccentricities from the proximity of Earth and Mercury to the Sun at different times.

When referring to Table 2 for long-range planning or for increasing your awareness of what is brewing on unconscious levels, you should first note that Mercury's retrograde pattern will emphasize a particular trigon in your horoscope. For instance, over a period of 20 months between February 1988 and September 1989, Mercury's retrograde cycle emphasizes the Air trigon. Houses occupied by the Air signs represent areas in your life that need repeated reflection at that time. Mercury activates those houses over a period of almost two years, insuring attention to the affairs of those houses. Being aware of this cycle offers the advantage of knowing where to concentrate introspection.

The entire cycle of elemental focus is repeated approximately every six or seven years. For example, the Water trigon was highlighted in 1973-74, then again in 1980-81 and so on.

The entire planet experiences retrogradation according to the element, but you as an individual bring it into personal focus through the lens of your own chart, refining the experience within the houses being transited.

Mercury represents the teacher. Within the subtle movements of the retrograde cycle, much can be learned, journeying from the known into the place of the unknown, where you may do battle with forces foreign to you. It is in this threshold place that the wisdom of the unconscious surfaces, teaching from the most intelligent source, the intuition. When you struggle against the inevitable and unavoidable timing of Mercury, you are fighting the *tao* of existence. Understanding the principles of transiting Mercury retrograde as it moves through the elements will help maximize your potential and conformation to natural rhythms. These rhythms are best expressed in question form. As each element in your horoscope is highlighted, a question arises that can act as a meditation guide.

WATER: What is the emotional quality of my life?

Mercury retrograde in Water signs gives an opportunity to rethink old habit patterns and emotional responses. The desire to retreat is strongest when the Water element is being emphasized. During this cycle, you will have three to six opportunities to hone in on your reflex responses. This is the best time to analyze patterns based on inherited psychological traits. It may be necessary to hold back from overreacting to moods, feelings and free-floating anxiety. Subliminal messages in your environment may need attention; it is time to learn more about your psychological needs and their physiological manifestations.

Dream analysis and journal writing are particularly effective at this time. By paying close attention to the symbols that arise spontaneously from your unconscious, you will be alerted to issues that remain unresolved. Water represents the greatest depths and the stagnant ponds of our most sensitive, private areas. Your emotional needs in connection with others may require some revisioning. Only through time spent alone can you unfold the complex web that has become your habit in relationships.

Since Mercury in the Water signs denotes the feeling

function, if you have been ignoring it, it will now require your attention. Many feelings will arise demanding equal time because the previous retrograde cycle in Fire did not allow for much analysis of emotion.

It is wise to be candid with all your associates at this time because the tendency is to escape from responsibilities; if not dealt with now, they will resurface later. Old friends, lovers and people from the past will appear to remind you of who you used to be. Thus, this is a great time for self-evaluation. Emotional and spiritual growth become pressing issues and can come disguised as practical matters even though the source is deep within you and related to the submerged past. When Mercury turns direct, you may leave these issues behind for a few months, but keep in mind that any unfinished business can resurface three months hence.

AIR: How shall I reorder my relationships?

This can be one of the most amusing and frustrating retrograde Mercury cycles. The thinking function is associated with Air and the next 18 to 24 months will give you plenty of opportunities to understand the meaning of the relationships in your life. You may find yourself absorbed in the affairs of the houses with Air signs on the cusps.

Mercury in Air signs is not particularly emotional, so this cycle concentrates instead on the patterns you employ in relationships. It is important to pay close attention to your associations with others. This is the time when acute dissatisfaction within your social and personal milieu can arise. Over the last three months your relationships may have been confused. Much unconscious stress may be resolved by airing old problems and working out difficulties with friends, family or associates.

Minor irritations may arise—unkept appointments, lost documents, faulty machinery, broken promises, well-intentioned but misleading information, and so on. These are all traditional signals to pay attention to a greater message: check your attitude toward and your use of time, assess your productivity, evaluate your goals and priorities. As Socrates said in his defense speech to the Athenian jury, "An unexamined life is not worth living."[17] There are times, however, when a thinking person doubts even this simple profundity, and the examined life can become a nightmare of doubt.

This is the worst possible time to buy machinery, cars, typewriters, computers, telephones, answering machines or anything that is normally a mechanical extension of your mind or communication network. However, it is a good time to research your needs for these mechanical appendages. When Mercury turns direct, you'll find what you need. Also, pay attention to the old warning: avoid either contractual or tacit agreements unless you are prepared to accept a change of events when Mercury turns direct.

It is better to clear the decks of complications and list long-range goals at this time. By doing so, some important messages from a more intelligent source (your unconscious) will come through. What you expect may not be what you get, but what is received is truly needed. By listening to your intuition now, you can make changes when Mercury turns direct without surprising results.

EARTH: How can I realize tangible results in my life?

Matters based on security, practical concerns regarding your surroundings and basic needs come to the fore. This is a time when you may find fault with your environment, whether home, job, country or your physical body! DO NOT move, quit your job, emigrate or spend a lot of money. DO look for new opportunities and keep tabs on possibilities that could be more satisfying for you on the ego level.

Self-criticism is often uppermost on the personal level. Critique is okay, but a shredding of ego is not. Reassessing your contacts with the world of practical reality is fine, but it is unwise to invalidate the past. Look at your assets and liabilities as if they were someone else's, researching the kind of advice that you would give others. Objectivity should be maintained in this particular cycle.

Because the Earth trigon relates to the houses pertaining to all facets of worth including money, self-esteem, working conditions, your health, and all your functions as a human being in the practical world of form, it is necessary to become aware of the deepest values of those resources. If changes need to be made in these areas, even though they are the ones with the greatest resistance to change, make those changes willingly or they will be thrust upon you.

Becoming more organized frees you up to be spontaneous. Life is full of paradoxes, and this is one of them—orderliness results in spontaneity! Organization can alleviate any guilt you may feel about not attending to the fundamental details of life. The spirit is encased in the flesh, so attend to the flesh. Not a particularly inspiring time, great accomplishments can still be made while Mercury is retrograde in Earth signs, resulting in significant practical returns. By dealing with logical issues at this time, you will find it easier to zero in on what is truly happening because your life won't be cluttered with unfinished business.

FIRE: How can my inspiration create my future?

Astrological Fire symbolism is a very psyche/soma, soul/body relationship. As the body is the vehicle for the soul, the inspired soul is the very anima for creative issue. It is the inspirational force of the Fire function that closely resembles the Jungian intuitive function. Intuition in this particular instance does not mean psychic ability, but instead addresses the capacity to see the past, the present and the future possibilities in all things. In this way you can create the future. You are made up of not only your past but also your future.

The apparent lack of direction that often accompanies a repeated transit of the Fire trigon is Mercury's way of breaking up old patterns of creative function expectations. You may often make haphazard attempts to start "something," a poor substitute for true inspiration. Angst about the future can often operate creatively. Reaching a "stuck" place in development can bring pressure to a bursting point, forcing growth and allowing the emergence of undeveloped potential. Periods of spiritual entropy alert you to a need for change in creative production.

Our cultural attitude towards play is not very healthy. Creativity and play are closely aligned. Schiller says that man is at his highest level only when he plays, when there is no conscious purpose, when the inner urge is not tempered by the controls of the "civilizing agent" of externally imposed controls. This can be very evident in the period associated with Mercury retrograde in Fire signs. The need for play, creativity and spontaneity may be preceded by a depression, and the retrogradation can provide the opportunity to descend into the awareness level of the mind, with no ego consciousness, and out of this can emerge true inspiration.

In her book *Creation Myths,* Marie L. von Franz deals extensively with this concept of play. She believes that the teleology of depression is to bring the consciousness down into the *nigredo*, the darkness of the unconscious, in order to release the creative spirit.

When Mercury is retrograde in the Fire trigon, it may indicate that you are going through a transition in creative outward direction. Relearning how to play adds a dimension of creativity to your life. Creativity does not just consist of painting, music and the various attributes of the fine arts.

It is a life style. How do you respond to crisis, for example? With anger and resistance? Or with a renewed vision and the consequent increased awareness of the ever shifting of gears? This cycle tests your ability to respond to life with spontaneous energy and enables you to make more creative changes.

On a practical level, awareness of sedentary habits can provoke a fitness urge. Psychosomatic illness may point specifically to an area of the psyche that is cramped or underactive. An artistic block may be the very symptom that indicates a change in technique or style. This Mercury position accents the need to experiment with new forms of being, new forms of thinking about yourself and new ways of relating to inspiration sources.

By assessing the affected houses, the source of your restlessness can be pinpointed. The revision of interests and creative focus over the next couple of years can drastically alter your future direction in a more appropriate way. It is the perfect time to lighten up!

MERCURY RETROGRADE THROUGH THE HOUSES

In what specific area am I undergoing reevaluation?

FIRST HOUSE: Is my persona really me?

Mercury has transited out of the 12th House where impressions were registered on the unconscious level. As it stations and turns retrograde in the 1st House, it provides you an opportunity to reevaluate your personal priorities. If it retrogrades back into the 12th House, you are being given a second chance for your unconscious mind to digest your attitudes and directions as a "personality." Further mental clarification is needed before forging ahead with renewed personal and physical vigor. Conscious intent should be focused on directing the energy into the 2nd House. When Mercury turns direct, it will move into the 2nd House, and without this reevaluation time, you would not be able to make the best of your personal resources in the future.

SECOND HOUSE: Is my self my worth?

If your actions were impulsive while Mercury transited the 1st House, this may be a questioning period. There is a very strong message to underplay ego gratification until your feelings have stabilized. The retrograde period implies the need to evaluate your resources, but do not attempt to perform an objective self-analysis. Self-criticism at this time can be more destructive than helpful. Instead take stock of your assets to see a clear picture and take the right path. When Mercury turns direct and moves into the 3rd House, it will bring a sense of new found security.

This time is for reexamining your personal finances, material assets and your attitudes toward these matters. It is not a time for speculation or wild spending but for very conservative action. Feeling unsure suggests an unconscious obligation to clear out any false personae not conducive to your personal honesty. Ignore the insecurity and concentrate on your positive assets because this is the time to reaffirm self-confidence in order to act quickly and communicate without hesitation when Mercury enters your 3rd House.

THIRD HOUSE: Am I what I think? or *Cogito ergo sum.*

Since this transit only happens a couple of times in a two-year period every six or seven years, it is a perfect time to be uncommitted, vacillating and difficult to contact. Break your old habits and allow some new input into just simply BEING. During Mercury's transit in this house, the meaning of its station is often obscure.

This transit is full of intellectual surprises; whatever you think is going to happen doesn't. To use this experience to your greatest advantage, make NO long-term commitments, either verbally or contractually. Much of the reconsideration that will preoccupy this time will be based on issues that recently arose when Mercury was transiting the 2nd House.

It is not uncommon to have serious breakdowns in communications and be forced to rethink most of your ideas. It will affect those of you in the information fields most strongly since that is where your vested interest lies. These breakdowns may work as blessings in disguise, bringing many opportunities over the next few years to completely revamp your focus on valid concepts that have all but lost their meaning.

The real purpose of this transit is to eliminate all the useless and ineffective data from your life in order to regroup and set new foundations. Struggling against this necessary mental housecleaning can only result in confusion and the traditional communication failures associated with Mercury retrograde. Ideally this is a time of no-think and nonlinear purity. Verbal communication can be problematic because symbolic images are more appropriate. The ideas that emerge from your unconscious will help you set the new foundations necessary when Mercury turns direct and heads over the IC (Imum Coeli).

FOURTH HOUSE: Is anyone home?

This is housecleaning time, especially the basement. Strong memories from the past, ghosts of old relationships, places, things and actions can haunt you. This 4th House transit may not be without emotional pain. The point is not to torture yourself about past mistakes but to develop a method of successful survival.

The Water houses are houses of memory, but they are

also houses of birth. The reclusive tendencies that predominate with this transit can be healthy because it brings an opportunity to regroup and heal from the heedless activity of the last three months . . . it is truly a time for rebirthing. The inherent psychological traits that run through the family may need to be transformed through your psyche. Although not necessarily comfortable, this housecleaning insures that you are not carrying someone else's load. It is the perfect time to retreat, sort out domestic issues that have been suppressed, and spend time in soul-searching. Long-disregarded matters about your immediate environs can be cleared away in preparation for the emergence of Mercury into your 5th House.

Any unfinished emotional business will resurface in about three months when Mercury stations in the next sign. Even so, this is the time that the roots of your existence need securing along with a reevaluation of just what home means to you. It may mean reconciling your early home environment patterning with new home environment realities.

FIFTH HOUSE: Am I having fun yet?
The entire concept around recreation needs to be examined when Mercury stations and turns retrograde in your 5th House. You need to focus on your creative powers and sources for inspiration—the archetypes that are the very heart of your being. If you are stifled/stifling, limited/limiting or bored/boring, your heart may be constricted. Learn to understand play in the most boisterous way.

What greater investment can you make than in yourself? Because this house is so intimately tied in with solar symbolism, it functions as a house of life and death. Examine just what your investments in love and creativity have produced. Do you give too much? Are your expectations not great enough? Do you feel that there is some repression seriously affecting your capacity for giving and receiving love? These are all pertinent questions for research now.

This introspection into matters of the heart may help loosen any ego knots. Try to lighten up on your personal expectations and goals. The new creative impulse that is trying to surface needs fewer restrictions. Trying to force yourself into a conventional mold could result in missing a significant unconscious message. Listen to your heart, but be prepared for a change of heart. Listen to the child within, nurture that child and discover what it wants from you the adult. Any unhappiness or serious flaw in your creativity and productiveness can result in illness when Mercury enters the 6th House. Whatever the psyche cannot process becomes somatic.

SIXTH HOUSE: Is my body doing what it wants?

This is a fantastic time to reevaluate your usefulness within your job, but it is probably the worst time to leave a position. Following Mercury's passage through the 5th House, you may be overreacting to sudden down-to-Earth demands being made upon you. Because the 6th House is the polarity of the 12th, the psyche/soma balance, if your body is not doing what your psyche wants, it will rebel. We now recognize the "illness as metaphor" doctrine as being a literal condition. When Mercury is retrograde in your 6th House, check out your body and its messages.

For about a month, there will be attention focused on systems from your bodily to your organization skills; systems of thought and management will undergo spontaneous overhaul. By attending to the minutiae of your life, you will be attending to your health as well. Health habits may cause physical rebellion because your body, as the vehicle for your soul, seeks balance. Sleep patterns may change; more dream time may be needed to compensate for the tension of conscious and stressful review that is common when the 6th House is magnified.

Rethink your activity program and research new work habits as Mercury moves into your 7th House. If you have developed greater efficiency, you will have more time for the joys of relating.

SEVENTH HOUSE: Do I see my lover in myself?
Mercury here suggests the preparation for externalizing the symbols of relatedness in your life. Sharing concepts will undergo a review and old perspectives in relationships are rehashed in order to establish a firm base for one-to-one commitments. It is as if the 7th House represents a trial run of the balance between you and the outside world.

Feedback becomes especially significant during this period because opinions and viewpoints of others have great impact on you. There has been an unconscious buildup of impressions (both *by* you and *of* you) which need to be aired. This is an opportunity to achieve depth in intimacy by looking into the mirror of relationship. This mirror may be somewhat dark during the retrograde period because of the "loosening" effect. You may not easily articulate your deep feelings . . . let them develop in silence. During this retrograde period, *vis-à-vis* relationships should only be reviewed. These feelings will emerge in a balanced way when Mercury turns direct.

Because of the legal implications of the 7th House and because it governs any person who represents you, this is usually a particularly poor time for litigation. When Mercury moves forward into the 8th House, all unresolved matters of an interpersonal nature will have to undergo analysis of the deepest kind.

EIGHTH HOUSE: What is the big mystery?
This is a "high risk" house. I have always been fascinated (at least for the last 20-odd years) by the amalgama-

tion of sex, death and taxes. Sex is taxing, and it should involve *le petit mort* if it is to be transcendant and successful as an act of creation; there is always a "tax" when one merges oneself with another; death is the final tax on life itself. If astrology is anything, it is mysterious in this way.

During the retrograde in the house of mystery, you may be absorbed in trying to find meaning in the most obscure symbol of truth. The layers of your mind can unfold and bring to the surface long buried fears and dreams. Everything has an ending; this may well coincide with the end of a cycle for you. Ghostly images in dreams and old fears that do surface are simply signals to do some deep analysis. Do not avoid confrontation with these old fears.

There is often a strong need to undergo a death of some type, either ritually or symbolically. Usually it is an "ego death," a letting go of an anachronistic persona or vested interest in an image. If you have money tied up with others, it is an excellent time to review those partnerships. In fact, a review of all investments of time, love or money is in order. It is the perfect moment to let unviable and risky ventures die a natural death. This is a very poor time to throw your lot in with others since the implications and motivations will not be clear; when Mercury turns direct, consider mergers.

Psychotherapy sessions can be rewarding as they offer an opportunity to view some of the dank and unaired components of your psyche in order to overcome any resistance to psychological growth. Delve into your mind in great depth to relieve fears and compulsions and to gain greater awareness of your unconscious motivations in life.

NINTH HOUSE: Did my karma run over your dogma?

This transit often finds your faith or belief wavering, and your belief systems may need a revision of some kind. Reassessment of your ideas and ideology should be a vital part of your spiritual growth. A sudden awakening or questioning of these values signals a healthy state of mind. Undoubtedly, you should reconsider perspectives on life; part of the preparation for enacting your beliefs in the world is a philosophical overhaul.

This overhaul frequently involves your attitudes toward education, and you may rethink its advantages and disadvantages. You may feel that any gaps in your academic history are impeding the development of your potential. If so, examine the possibility of furthering your schooling. On the other hand, feeling that a lack of travel has limited your horizons, now is a good time to spread out more, to listen to the inner voice of your higher mind and to disregard the doctrines of previous days. All that is substantial and valuable for your future can remain, but a severe paring of nonessential beliefs is necessary.

These beliefs will be tested in the 10th House where you must be prepared to act upon and uphold your personal ethics.

TENTH HOUSE: Is it lonely at the top?

It isn't really lonely at the top; the person who started that rumor just didn't want anyone else to arrive there and compete! This retrograde period is a competition of mind over matter. The struggle to maintain status and image at all costs can become tiresome and wasteful. If you find this a difficult time to gain ground, take a less aggressive tack.

This 10th House transit begins a new cycle of social obligations and awareness. What used to be attractive on the social or material plane may seem to be out of control, but it is only a reflection of the inner need to let go of old realities or the expected rewards may go unreceived, or worse, unnoticed.

If you lose your job during this period (and it happens surprisingly often), it may be a blessing in disguise. Have you been clinging to outmoded security patterns and allowing your unconscious to take over and externalize itself in the form of social rejection? Have you been looking in the wrong place for your worldly or status returns? If so, move on.

Acting against your professed beliefs in the recent past may have caused you to incur a "karmic kickback." It is best to reorganize work habits and social life in order to understand your true priorities now. Let the important issues rise to the surface naturally, without force or aggression, and you will find that your attitudes toward success will be remarkably different by the time this transit has been absorbed.

ELEVENTH HOUSE: How can I win friends and influence people?

Feeling insecure about your connections to humanity is often a part of this transit. Probably you are too preoccupied with what *seems to be* rather than what *really is*. Because the 11th is the house of hopes and wishes as well as "just deserts," your life expectations can undergo examination. Your needs and hopes increase proportionately to your relationship output. It is a good time to test material on small groups before heading out into the world with great expectations.

Introversion is natural now and it is advisable to flow with that urge. Mercury's unconscious message is: clear up any unfinished social and occupational business that stands in the way of gaining ground in the immediate future. When Mercury turns direct, new horizons become apparent. Its entry into the 12th House carries with it the results of past efforts, so it is advisable to be very clear about your obligations to others. Phoney relationships and false images (especially in the realm of superficial social conduct) may lead to self-undoing as Mercury moves into the 12th House.

This retrograde period should include quiet time and goal setting in order to assure optimum rewards in achieving life objectives. Include what you expect from friends as well as how much you can offer them. By being honest, you can avoid fantasy situations and dreadful disappointments when others don't do what you want.

TWELFTH HOUSE: Am I the dream or the dreamer?

Nothing is as it seems to be when Mercury turns retrograde in the 12th House. There is a romance to life, a mysterious ambience that allows the unconscious mind to function at an observable level. Your dream life is particularly revealing, and this is the best possible time to do dream work and journal keeping. Writing might reveal some hidden patterns to your thinking, allowing a healthy outflow of a steady stream of consciousness. Hypnotherapy or regression work can be rewarding. This is the most reserved time for you in a six-year period since you are in a natural state of unconscious contemplation.

Sensory perceptions are of great value in interpreting symbols now; however, do not engage the intellect too readily. Simplify and purify. Heighten your state of awareness. Avoid overinterpretation and confusion. This is not the time to intellectualize . . . it could manifest as paranoia. You must be careful not to let spillover emotion and unresolved conflicts result in confrontational experiences. This is a time to go on a retreat, to isolate yourself, to act out ritual so you can reengage with your unconscious impulses and become more at one with Nature as Mercury moves into your 1st House.

The high degree of sensitivity inherent with any 12th House transit is magnified when Mercury the Messenger is there. Less protected from the influences of other people's psychic fields, you may be susceptible to overstimulation. The boundary between the self and others is not so very clear during this period; therefore, it is healthy to be aware that even though spiritually we *are* all One, we are also singular and unique and need a separate identity.

Footnotes

1. Franz Cumont, *Astrology and Religion Among the Greeks and Romans.* Dover Publications, 1960. This little book should be read in its entirety for a capsule of the history of astrology as seen from the world view of a classicist with good knowledge but little empathy for the current (or ancient) practice of astrology.

2. *Classical Mythology.* "The Homeric Hymns. The Homeric Hymn to Hermes: Number four." Translated by Morford and Lenardon. Longman Press, 1971, pp. 179-92. (There are many translations of the Homeric Hymns, but one of the more popular and poetic is by Charles Boer.)

3. *Ibid.*

4. *Ibid.*

5. *Ibid.*

6. Homer, *Iliad.* 24.344 ff. Translated by R. Lattimore. University of Chicago Press, 1951.

7. *Ibid.*

8. Karl Kerenyi, *Hermes: Guide of Souls.* Spring Pubs., 1986, p. 88.

9. Arthur Koestler, *The Act of Creation,* Macmillan, 1967.

10. Homer, *Odyssey.* 23.1 ff. Translated by R. Fitzgerald. Anchor Books, 1963.

11. *Collected Works of C. G. Jung: The Archetypes & the Collective Unconscious.* No. 9, Pt. 1, 2nd ed. "On the Psychology of the Trickster Figure." Ed. Gerhard Adler, et al. Translated by R.F.C. Hull. Bollingen Series, Princeton University Press, 1968, para. 456.

12. *Ibid.,* para. 469.

13. *Ibid.,* para. 469.

14. F. David Peat, *Synchronicity.* Chapter B, Bantam Books, 1987, pp. 222-24 in particular.

15. *Ibid.* para. 479.

16. John Lilly, *Communication Between Man and Dolphin.* Crown Publications, 1978, p. 54.

17. Plato, *Apology.* 38A. Translated by W. H. D. Rouse. Mentor, 1956.

Robert Glasscock

Robert Glasscock has been one of the most prolific astrologers on the West Coast since 1966. In addition to personal and tape-recorded consultations for clients from more than 60 countries, he has written for leading astrological publications and conducted hundreds of workshops and classes in Los Angeles, San Francisco and San Diego.

For a number of years he published over 250,000 words a year in the Annual Digest and monthly Sun-sign columns of *American Astrology*, his weekly column for the entertainment newspaper *Drama-Logue*, and his lunations forecasts for *Aspects* magazine.

In the early 1980s he focused on screenwriting.

He's written industrial/commercial films for corporate clients such as GTE, Trainex, and the 1984 Olympics Committee. He was on the staff of NBC's *Alfred Hitchcock Presents* and has written films for TriStar, Paramount, and network and cable television.

He continues to teach and consult whenever possible, though films now consume most of his time. "My joy is knowing I've sparked a lot of students and clients who've gone on to become excellent professional and amateur astrologers."

VENUS

There is a temptation to shortchange Venus in astrology. Venus is regarded as the planetary symbol for Love and Art. The "major" planets—Jupiter through Pluto—seem to carry much more weight and significance than the "Lesser Benefic" because they stay longer in a sign or house by transit.

But nothing is more important than understanding Venus in the chart—natal, progressed, solar arc or transiting. Venus alone shows what one *loves* or *values* (one's innate value system in the birth chart and one's value system at the moment in progressions and solar arcs) and how one *relates* to others. *One*, as opposed to the many, the group or the collective. Venus represents a *personal* archetype; the major planets, more social or collective archetypes.

ARCHETYPES AND PHYSICAL REALITY

Archetypes are not man-made ideas, not concepts coined by Carl Jung. They're living entities that pre-exist physical life. If that sounds far-fetched, please read Dr. Anthony Stevens' *Archetypes: A Natural History of the Self* (Quill, 1983) in which this remarkable British psychiatrist states what astrologers and metaphysicians have realized for a long time—archetypes are conscious living entities. According to Dr. Stevens and other scientists, speaking, walking, health, fighting, working, parenting and so on *exist in our genes* the way the pattern for a particular kind of tree exists in its seed.

Physical reality is formed around archetypal patterns or matrixes. The archetype for *table* might be "a surface paralleling the ground, supported by at least three legs." With only two legs it would fall over. All tables, elaborate or primitive, are formed from that archetype no matter how different or unique any given table may be.

Human beings are formed from archetypes in the same way. So are solar systems. And universes. Astrology is the science of understanding the archetypes of our solar system—and relating these archetypes to human earthly life. This means understanding that our solar system is an archetype of profound meaning. Bodies or entities (people) rotating on their axes (centered and capable of turning in all directions) are orbiting a central life-giving star (God, the Ego, a leader, the King, the President) in cyclical patterns (seasons), held in orbit by gravity. Gravity is another name for attraction. And attraction is another name for love. Quite literally, the planetary orbits of our solar system are maintained by a form of love we're pleased to call gravity. And love—in all its profundity, comedy, tragedy and ecstasy—is symbolized by Venus. So let's not shortchange her in our work with clients.

SOME BASICS

Astrology depicts our genetic archetypes, or living pre-physical entities, through the planets, signs, houses and aspects. It is crucial to distinguish these clearly.

The **twelve houses** are imaginary lines extending from Earth, dividing the 360-degree whole of space through which the Earth (the person) rotates. The houses are established by the Earth's rotation and one's location on it at the time of birth. So the houses are Earth-centered archetypes for what are essentially *externals*—physical appearance (Ascendant), spending habits (2nd House), communications

(3rd House), home and family (4th House) and so on. The sign on a house shows the *external conditioning* one receives with regard to matters symbolized by that house. Imagine yourself standing in the center of your horoscope looking out, turning to face the various houses, looking through the lens of the sign on the house cusp. You'll be conditioned to see the world of experience ruled by each house through those lenses. This conditioning comes from outside.

The **signs** are like scripts or modes of expression through which the planetary energies act. Remember that signs are actually shorthand for Earth/planet relationships. If you're born an *Aries*, that's shorthand for birth within 30 days following the Vernal Equinox, which is a particular Earth/Sun relationship. In the fall, the Earth/Sun relationship is quite different, and astrology expresses that relationship in the shorthand *Libra*. The signs represent seasonal relationships between the Earth and the other planets, the Sun and the Moon.

The **planets** represent archetypal *energies* that act through signs in particular ways in houses of particular areas of life. The planets are emissaries of the psyche, which in astrology is symbolized by the Sun.

The ancient concept of the planets as gods is closer to the truth than our simplistic materialist's view of them as lumps of matter orbiting the Sun. Science makes an excellent case for Earth being a living, conscious organism since it fits some 20 scientific criteria defining such organisms (*The Global Brain: Speculations on the Evolutionary Leap to Planetary Consciousness,* Peter Russell; J.P. Tarcher, Inc., 1983). The same can be said for the other planets and, by extension, our solar system and the universe. It's convenient to think of the planets as "gods" acting out scripts or archetypes (the signs they're in) in relation to matters shown through the houses, with aspects indicating ease or tension.

The Sun is the archetype of the Source of life, the life force, the psyche, the whole. Its symbol is a target—a circle with a dot in the middle. It is what we are aiming for, not necessarily what we are. The other planets orbiting it are various archetypes for divisions of the whole into more specialized energies. When you're angry or assertive, you will behave according to your Mars archetype. When you're in love, your Venus archetype emerges. When you're being rational and intellectual, your Mercury archetype becomes apparent. These planetary energies are the archetypes for your *inner nature*. The houses are the archetypes for the world as you see it and encounter it. You will have to use a particular planetary energy in matters ruled by the houses where its sign(s) is/are found.

Your innate nature (planets in signs) may or may not harmonize with your conditioning (signs on houses). You may have Aquarius on your 2nd House, for instance, indicating that you've been *conditioned* to regard yourself as different and distinctive; to equate money with freedom; to be erratic about earning and/or spending; to make money through your ideas (Air sign) or through groups, communications, science, astrology or psychology; and to buy electrical conveniences and recreational machines like televisions, cars, computers, cordless phones, connecting them somehow to your work. All of these traits and more come through the archetype of Aquarius. But your inner nature regarding money and self-worth, shown by Venus' placement, may be in a conservative sign like Taurus, oriented toward making and accumulating money in usual ways and desirous of "fitting in" vocationally, far less risk taking and more security-oriented than the Aquarius conditioning on your 2nd House might suggest. Thus conflicts often exist between your conditioning and your response to a given situation or house matter.

You may have Capricorn rising and be raised in an

environment that conditions you to expect trouble in life but to conquer it or rise above it ambitiously; to demand respect; to focus on status, prestige, material success; to project a worldly, wise-beyond-your-years personality; or to appear snobbish, cold or preoccupied with work and career. If your Saturn (ruler of this Capricorn Ascendant) is weak by sign, the portion of the psyche devoted to security, self-defense, position, ambition, attainment of status, etc., will conflict with the demanding, social-climbing conditioning you've been born into with the archetype on your Ascendant. If Saturn is in a sign like Scorpio or Taurus which harmonizes with Capricorn and tends to reinforce its positive qualities, you are more likely to exhibit a harmonious, less compulsive personality, at least with regard to ambition, status, and the like, than if Saturn were in Aries or Cancer.

There are two kinds of **angles** between planets: so-called soft aspects like trines and sextiles and hard aspects like squares and oppositions. **Trines** and **sextiles** are archetypes for harmony, constructiveness, preservation, ease and passivity. Hard aspects are archetypes for conflict and action. The basic aspect of birth and life on Earth is the **square**—the cross formed from the Ascendant-Descendant axis intersected by the 10th-4th cusp axis.

The Ascendant is the most personal point in the chart, the point of birth, individuation, initiation into earthly form. It represents the soul's choice to clothe itself in one form and personality while clothing others (7th House) in the form and personality of the opposite sign. Since these archetypes exist in our genetic code, we gravitate to people who fit our Descendant archetype in one way or another. Without The Other, one arm of the cross is missing. This doesn't mean that one isn't complete unless married. The 7th House rules all close ties, whether friends, associates or spouses. One arm of the cross *is* missing if there are no close relationships whatever, according to the archetype. In other words, close ties are essential to the archetype of life itself.

The 10th-4th axis squares the Ascendant-Descendant line. Thus the mother-father constellation conflicts (squares) the archetypes for identity (1st House) and relationships (7th House). This cross suggests *the* fundamental reality: to be born is to square one's origins (parents)—to individuate from the All That Is. Birth means leaving the collective to become an individual. This cross, this square, this conflict is *natural*. Without conflict, we don't develop. Nothing changes. Thus squares represent not just conflicts between planetary or psychic energies, but developmental conflicts without which we would neither be born nor die.

We are meant to be in conflict with our families. According to Luke 14:26, Jesus Christ said, "If any one comes to me and does not hate his own father and mother and wife and children and brothers and sisters . . . he cannot be my disciple." Jesus was an emissary from the God of love, sacrifice, redemption and resurrection (Venus and its higher octave Neptune/Pisces seen in Christianity's fish). Christ's New Testament with God was literally a new archetype to replace the capricious, judgmental, punishing and vengeful Jehovah, archetypally symbolized in all that is primitive in Saturn and Capricorn. Forgiveness was to replace vengeance as the archetype for religion and spiritual enlightenment. How successful Christ's living archetype was can best be assessed within oneself. Collectively, certainly, it has failed miserably as witnessed by everything from the Crusades to the Spanish Inquisition to present-day Irish "troubles" to the Middle East to Hitler and Stalin to all of Africa and South America—to the repugnant would-be tyranny of fundamentalists of all religions whose worship of the old God of vengeance still holds more power than their professed "holiness."

Trines, the aspect of the pyramids—the most solid architectural form—represent the archetype of preservation of form, experience, knowledge, marriage, job, whatever. Trines also represent energies we've learned to work with positively in other life experiences, energies which are "preserved" in this life as strengths, talents and gifts. These two symbols, the cross and the trinity, are archetypes that have powerfully manifested in Christianity whose two strongest precepts are sacrifice and compassion, solely the qualities of Venus and Neptune.

Now we can examine Venus as the energy of our psyche directed toward the impressive, pervasive and profound archetypes of Love and Art by studying Venus' linkage with Taurus and Libra and the 2nd and 7th Houses, its exaltation in Pisces and its classic relationship with Neptune, Venus being the lower octave of that enigmatic planetary symbol for collective compassion and sacrifice.

VENUS' SIGNS AND HOUSES

Astrology's cues are as obvious as its implications are deep. In the archetype of our solar system as perceived from Earth, Venus "rules" Taurus, the natural 2nd House sign, and Libra, the 7th House sign. Venus and these houses are our archetypes for **self-worth** and **relating.**

Venus represents the *valuing* or *attracting* energy that draws us toward anything (or away from something else). Note that the attracting energy comes from within ourselves rather than from the desired person or object. We may say we love someone or something because of its beauty, intelligence, and accomplishments. But we're really drawn because we *value* what we perceive this person or object to embody. Falling in love—that hallowed sacrifical metaphor that implies we're doomed before we start—means feeling a gravitational pull toward our own value systems reflected in another or some object. This isn't to say that the beloved may not actively pull us toward them through flirtation and seduction, but all the flirting in the world won't attract someone who doesn't value what is being offered.

We value the archetype of the sign Venus is in. We literally love that sign's mode of expression and are attracted to it, finding it pleasurable and irresistible. Venus feels good in the immediate, pure, compelling way that a baby's eating and excreting (Taurus-Scorpio) feels good. Venus has to do with taking in, obtaining, acquiring, ingesting, amassing just as the archetype of Mars has to do with throwing out and putting out (in the sexual as well as assertive connotations). And what we take in, obtain, amass, possess, etc.—what we love—is dictated by our genetic value system.

We value the externals shown by the house where Venus is positioned at birth. We are drawn to these areas as if by gravity. In these areas we exercise whatever capacity we have for charm, sociability, tact, beauty, diplomacy, flirtation, pleasure, art, refinement, love, compassion and relationship. Or, we show our lack of these qualities if Venus exhibits the negative side of its sign or conflicts other planets by aspect.

Venus also rules the 7th House of relationships. Again, the astrological archetype is obvious: there is a direct link between our self-worth and our relationships. The cliché "You have to love yourself before you can love others" stems from this pre-physical archetype of Venus.

The sign on the 7th House, its ruling planet and the sign that planet is in point to the living archetypes we have chosen to experience through our close relationships. This sign is opposite the one on our Ascendant. It is our "shadow persona," the parts of ourselves we turn away from in order to express those qualities we've chosen as our Ascendant.

Thus we project these shadow qualities onto others and seek to engage them in the instinctive drive for completion through interaction. We seek to complete our Ascendant-Descendant axis by courting, marrying, and forming close friendship and business ties with people whose own gestalt advertises our shadow qualities. This archetypal process is embodied in the planet Venus, whose glyph has been compared to a hand mirror, suggesting that what we love is a reflection of ourselves.

So we can now begin to see in Venus the archetype of the 7th House opposition or the idea that completion depends on interacting with one's opposite. The opposition is the aspect of both marriage and war. Pallas Athenae's (Venus) seemingly contradictory dominion as the goddess of love and war makes perfect sense when it is understood to be another manifestation of this pre-physical Venus archetype.

The sign our Venus is in shows how we innately handle 2nd and 7th House matters. The actual signs on those cusps in our charts show how we're conditioned to handle them. Again, the qualities we bring to Love and Art in ourselves may conflict or harmonize with the world as we see it.

It is because we idealize the qualities of the sign Venus is in and the matters shown by the houses it rules that we tend to experience happiness and success through them, all else being equal. When we value something or someone, we act nice and court him or her. We put our best foot forward. And because we're on our best behavior there, we often come out ahead, which reinforces the belief that we're good in these areas in these ways. This reinforcement of belief is cumulative—Venus is the builder. The more success and happiness we experience, the more confident we are. And confidence breeds success the way distrust breeds failure.

Venus rules the talent we believe we possess or don't possess if challenged. *Talent* is an old word for money. Venus' sign and house position show the kinds of talent we have and where we are meant to express them. The sign on the 2nd House (and its planetary ruler and sign) show the talents we are conditioned to develop in this life—additional talents we may nurture in connection with our Venus natures.

As an example of how this works, a woman with Aquarius on her 2nd cusp will have a chance to develop her talent for communication, intellectual and scientific understanding, her sense of humor, her ability to work with groups, and her facility for linking state-of-the-art techniques, tools and philosophies with ancient tools, techniques and philosophies. She may gravitate toward the sciences. There will be a potential for contributing something to the masses—she will have been somehow conditioned to believe that she has that mission in life.

All this may contrast with her Venus in Taurus, which shows a talent for motherhood and wifehood and making money through traditional, conservative means like real estate, banking and finance, or business. Venus here also indicates artistic or creative talents with a facility for touch, taste, texture, proportion and color that can make for an excellent cook, beautician, architect or artist.

Despite these and other gifts suggested by Taurus and Aquarius in this woman's chart, she may have a difficult time resolving the conflicts between these two signs. How does she resolve the side of her that values domestic life, home and children with the side of her that values excitement, variety and stimulation? She may find her life going through distinct periods of conservative calm with everything running along predictably until a sudden explosion of pent-up energy drastically changes things overnight through divorce, loss of job, deaths in the circle, winning the lottery, falling in love, etc.

The way she can resolve, harmonize, *own* her conflict is to use the Venusian principle of balance. The midpoint axis between two conflicting (square, opposition, semi-square, quincunx) houses or planets is the solution axis. This woman, for instance, would be counseled based on the midpoint between her Aquarian 2nd House and her 5th House Taurus Venus. In other words, you would spend time explaining the archetypes of the 3rd-9th Houses in her chart and their cusp signs of Pisces/Virgo. Consciousness of higher aims (9th) and organization and execution of details and priorities (3rd, Virgo on the 9th) may be allowing her home to get a little disorganized and chaotic (Pisces on the 3rd) rather than letting domestic routines interfere with her higher long-range aspirations. By consciously paying attention to the Pisces/Virgo, 3rd/9th life scripts and applying them in 3rd/9th matters, she can conquer the conflict presented by her square.

Self-worth and close relationships (Taurus-Libra) are quincunx in the astrological archetype. The quincunx is essentially a 6th/8th aspect since the 6th and 8th Houses quincunx the Ascendant. So Venus carries within its supposedly harmonious archetype the peculiar energy of the quincunx.

The quincunx between Venus' two signs, Taurus and Libra, is essentially an Earth-Air dilemma, a body-mind conflict. Something in the thinking—the value system—is struggling with physical reality. This is the dilemma between the ideal and the work and readjustments (quincunx) necessary to materialize the ideal.

Venus' signs Taurus and Libra also embody a fixed-cardinal dilemma. The archetype of love contains both preservative (fixed) and initiating (cardinal) elements. Part of Venus wants love and marriage to last forever. Part of Venus wants to be eternally seduced by someone new, an assertive cardinal action that comes through another by the

7th House—allowing one to proclaim innocence to one's spouse. How to make love last yet keep it new is an archetype for self-development through relationships. Even hermits have relationships with inner figures—Higher Selves, God, the Demon or the Divine. These are often more intense and intimate than outer relationships.

What happens to Venus, Taurus, Libra, the 2nd and 7th Houses when the individual is primitive, unconscious, negative? First, the principle of valuing is reversed and becomes an urge to *de*value. These people devalue themselves and others, according to sign and houses, so that there is no hope of attaining happiness, stability, material and marital security in those areas of life without some pain and its opportunity for growth. Second, the perception that loved ones (7th) are in conflict (quincunx) with one's self-worth leads to a primitive decision that one must somehow protect oneself against others. A more adult development is to recognize that the quincunx implies that love means constantly readjusting to the other, finding the Libra balance and compromise between self-worth and other-worth. This means identifying "both-and" solutions to seemingly "either-or" conflicts by working with midpoints.

VENUS IN CONFLICT

Hard aspects to Venus from other bodies presuppose a reversal of this valuing archetype that the individual must struggle with. All aspects are karmic in the sense that this life is an extension and reflection of other lines of development. Hard aspects suggest areas where our karma is negative, difficult, challenging. Soft aspects show qualities we've earned and learned to use well which are now karmic gifts we can build on in the present. The word *karma* means "results of past choices," whether these choices are made in this life or some other. Squares present us with negative or conflicting manifestations because of choices we made in the past—or, to those who've surmounted the illusion of time, negative choices we make in any of our simultaneous existences.

Venus/Saturn

Karmic indications are quite graphic in astrology and highly productive in work with clients. A man with Saturn in Capricorn square Venus in Aries may have experienced in other lives the loss of love (Saturn square Venus) through his own actions (Venus in Aries) and through harsh circumstances (Saturn in Capricorn of the outer world of achievement and status).

Such loss (Saturn square Venus) produces the deepest feelings of tragedy, sorrow and longing. Often a vow was made by the soul to love someone "forever" in the face of loss. Returning to a new incarnation, such a vow may carry over in the desire to reunite with that soul in a new life. But the old experience of loss of love through one's own action, or through tragic circumstances, returns to haunt the present.

A fear of repeating past tragedy consumes the love in the present. Suspicions arise out of jealousy and possessiveness. "Didn't we vow to love each other forever?" Mistrust at the loved one's slightest action, overprotectiveness out of fear of loss, control and manipulation—all these archetypes must be dealt with in the present life when Venus and Saturn conflict.

It begins with mother who will be absent through divorce or death, incapacitated through physical or mental illness, controlling and manipulating and overprotective, or cold and devoted only to worldly matters (namely money or the lack of it), etc. This experience of mother activates the archetype in our man's psychic DNA.

His Venus in Aries reacts to this fear of loss in its own assertive, independent way—he joins the Army at the earliest possible age to get away from Mom and to feed his love of combat. He falls in love readily and often and may marry too young, only to fall out of love again because he bores quickly or because she starts acting like dear old Mom. His conflict is between independence and freedom versus responsible relationships, marriage and parenthood. His "both-and" resolution will be along the midpoint axis—his Aquarius/Leo axis.

Like all oppositions, the resolution axis contains its own challenges. He can resolve his love conflict by learning to love (Leo) as a friend, nonpossessively with detachment (Aquarius). He needs to love (Leo) someone who's a friend (Aquarius) instead of a competitor and marry her. Maybe it'll be someone met unexpectedly at a group or convention (Aquarius), at a recreational resort or during a creative endeavor (Leo), and so on. Until then, his conflict is likely to be resolved through divorce, a legitimate Aquarian option, or having children (Leo) in the hope that he'll settle down, or finding Aquarian-Leonine excitement and sexual outlets through affairs. Or he may withdraw from sex (Leo) into intellectual pursuits and platonic friendships and groups (Aquarius) or become celibate. The Aquarius/Leo resolution axis also implies a need to learn to give (Leo) without an expectation of obligation (Aquarius doesn't feel obliged anyway) on the part of the receiver. Much more is contained in these archetypes, but this shows how valuable an exploration of karmic indications and midpoint solutions can be.

In the most tragic cases of Saturn in Capricorn square Venus in Aries (and to some degree, Saturn square Venus anywhere), one has been either directly or indirectly responsible for a loved one's death in another life. Thus love relationships in this life bring with them powerful fears of death and destruction or violence—until the source is understood and resolved within the individual. Such people need to know that God, or All That Is, in granting life also grants freedom of choice. It is not God who says we must come back and repeat experiences to atone for our sins, but it is our own choice to feel guilt and remorse or to believe that we must pay in this life for deeds in former lives. It is equally possible and valid to believe that we don't have to keep on paying for our sins. That, in fact, is Christ's message: we *are* forgiven—in the present. It is His gift—a gift from All That Is—given freely and to free us. Since Venus rules both the Christ-concept and gifts, there is much to explore in this gift of forgiveness given us in the New Testament.

That there are aspects of God that are not Judeo-Christian and do not exact retribution or demand self-flagellation seldom occurs to those unwilling (too fearful and mistrusting) to go beyond their Saturns. It usually takes awhile to evolve this realization that God creates a universe of thunderous abundance and grants freedom of choice to all forms for us to make *positive* choices now for positive karma. Few are born knowing this. It is the nature of institutional forms—all ruled by the Saturnian archetype—to want to control and maintain power.

In fact, where we find Saturn in our charts and the houses it rules are the areas where *we* want to be perfectly free but wish to prevent others from having the same freedom. We want to control others of this house out of fear—which is to say, lack of respect for them. If Saturn is near the Ascendant, it is *ourselves* that we fear, that we may not respect, that we must control. Lack of empathy leads to lack of respect, to fear, to a desire to avoid or control. A misunderstood, unanalyzed Saturn prevents us from empathizing with others fully, from really connecting. We fear in them the qualities of the sign where our Saturn is positioned. We may form relations with people far "beneath" or "above" our status, depending on whether our charts show an overall need to dominate or submit.

Through learning to empathize with people in accord with Saturn's archetype by sign—walk a mile in their shoes—we can respect them (which isn't to say we agree with them). Respect leads to treating others as *equals*.

Libra is the sign *par excellence* of this sense of equality and ability to relate to people from all walks of life. It is no accident that Saturn is exalted in Libra and accidentally dignified in the 7th House. Relationships are where the Saturn archetype can best manifest. Quite simply, Saturn forces respect for others. Initially, this respect often occurs through a series of failures and rejections, particularly in romance.

The clear message in this exaltation/dignity scheme astrology affords us is that we must be responsible to our close ties in love, friendship and marriage. These ties carry obligations. Commitment requires maturity, discipline and hard work. Relationships are scary. If they're not scary, at least in the beginning, no Saturn is involved, and they're less likely to last or be as deep.

Once you know you can make positive choices in the present—evolve past your Saturn—you can change your karma in any area of life by exploring your hard aspects with an eye to uncovering their potentials for constructive action. This often entails breaking ties with old beliefs and the people who've embodied them in your life. There is nothing wrong with such breaks, whether they occur through tender partings, bitter divorce, or death. Indeed, for someone with Saturn square Venus, such separations are practically required before s/he can change belief systems through this deepened understanding and go on to new and positive relationships.

It pays to study Saturn in connection with Venus because of Saturn's importance in stable, lasting relationships. The sign it's in clearly depicts an inner archetype we need to work on in this life in order to improve personal and business relationships—our overall fulfillment and success.

Speaking of business, Venus/Saturn configurations indicate latent business and financial talents in need of development if the contact is a hard aspect, coming more naturally if the contact is by soft aspect. Venus/Saturn people love and are drawn to careers involving control, order, discipline, hard work, sometimes low pay, long hours, management and authority. Professional and financial respect are important—perhaps overly important in the case of the square.

In the negative or primitive type, Venus/Saturn configurations show a negative belief system, a sense of financial powerlessness, envy, greed, low confidence, skepticism, lack of discipline and focus, and avoidance of responsibility. At its extreme, this results in a love of poverty and misery so that even if the person won the lottery or met the person of his or her dreams, s/he wouldn't know what to do because of the belief that s/he doesn't deserve happiness to begin with. Within a year, winnings would be misused and love abused, causing poverty and loneliness.

Venus/Uranus

Venus hard-aspected by Uranus tends toward earning money and spending it in Uranian modes. These people may value science, freedom, excitement, mental stimulation, communication, the new, experiments, social causes, and so on. This can draw them toward self-employment, a checkered career, hard science or social sciences, ancient careers like astrologer or inventor, modern careers in high-technology or space science and the like. People who haven't explored and understood their Uranus/Venus archetype are likely to exhibit more primitive qualities like erratic earning power, impulsive spending, and rapid boredom with their current jobs. They may dabble in this and that, unwilling to commit to the study and effort necessary for success, often quitting a job or relationship precisely when a little further dedication would have yielded lasting positive results.

Venus in hard aspect to Uranus presupposes stress between the idealized notions of love and romance and the need for variety and excitement. Notice how collective forces impinge on such people. They may be born with a conservative Venus into a generation that collectively embraces free love. Or they may be born homosexual in a heterosexist society, be drawn to sudden compelling attractions that end just as suddenly, be prone to divorce or loneliness, or be unable to combine friendship with love successfully so that friends interfere with romance and vice versa. Challenging aspects from Uranus to Venus imply a karmic choice to be a loner at some level, whether for positive or negative reasons. In this life, they may experience a lack of intimacy out of a remembered desire to avoid entanglement in any one relationship or to avoid relationships altogether.

Venus/Uranus hard aspects tend to intellectualize love and emotions. This detachment can develop in negative types into sadism and cruelty, often in the guise of teasing. Such types like to act out provocative behavior to stir up controversy and turmoil. These negative Venus/Uranus types are particularly capable of sudden violent emotional episodes and explosions with extreme types committing impulse beatings and killings. They are *always* sexually magnetic, even when physically unattractive, to people who value and seek (consciously or unconsciously) violent emotional and/or physical assault. Their intellectualizing of feelings can lead to sexual games involving sadomasochism where one partner plays Uranus the sadist to the Neptune victim. Always examine such dimensions when

Venus and Uranus are in hard aspect or when Uranus rules or is in the 5th, 7th or 8th Houses and afflicting Venus or Mars (the planet of lust).

Stressful aspects from Uranus to Venus also presuppose choices in other lives to seek overstimulation of the emotions and senses through experimentation with love and sex. In this life, there are similar patterns of "going overboard" or charting new territories in these areas, especially with the hard aspects. These binges involve any sort of pleasure—love affairs, sex, food, drink, drugs, religion, making money, whatever—since Venus is the archetype for what feels good. Swings from extreme promiscuity to serious religious celibacy are not uncommon in such lives because their value systems are subject to sudden, seemingly unpredictable shifts. Thus they seem unreliable in matters of love and money and often go from job to job and lover to lover until they solve their need for excitement, change, variety and freedom within relationships by studying the midpoint axis between the Venus/Uranus aspect.

Basically, there is a conflict between the personal love nature and the collective with Venus/Uranus. One somehow feels odd man or woman out. Notice how the Taurus qualities of Venus actually value being odd man or woman out. Remember that it is always Venus' nature to love what it touches or what touches it, whether pleasant or frustrating. This is why bad habits are so hard to break. This Taurean quality of Venus is fixed, compulsive, self-indulgent, stubborn and resistant to change. Strongly Venusian types typically try to break bad habits for other people—a child wants Mommy to stop smoking, a husband wants his wife to lose weight—or look for the one who is going to *make* them change: weight loss clinics, an acupuncturist, a spiritual guru, etc.

The secret to changing any habit is to learn to love its opposite. This takes a great deal of continuing work on the inner self, primarily through observation and awareness of the motives behind one's compulsions. But habits and addictions and idealistic quests for health, love, harmony, beauty and success naturally bring us to Neptune, the higher octave of Venus.

Venus/Neptune

Neptune is the archetype for that portion of the psyche's energy known as the collective emotional unconscious. Uranus is the collective mental unconscious—the realm of free-floating ideas waiting to be seized, rabble-rousing political rhetoric, and television and communications media.

The collective emotional unconscious has to do with feeling that we belong to the group emotionally, that we are loved by the group as a part of it. Its energy has to do with sacrificing our differences (Uranus) in order to blend and vanish into the group. People who have problems with this emotional identification and participation with the group (i.e., stressful aspects to Neptune) often seek to experience Neptune through alcohol and other recreational drugs. Only when drunk or stoned do they lower their Saturnian inhibitions and feel a part of the herd.

Neptune mixes and dissolves our notions of duality of love and hate, good and evil, night and day, and so on. It is the primordial soup of the psyche, the All That Is, the sea of infinite possibility. It is the archetype of empathy, the capacity to feel what others feel because one does not perceive oneself as separate. Developed to its highest level, this archetype allows individuals to walk into lions' dens without fear, to communicate over great distances through trees, and to have a "way" with animals or people. On its primitive level, Neptune's ability to instantly "know" the other is used to con people and make them victims.

The archetypes are meant to be explored and experienced in order from the Moon through Pluto. Exposure to too much Neptune before one has learned Saturn's lessons of grounding, self-protection and discipline can literally wreck the psyche and the life.

The hard aspects of Neptune to Venus show that one's natural mode of love conflicts with the collective emotional pool around one. These are the people forever being disillusioned by loved ones who break promises, lie, cheat, steal, drink too much, play around, or wear them out emotionally. The pleasure-loving side of both these archetypes can take over in the hard aspects so that one becomes addicted to people and objects that give pleasure and takes pleasure and love to extremes of high and low.

A common resolution of the challenging aspect of Venus/Neptune is to "sacrifice" oneself to love in one way or another. Raised to its highest level, this archetype of "loving the victim" can lead to the kind of selflessness where one devotes life and love to the unfortunate—a Mother Teresa, physician, nurse, minister, psychologist, social worker, or public defender. This is not seen as sacrifice but as fulfillment of one's highest beliefs and intentions.

Another common pattern is to sacrifice to art to find one's highest emotional involvement through music, painting, writing, dance or acting. Or one may fall in love with people who are doing this.

The Venus/Neptune individual wants to be swept away by love. Overwhelmed. Bewitched. Enchanted. Seduced. Plain old everyday mortal love with its hairs in the sink and the garbage waiting to be taken out won't do. *They want magic.* The discrepancy between what is idealized and what is manifested physically is too much for the excessive idealism of the hard aspects between these archetypes.

Neptune does seek perfection of form. It is the archetype of higher mathematics (Einstein was a Pisces, remember) and rules the "music of the spheres" that Kepler studied in the orbits of the planets. Neptune's archetype is meant to lead one toward what is valued, especially the higher values since it is Venus' higher octave. But by the time the other portions of the psyche have done their part in creating reality, Neptune's vision has been altered through collaboration, and "reality" never matches the ideal, or there'd be no point to ideals. This eternal frustration drives some people to drink. Venus/Neptune in its best development produces Michelangelos and Bachs, great surgeons who "sculpt" out illness to leave health , and great architects. The museums of the world would be empty without this archetype. So would churches and hospitals.

Notice too how Neptune plays a role in career and financial choices of these people, as does any planet that touches Venus. Remember, difficult aspects always denote a need to actively interact with the archetypes involved. Venus in adverse aspect to Neptune shows a need to act in ways that are artistic, creative, spiritual, healing, compassionate, emotional, theatrical, beautiful, refined, and pleasurable. Thus these people are drawn to the arts, magic, cosmetics, interior design, art objects, religions, beautification, spiritual careers, medical careers, psychology, and the healing arts, catering to the public's need for entertainment, decoration, pleasure and recreation.

In primitives, Venus/Neptune stressful aspects lead to the attempt to acquire as much as possible for as little effort as possible. Apathy, lethargy, sloth, laziness, and the inability to commit oneself must be fought. These people don't really commit to anyone or anything because commitment means giving up on the possibility that "anything can happen." Rather than accept the job or lover right under their nose even though they're less than perfect, these types prefer to believe that something or someone better could come along and don't wholly engage, creating mistrust and suspicion in their relationships.

The lesson with Neptune is always one of *trust*. People with hard aspects to Venus secretly don't trust themselves, though they don't admit it, and project this onto their relationships. They choose people who either turn out to be untrustworthy (thus proving their belief system) or who leave them because of their paranoid suspicion and doubt. No healthy adult wants to act out the role of persecutor to someone's victim.

People who cannot trust love have been deeply hurt. All these painful aspects with Venus to the outer planets imply deep hurts in childhood, whether remembered or acknowledged or not. It is always essential to explore these early areas with clients to help them examine what could possibly be *gained* by choosing to be born into poverty, or early ill health, to cold, abusive parents, to parents who die, or to manipulative controlling parents. All these archetypal experiences confront such individuals with an early sense of deep hurt, rejection, cruelty, coldness, seduction, alcoholism, drug problems, violence, competition, incest, guilt, anger and rage, depending on whether it's Saturn, Uranus, Neptune or Pluto aspecting. But somewhere in these people's backgrounds are clues in the environment and events that are metaphors for their particular Venus-outer planet archetypes. Until they understand that they can outgrow these hard, primitive events and environments, they're doomed to repeat them over and over in relationships, usually with escalating desperation, unless they withdraw altogether from relationships and devote themselves entirely to work or suicidal self-destruction.

To conquer any of these outer planet aspects to Venus requires the conscious development of spirituality and metaphysics symbolized through Neptune. While Venus is pleasure, Neptune is ecstasy. It can only be found permanently in inner spiritual states, which can literally dominate one's waking and sleeping hours with a conscious awareness of how beautiful it all is. When one comprehends meaning even in beauty and ugliness, there is a physical reaction in the glandular biochemical system (ruled, not incidentally, by Neptune) that produces a more or less continual feeling of ecstasy. This is what less developed types seek through alcohol and drugs. Dramatic turnarounds are possible by working with Venus/Neptune's metaphysical truths and spiritual energies.

Incidentally, since Neptune rules the immune system, Venus/Neptune hard aspects predispose to venereal diseases including AIDS and to illnesses resulting from excessive intake of food, drink or recreational drugs. With these aspects, there is a very real need to be discriminating in one's social and sexual partners due to sensitivity to physical, emotional and mental illnesses.

Venus/Pluto

Pluto challenging Venus is perhaps most difficult to discuss since this archetype is utterly nonrational, nonverbal and nonintellectual. In common with Venus stressfully aspecting the other outer planets, there is a collision between the personal archetype of love and the collective archetype of death/rebirth or the transformation from one reality to another. Like Pluto orbiting the deepest reaches of our solar system, transformation occurs at the deepest reaches within us. Pluto is the archetype of "surfacing" deep-seated, usually hidden talents, leanings, longings and awarenesses from the soul's unrealized depths to be incorporated into the self.

Pluto concerns sexual energies, compulsive-obsessive energies, devouring and destroying energies, rebirthing energies, kundalini, passion and the Root Chakra. It also carries with it the meaning of the 8th House and sign—other people's self-worth. So again one of the keys to understanding and working with Pluto lies in how we value (or devalue) others.

People with Venus in adverse aspect to Pluto value intense, transformative emotional and romantic experiences which seem tinged with great tragedy or which contain potentials for great violence and destruction. Pluto/Venus means love on the edge along with one's money and finances. These people seek peak transcendental experiences through love, art and money. Pluto represents the emotional-sexual power of the other, predisposing one to extreme passionate romantic and sexual ties with people with whom one unconsciously competes and also hates. Pluto isn't Donna Reed or June Cleaver; she's more like Glenn Close in *Fatal Attraction* or Medea.

Because of Pluto's rulership of extremes, people with Venus in hard aspect tend to go to extremes in love, romance and sex. They either have lots of it or none at all. The same goes for food, drink, drugs and pleasures. Venus/Pluto (and Venus/Neptune) conflicting aspects can indicate rampant self-destruction of some kind. Self-destruction is the opposite of other-destruction, which is what self-destructive people really want to do but won't acknowledge. It is important to find out where the rage behind Venus/Pluto stems from—whom they "unconsciously" want to destroy, to pay back or to dominate. It's usually a parent, often the one they think they love the most. It's also important for them to learn to fight for what they want, rather than against what they don't, and to destroy in themselves whatever negative personal habits, attitudes and patterns they can identify, rather than trying to force others into being "better" human beings.

Karmically, with Venus/Pluto there is the clue that other lives involve jealousy, possessiveness, emotional and sexual manipulating and perhaps violent overtones. In *this* life, love must be dangerous on some level to be attractive to these types. It must threaten the self in some way if it is to appeal and hold. There must be an unspoken need to devour and possess. Otherwise, why bother? Because the loved one is also perceived as dangerous or threatening, there is a life-or-death need to control through money, mental and verbal dexterity, feelings, or dominance. Thus these people make various attempts to "buy" love, arouse guilt, and manipulate indirectly through verbal or psychological power plays and a series of ever escalating ultimatums in the face of increasing threat, real or imagined. They are torn between a fear of being possessed by the loved one and a fear of losing him or her.

The uppermost emotional and sexual highs accompany Venus/Pluto positions in contrast to the deepest emotional and sexual lows. The soft aspects between these archetypes often experience many of the same extremes of the hard aspects but are far less likely to form destructive reaction patterns. Flowing Venus/Pluto contacts give potential for achieving lives marked by extremely constructive, profitable actions and choices, all else being equal.

Classically, the driving aspects of Venus/Pluto involve enslavement; this enslavement , usually sexual, can also be spiritual or financial. One's passions control one, rather than the other way around. There is typically one great love (more if Venus is in a mutable or cardinal sign) which ends sorrowfully and agonizingly, never to be forgotten. Such an experience can actually "kill" love for that person from then on. They carry this lost love around with them the rest of their lives, secretly of course, since Pluto is never open. This means they carry the pain, too, which is inseparable from the love that was lost. Thus romance in the present activates this archetype of agonizing pain through love, the potential for devastating loss.

Yet if such people are honest, they can ultimately come to admit that the relationship should have ended when and how it did. If they are extremely aware and developed, they will be able to recognize that had the relationship gone on it would have led to an appalling, horrific mutual destruction. Venus/Pluto aspects are common in charts of "crimes of passion." People with these aspects literally or figuratively want to kill and be killed by the loved one. Ultimately, one must die in a literal or figurative sense to be transformed.

If there's a lesson to be learned from Venus/Pluto conflicts, perhaps it is that one cannot own or be owned by another. The power plays and struggles common to lovers with these configurations are externalizations of this inner archetype that seeks to be completely transformed by the other while simultaneously transforming that person. These aren't the manipulations of Mercury or the wiles of Venus or even the bullying of Mars. The energy behind a conflicted Pluto is so diabolical that it cannot be admitted to the self, for it involves the total domination of another human being or the converse. At some point in such love ties, the face of true evil will be perceived, however briefly, in the other. It is one's own evil projected, and that is the lesson of Venus/Pluto disharmony.

One of the important meanings behind Pluto's archetype is that other people can die on you, divorce you, play around on you, go mad, get sick, cheat you, lie, and devastate you. Those externals (people or things) we love most and want to last for eternity seem doomed to pass away. People with Venus in troublesome aspect to Pluto are meant to learn a valuable lesson in letting go since they have held on too much (or in destructive ways) in other lifetimes.

The point of all the pain and tragedy is to turn one to *inner* love which is *eternal*. Once you develop an inner relationship with your Higher Self, God, Jesus, Buddha, Allah, Your Guide, you begin to realize that you're never alone, you're always loved and supported, and this inner relationship won't die, divorce you or prove disloyal. Scorpio and Pluto symbolize this inner union—which is every bit as private, intense, enjoyable and releasing as good sex. Intoxicated with the Beauty of All That Is, people transcend pain even in the face of life's sorrows by recognizing the meanings in the archetypes underneath the pain. One's sense of self is so large that personal pain (and joy too) are *contained* and experienced from a perspective that is more encompassing, compassionate and truly understanding than that afforded by the view from one's ego.

Venus/Pluto aspects (especially the difficult ones) are meant to transform others and be transformed through love. It is important for these people to identify what it is they love to do and do it for a living even if the initial period is full of hardship and struggle, which it often is for anyone who devotes oneself to a cause. Whether this love is artistic and creative, socially conscious, mystical and spiritual, or financial and material, it must be intensely personal almost to the point of a compulsion or drive. By loving what they do, they do it with love automatically. They'll succeed at it because others will respond to this Venus archetype constructively at work and love it (and them) too. The archetypes of the 5th House cusp and its planets offer indications of what we love to do. The archetypes of the 6th House show how to make money from it (2nd from the 5th).

In marriage and personal ties, Venus/Pluto offers the chance for the deepest, most profound romantic experiences of all the combinations. In the primitive type, love under this configuration is often seen as a yearning for a savior. It's fascinating to watch how often a new lover enters such people's lives just when they're on the brink of going under in some way or other. But invariably the savior "fails"—by being human. And the primitive type lashes out with the vengeful, undermining destructive force of this planetary combination.

But to the Venus/Pluto who is evolved and developed, there is no neediness, possessiveness or jealousy but a conscious joining of two whole human beings in a powerful metaphysical, spiritual and physical union, helping each other compassionately out of past losses or tragedies, giving each other rebirth through mutual support for new shared goals. This is living the true "life of passion"—passionate devotion to what and whom is loved. The passionate life, the hallmark of Venus/Pluto, requires fulfilling Libra's need for equality, justice, moderation and self-control and Taurus' need for peace, steadfastness and beauty.

VENUS IN THE SIGNS

Venus' attracting energy is the archetype of *bonding*. Bonding because one sees one's self-worth externally reflected in the other. This archetypal energy or law applies to electrons and molecules, tissues and organs, to human beings and planets. Venus is the glue of life. It embodies form, color, texture, taste, proportion—the so-called "decorative arts." It also implies that life itself is an art form and that one's "loves" play a profound role in it.

Venus relates to our emotional, glandular side of life, too. The Moon (the glands, liquids in the body, secretions) is exalted in Venus' sign Taurus. Venus' higher octave is Neptune, which is also associated with the glandular system, bodily liquids, and the metaphysical meanings of the immune system. So Venus' sign in a horoscope and its aspects offer indications of one's habitual emotional state as an adult and one's glandular condition—the emotional basis for action.

Venus in Mars' signs—Aries and Scorpio—literally tends toward a constant underlying state of arousal, stimulation, competition, drive, anger, hostility, bitterness, envy and conquest. Testosterone City, in other words. These people love these feelings, which is why they tend to have so many problems in romance and marriage. They are motivated solely by passion, which in Aries never lasts and in Scorpio can't be consuming enough. Venus' archetype is traditionally out of whack in Mars' signs because the energies which are natural to Mars are seemingly in conflict with Venus' gentle, nurturing, beautifying, peace-loving side. Seen from the larger perspective afforded by astrology, Venus and Mars can be viewed, *must* be viewed, finally, as ends of one polarity, the Aries/Libra and Taurus/Scorpio polarity, with all its attendant implications.

Venus in Mercury's signs—Gemini and Virgo—intellectualizes feelings, detaches from, objectifies, labels, analyzes, talks about, mimics and rationalizes them. Such people, though charming, usually intelligent, witty and fun or interesting, can also seem cold when you try to get close to them. They tend to be gamey in romance, which is to say that they play with their feelings and those of others. The essential duality and duplicity of Mercury often leads them into experimental, complicated romantic triangles or to the avoidance of love and romance through intellectual or social pursuits. The glandular state often vacillates from high to low since the dual impulse of Mercury leads to constant second guessing of the self. What would have happened if I'd chosen Millie instead of Tillie? What if I'd gone to Borneo instead of Cleveland? Even as such individuals act in one way, their nervous systems are sent contradictory messages to act the opposite. Thus, they can seem to be irritable, high-strung, restless, superficial, unreliable, never satisfied, petty and inconsistent, financially as well as emotionally. There is an innate love of variety and mental stimulation with these positions. Communication, or lack of it, is often the key to the success of their personal and business ties.

Venus in Jupiter's signs—Sagittarius and Pisces—triggers a glandular yearning for ecstasy that with hard aspects is mistakenly sought through alcohol, drugs, food, emotional dependency, self-sacrifice and enslavement. In the positive expressions, there is love of the ideal. The spiritual, philosophical, religious, and metaphysical realities can attract with a power and force that makes living in the physical workaday world difficult or impossible if the lessons of Saturn have been skipped. Positive manifestations lead to heights of fame, love, and professional attainment through focus (Virgo/Mercury) and discipline (Saturn).

People with Venus in Sagittarius or Pisces need to mythologize love, to seek someone or something to worship —a guru or religious, educational, medical or financial authority figure. With both signs there is impressionability—a need to be "impressed" by others—which presupposes a need to lessen the self by comparison. This is another variation on the self-sacrificing theme running through these signs. They need to learn to admire others without simultaneously putting themselves down, which trait produces anger and inner emotional-physical turmoil that over time manifests as accidents, skin eruptions, temper tantrums, nervous disorders, joint problems, eyesight problems and speech and hearing difficulties.

There seems, with Venus conflicted in Sagittarius or Pisces, an almost chronic dissatisfaction with the self and the world with a need to "prove" things to people, who are substitutes for parents. They're still looking for approval from higher-ups without realizing that they must approve of themselves. This feeds into the Fire/Water theatricality of Sagittarius and Pisces in the tendency of both archetypes to dramatize life and events.

As in all cases involving stressful aspects, the initial tendency is for the childish, primitive, undeveloped, unaware traits of the signs involved to show forth. Here, with Sagittarius and Pisces, a startling immaturity and childish temperament often accompany vast wisdom and deep insight. Variety and change in love and money are inherent in these archetypes as are divorce, separation, and periods of being single or celibate. Venus, like Jupiter, goes overboard when challenged.

The rules mean a lot to Venus in Sagittarius, whether s/he personally follows them or not. Venus in hard aspect in this sign can produce a moralistic type, a hypocrite, a fanatic. Sagittarius is religion while Pisces is God or the All That Is. We are meant to explore and understand (to the best of our abilities) the first 11 sign archetypes before we plunge into the Infinite and Unspeakable (in the sense that it cannot be verbally communicated) of Pisces. People who dive into Pisces' waters without a philosophical or religious system or Saturnian knowledge of their own limitations and sense of rigorous discipline are lost. But those who approach Pisces relatively sure of themselves in the preceding 11 archetypal experiences are destined to find the everlasting, internal ecstasy promised by every guru in every age and land.

In adverse aspect, Venus in Sagittarius must somehow learn to go beyond the rituals and objects of religious veneration. But as usual with Venus, it wants to accept and settle for whatever is offered unquestioningly. The Bible is the "Word of God" to such people even though it was written by all too human beings, passing the stories on through their own lenses and archetypes, successively translating and bastardizing the original words to fit each ensuing generation. It never occurs to these people that God speaks through the words and deeds of men and women. Venus in Sagittarius is an old sign of prophetic abilities and of success in religion or teaching fields.

There are two primary dangers inherent in Venus in Sagittarius. One is that the Divine Voice will take over and madness will result—hence the desperate adherence to rules and rituals and "right" ways and "wrong" ways in the hope that these will protect against the perceived threat of self-loss through possession. This same archetype operates in such people's love ties, too. They fear losing themselves when in love, avoiding real intimacy while upholding all the external props and rituals of the "happy marriage." The other grave danger is spiritual pride. This is the classic position of fanatics and fundamentalists who actually worship things other than God. The literal words of the Bible or Torah or Koran, and their vociferous and often violent defense, are more important than the striving for living union with God, or ecstasy, which was the original impetus for religion. Armed with spiritual pride, fortified by a belief system that says "I'm okay-You're subhuman," these Christian soldiers, Nazis, Fascists, Holy Warriors, Israeli soldiers, Islamic terrorists, etc., all share the same negative Sagittarian archetype of "My way or die" that results when the ego is mistaken for God. Religions are an egoistic and egotistic expression—man's attempt to communicate and codify the esoteric truths of the Unspeakable in Pisces.

Religions completely miss the mystical union they tout because they separate the All That Is into God and the Devil, giving themselves a hell of a time with the inherent contradiction between an all-powerful, all-good deity and the seemingly overwhelming power (to them) of the Devil in all its sinful forms. Does God not contain the Devil? Negative Sagittarian accents in horoscopes are caught up in this apparent dilemma to an inordinate degree, tending toward either holier-than-thou or sleazier-than-thou polarities of sexual and worldly behavior. Acceptance of things as they are without overlaying a moral judgment, or the acceptance of All That Is, never occurs to them. It is a stretch to see godliness in murder, torture, illness, death and destruction. But it is a stretch the whole individual will make if s/he is to safely enter Pisces and become whole and one with God.

Venus in Pisces literally means finding ecstasy by loving All That Is. At the Pisces level of consciousness, there is the awesome and wonderful experience of the relatedness of all things—Venus' prime archetypal energy at its most profound and moving. Christians need lions and Judas and Pontius Pilate and vice versa. Cops need killers and vice versa. Saints need sinners and vice versa. I need you and vice versa. Contained in All That Is is everything beautiful and ugly and true and distorted—an infinity of choice. The Devil is God in negative guise. God is what I like and therefore worship; the Devil is what I don't like. It is far easier to dislike something than to understand it. So belief in God and the Devil or duality is the easy way out. They are both aspects of something larger—of All That Is.

This is the deep end of the pool where we sink or swim. Infinite choice implies infinite freedom. If it all means the same thing no matter what I do, then why do anything at all? If fantasy and reality are equal, why not live in fantasy since it's so much easier? Pisces misunderstood leads to meaningless chaos. Pisces comprehended leads to meaning in everything. That in itself is a beautiful awareness that physically evokes ecstasy in *knowing* one is connected intimately to All That Is—each life form—each galaxy. We are free to choose and create from All That Is. God the Giver grants this freedom to his or her creations. This is the kind of love Venus strives for—the affection and delight and compassion in which the beloved is held, no matter what the beloved's choices—the limitless joy in watching all life be itself. When one identifies with All That Is (God), one is free to observe the results (karma) of choices on all planes of manifestation. One can then come back down to Earth with an enhanced awareness and understanding of where various choices will likely lead. This is the prophetic side of Venus/Neptune.

Venus is more at home in Sagittarius and Pisces (its exaltation) than in some signs. Sagittarius potentially guides Venus' energies according to a set of principles, teachings, laws, social or political causes and the like. Pisces gives Venus limitless scope for love and success as well as failure. Both positions demand an awareness of collective factors in working with Venus in the arts, business, money and romance. Such people are more prone to marry outside their own religious, racial or national backgrounds (as are people with Jupiter or Neptune aspecting Venus or Mars), or to "be different" and seek to distinguish themselves through their work. They may choose professional fields like health, teaching, social work or communications which affect collective populations.

The dangerous tendency of both Sagittarius and Pisces to put people on pedestals (only to attempt to topple them) can make for highly provocative behavior in love and money. These actions create chaos in these departments.

The ever upward aspiring nature of both these signs makes even the most vicious and primitive types end their lives more spiritually aware than they began them and gives the average human being a better-than-average chance at success in love and money once the lessons have been learned. The faith these people have in a Higher Being or a Higher Self lends an air of confidence and joy to their enterprises in the best manifestations. Others respond in kind so that projects can seem to fall into place almost without effort, or "luck" comes along at just the right moment. It's not luck but an underlying belief in an abundant, just universe that makes these types prone to happiness and fulfillment if they overcome their tendency to compare themselves with others. They *expect* miracles, and they get them.

Venus in Saturn's signs—Capricorn and Aquarius—operates quite differently as befits the ancient dual face of

Saturn. In Capricorn, Venus grapples with a blend of lusti-
ness, ambition, love of control, need for prestige and respect, desire for a traditional marriage and family (this position can make one of the best of all zodiacal parents) and the
dichotomy between one's personal and public lives, which
often seem to conflict in some way. With the hard aspects,
when love's going well, business and money may not be
and vice versa. In Aquarius, Venus functions as friendship,
which is freer and more detached than the sexual love of
Scorpio which squares Aquarius. Humanity as brotherhood
and sisterhood is an accurate Venus in Aquarius archetype,
and these people can be more successful in their public,
group relationships or friendships than in the one-on-one
intimacy of marriage. Jealousy is anathema to Venus in
Aquarius. This position seeks freedom, excitement, mental
and physical stimulation, and variety and change in love
and romance and money and career. Because of Aquarius'
fixed nature, energies tend to build up under pressure so
that the changes and variety they seek often come explosive-
ly. Then they settle back into new patterns and relationships
for a while before erupting again.

Both Capricorn and Aquarius have the capacity for
what seems to be cold, cruel detachment—Capricorn out of
preoccupation with work and material concerns, Aquarius
for experimentation or to see what you'll do if they poke or
prod. The Saturnian control-needs implicit in both archetypes can lead to power plays in relationships and sexual
games and kink. People forget that Capricorn is a lusty,
earthy sign. Like the other cardinal signs, its lust or love can
vanish as suddenly as it arises or be too quickly satisfied for
lovers who like the feeling to linger awhile. The airy nature
of Aquarius can point to problems in relating through
overintellectualizing life rather than experiencing and vali-
dating the feeling reality.

The ecstasy available through Pisces' archetype (sign of Venus' exaltation) is first mental (Aquarius), then emotional and glandular (Pisces), leading to personal actions (Aries) chosen out of the All That Is, which creates results or "karma" in the outer world (Taurus). Taurus and Venus teach us to love the results we get, our karma, by loving our self-worth. We *will* love life in the Garden of Eden if we love our planet, our Earth, listen to Venus—to what we love by *nature*—and listen to our 2nd House which is what we've incarnated to learn to love and value on Earth.

Johanna Mitchell

Johanna Mitchell is a successful professional astrologer with an extensive consulting business based in Eugene, Oregon. With her Aries Sun and Gemini Ascendant, she has a reputation as an excellent counselor, teacher, lecturer and innovator.

Her field of expertise is combining the spiritual with the practical. The emphasis of her work with clients centers upon the utilization of astrological and Tarot symbolism in order to help them discover potential, solve problems and attain inner peace.

In 1969 books by Linda Goodman, Dane Rudhyar and Alan Leo inspired her endless exploration into self-discovery. Johanna considers her four-year participation in Marion March's Master Class the highlight of her astrological training.

As an astrologer, she is well known for her lectures at various conferences, including UAC '86 where her videotape *"Planets Part I & II"* (Video Lecture Series) was produced.

MARS

Conversations With the Inner Warrior

Hot, dry, male—force, competition, passion—anger, war, hate—sex—**MARS.**

These key words for Mars represent the basic drive connected with the red planet. For centuries, Mars was called on in the fight for survival and the defense of hearth and home. With this as our human heritage, it is no wonder that Mars' energy has come to be associated with force and violence. It is either/or with Mars—passive or aggressive, kill or be killed, win or lose, love or hate, fight or run.

In our society, we have many examples of Mars as the violent warrior: Sylvester Stallone as Rocky, Clint Eastwood as Dirty Harry and Arnold Schwarzenegger as The Terminator. But what about Mars as the peaceful warrior? We have lost touch with our inner warrior and now struggle for nondestructive ways to embrace its power. It is time to learn to utilize Mars as *the driving force to achieve our goals.* Without integrating this planet in a healthy, active way, we will be doomed to project Mars outwardly and continually precipitate crises. True harmony, peace and cooperation can be actualized through the acceptance of Mars on the individual level.

The role of an astrologer is not to analyze the character of the individual but to help that person discover his or her life path and purpose and to offer clear, useful and understandable solutions to the problems presented in the birth chart. In discussing Mars with clients, the challenge of the astrologer is to guide others to a positive use of Mars' energy and to help eliminate negative projection, fear, and emotional paralysis. Many people do not recognize their Martian energy. Areas connected with assertiveness, passion, achievement, competition, anger and sexuality are sometimes categorized as negative, impossible and/or evil. In our quest for unconditional love, we have lost the connection with our inner fire . . . our inner warrior.

The key to solving the Mars dilemma is an understanding of this planetary energy in a new context. Examining the lives of individuals and how they utilize Mars provides an opportunity to develop ways to counsel others. The following biographical sketches along with astrological correlations illustrate the diverse ways that individuals set in motion their inner warriors.

MARS' ASSERTIVENESS

At age two, we have our first Mars return. This is the time when we learn to say our first Mars word—"NO." We begin to assert ourselves against the authority of our parents and siblings. The reactions we receive are not always favorable; often we get the message that disagreement is not acceptable. It is at this time that we may give up the connection with Mars in order to gain love and acceptance. Family patterns, expectations and circumstances are contributing factors to the health and well-being of our natural assertiveness. In some cases, we force our way through the objections of others and utilize Mars to get what we want. Aggressive behavior develops when there are no limits to the child's use of the assertive Mars function.

Mars in Virgo

Ellen has Mars in Virgo intercepted in the 9th House. It rules the 4th House and Uranus is placed there. Mars makes a quincunx to Uranus, so disruption, dissension and anger are indicated in the early family life. Mars also quincunxes Saturn in Aquarius in the 2nd House, thus a Yod is formed. This configuration indicates that the fear of asserting herself could become a chronic situation. There is no planetary square to Mars to challenge her to be strong enough to push out of the situation. She learned at an early age that it was not permissible to assert herself; her Mars energy lost an appropriate outlet.

Astrologer: What were some circumstances in your early childhood in which you learned not to be assertive and disagree?

Ellen: I was always the loser when I was a child, no matter what the circumstances. I did try to raise a fuss, but it never turned out to my advantage. My half sister was three years older and smarter. She always won and I always lost. I was never allowed to express my frustration without being called a poor sport or a baby.

Astrologer: How do you see that early childhood behavior reflected in your present life?

Ellen: I avoid anything competitive because it brings up that old anger. I learned that my assertiveness resulted in punishment. I rarely ask for what I want because I don't know how. If I try to ask, I feel guilty and selfish, so I pull back. It's a never-ending struggle.

Astrologer: Mars in Virgo has a drive to serve. In the 9th House, the drive can be expressed through teaching, writing and physical activity such as travel which will broaden your perspectives. Because Mars is square your Sagittarius Ascendant, you can become more assertive in areas that you feel offer the spirit of adventure. Finding an area where

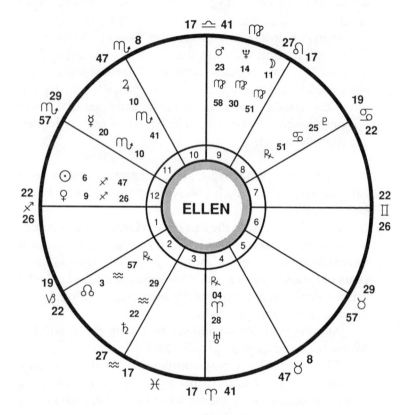

Natal Chart #1
Koch Houses

November 29, 1934 8:46:0 AM PST
13:05:14 ST
44N05'00" 123W04'00"
Eugene, Oregon

you can break rules without recrimination will help you understand Mars.

Ellen: That makes sense to me. I have kept a journal for the past seven years where I say whatever I want, no matter how harsh or seemingly unfair it is about the situations around me. It is the one place I feel safe to express my anger. The energy just flows out of me, and I don't stop until I feel vented.

Astrologer: Could you use this same technique to prepare yourself to face situations in your daily life?

Ellen: Absolutely. I find myself saying the very things today that came out on the paper yesterday.

Astrologer: When you become conscious of your ability to assert by organizing your thoughts, you are using your Mars in Virgo in the 9th House in a productive manner. The combination of Saturn sextile Uranus as the foundation of your Yod can be utilized by organizing your need for responsible freedom and independence in your communication. Because Mars also squares your Ascendant, you will also need to find physical outlets. If the Mars energy is held within, there can be health problems. One of the manifestations of an underactive Mars is physical tiredness and lack of energy.

Ellen: I had chronic health problems as a child and a nervous stomach. I vomited every time I was upset or there was excitement in my life. As the mother of five children, I suffered from exhaustion, which I attributed to overwork. Now at age 53, I'm still tired. I have lots of work energy but little left over for other things.

Astrologer: The sign Virgo rules nutrition and health care. Examine your diet and exercise programs to find ways to increase your physical energy level, which can have positive results in your emotional nature.

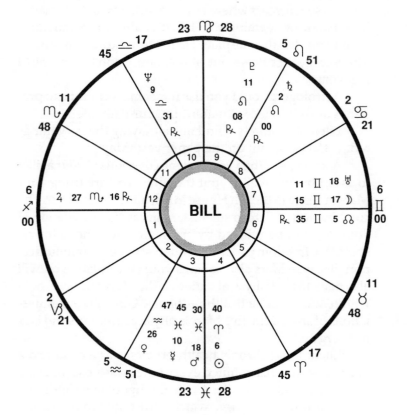

Natal Chart #2
Koch Houses

March 27, 1947 11:43:0 PM EST
11:36:00 ST
41N05'00" 81W31'00"
Akron, Ohio

Mars in Pisces

Bill has an Aries Sun in the 4th House with Mars ruling his 5th House. His Mars in Pisces in the 3rd squares the Moon in the 7th. He is a veterinarian with a reputation as a gentle, caring and competent healer. He has built two successful private practices and is actively involved in the business community in his city.

Astrologer: You have Mars in Pisces. Traditionally, that's not seen as an assertive Mars placement. How do you deal with a situation in which you need to be assertive?

Bill: A lot of people look at me and think I am passive. There are two ways to be aggressive and strong. One of them is vocal and showy and the other is quiet. I make sure I set up situations at the beginning so I know what the rules are. I'm pushy in a lot of ways in terms of getting what I want, but I don't necessarily do it in an aggressive manner. I don't tend to be flashy. If I get backed up against the wall, I generally get my way, but I don't like that position.

Astrologer: How do you set up those rules?

Bill: I'm clear about them and I decide what I want. For example, if one of my secretaries came to work wearing jeans, I'd hate to go up to her and say "Don't do that." When someone is hired, I inform them of the dress code so I don't have to be assertive later. I'll be straightforward in the beginning so things go my way.

Astrologer: Do you think you are competitive?

Bill: In some things I am. In sports I'm extremely competitive but not obnoxious about it; if someone beats me, I'm gracious and they may not know how competitive I feel. I rarely show it outwardly. In business, I work hard and am honest about what I do. I am very competitive about things that are important to me.

Astrologer: Mars in the 3rd House usually verbalizes anger. Because Mars squares your Moon/Uranus conjunction, you could become extremely emotional in an argumentative situation. How do you get out your anger?

Bill: It depends on what kind of anger it is. At home I won't argue just for the sake of argument. That bores me. If I am angry in sports or at work, I'll talk it through. I'm not showy—I don't ever put my fist through a wall; I'm not that kind of person. I steam inside and vocalize anger but not in a flashy way.

Astrologer: Mars ruling the 5th House and stressfully aspected often gives a strong sense of sports competition. How does this apply to you?

Bill: I play golf with guys who are as competitive as I am, but they will pout for two or three holes and aren't fun to be with. They throw clubs. I throw a club every now and them, but I'm embarrassed when I do it. Even when I'm mad at myself, I can still enjoy the game. I do not show aggression unless it has something to do with my kids or when people will be hurt if I don't take control. Then I can show my aggression vocally, externally, every way.

Astrologer: Mars in Pisces can be just as assertive as Mars in Aries or Leo but in a quieter, less obvious way. Do others accept your quiet assertiveness?

Bill: Not always. People tell me to be more aggressive. "Why don't you do this?" "Why don't you do that?" I start thinking I'm Wally Wimp, but that's not true. I just don't show hostility or assertiveness outwardly. If that's not acceptable to others, that's their problem.

Mars in Capricorn

Christina has the Sun, Mars and her Ascendant in Capricorn square Neptune in Libra and quincunx Saturn and Pluto conjunct in Leo. Her Moon is in Aries.

This is a forceful combination. Christina projects an image of toughness and appears unapproachable to some people. These strong planetary placements indicate the chart of a high achiever. When Christina was a year old, she had her first and last temper tantrum. Her mother threw a pot of cold water on her that took years to evaporate.

Her assertiveness began to return at age 13 when she got her first job. Capricorn needs to work to achieve results. The money she earned provided the incentive to combat the shyness she had expressed as a young girl.

Christina: My first career position was teaching handicapped children at a special school. It was a position where I could express my autonomy. As teachers we were allowed to express our individuality in the classroom.

Astrologer: What did you like best about teaching?

Christina: It was easy for me to play the role of teacher. It was cut-and-dried, black and white. After my success in that role, I was able to take one of the first classes of severely handicapped children into the public school system. I was proud to be involved in such an innovating, pioneering opportunity.

Astrologer: Saturn conjunct Pluto in Leo functions well when in control. The quincunx to your Capricorn planets shows your willingness to serve and help children who present difficult challenges. Why did you decide to leave that career and open your own business?

Christina: I was tired of teaching. I had proven that I could do it and I wanted another challenge. I wanted to be my own boss. I didn't know anything about business, but I wanted to go out and set the world on fire. I decided to buy a clothing resale shop. It was a business I could afford, but the woman I bought it from lied to me about the profits, and I didn't do well. I want what I want, and even though it might not be in my best interest, I go for it anyway. What have I got to lose?

Astrologer: Your Moon in Aries symbolizes the need for emotional excitement and the inclination to jump in

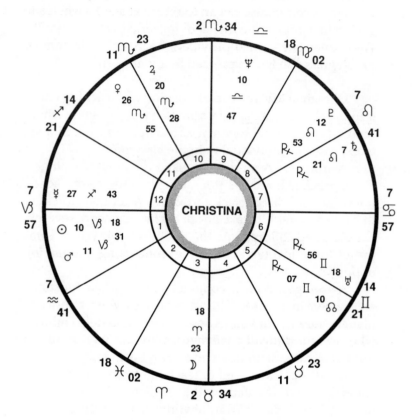

Natal Chart #3
Koch Houses

January 1, 1947   7:25:0 AM CST
14:01:30 ST
40N49'00" 91W14'00"
Burlington, Vermont

head first. Capricorn, on the other hand, is quite practical. The square from Neptune to your Mars can make things appear better than they are. Neptune can cloud the good judgment of Capricorn. What happens if you don't get what you want?

Christina: I always get what I want, at least at first. I choose goals that are glamorous and fantasize about them. I bought a restaurant without knowing anything about the food business. I figure I can make anything work. I worked hard to get my café; it took a long time and finally it happened. Then reality set in, but I didn't know when to quit. As I mature, I hope I will gain more wisdom about when to push and when not to push.

Astrologer: On one hand, Mars in Capricorn indicates tenacity. It also signifies obstinacy. Mars conjunct the Sun can identify with action and is reluctant to separate the self from the deed. The square to Neptune provides the illusion that the grass is always greener elsewhere. How does this operate in your life?

Christina: When I am disenchanted, I cut my losses and seek a new challenge. I learn so much about myself, the world, people and how to manage them. I have incredible drive and ambition I have to put somewhere.

Astrologer: Does the challenge have to look insurmountable before it seems exciting?

Christina: I never see anything as insurmountable.

Mars in Capricorn

Mark has the Sun, Mercury, Jupiter and Mars in Capricorn. Mars opposes the Ascendant, quincunxes Pluto, trines the Moon and squares Neptune. It rules his Aries Midheaven and co-rules the 5th House. The Moon is in Virgo widely conjunct Saturn and rules his Cancer Ascendant.

Last year, Mark consulted an astrologer to discuss

health issues. A student of astrology, he has a basic understanding of planetary symbolism. During the year, his health
has improved. However, this year he is frustrated with his
work and wants to make a change. He wanted to better understand his powerful 6th House and Mars in Capricorn.

Astrologer: Can you take the assertive plunge and quit
your job?

Mark: It would be extremely hard. The lack of security
scares me.

Astrologer: The need for security represented by your
Cancer Ascendant with the Moon in Virgo trine Mars explains your acceptance of unpleasant circumstances. Are
you staying at your job for financial reasons?

Mark: I don't have a lot of debts, nor do I have a lot of
money. Financial security is important to me because I
grew up in a home where money issues were always significant. I'm comfortable now, and the thought of giving that up
is stressful. That's one thing that holds me back; the other is
fear of the unknown. But I hate my job.

Astrologer: Mars in the 6th in Capricorn quincunx
Pluto indicates the dread associated with the loss of a specific
job. Mars square Neptune mirrors the fear of the unknown.
What are you doing to combat all the frustration?

Mark: I scream a lot. I drive home on the freeway and
yell. It's a new thing for me. I am a different person this year.
I'm a lot more in touch with my Mars. I have more energy
and strength and personality, and I like it. My reactions are
a lot healthier than they were a couple of years ago.

Astrologer: Mars in Capricorn opposing your Ascendant needs an outlet for emotional stress. You explained
that you have more energy. Has your physical health improved?

Mark: Yes. I'm still dealing with a fatigue problem, but
I'm a lot healthier.

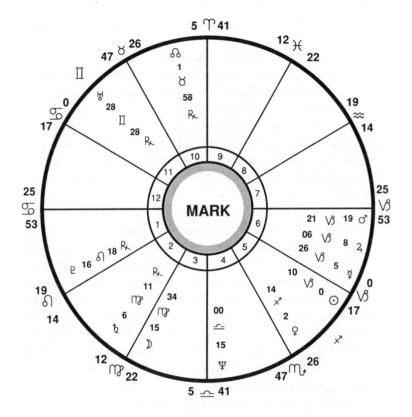

Natal Chart #4
Koch Houses

December 21, 1948 6:30:0 PM PST
0:20:51 ST
45N09'00" 122W51'00"
Woodburn, Oregon

Astrologer: Transiting Neptune in your 6th House for the past four years shows your struggle to maintain your energy. Uranus and Saturn entering this house will provide opportunities to break through physical limitations. To activate your Mars, you need involvement that stimulates passion.

Mark: True, because when I feel passion I feel alive.

Astrologer: How can you combine work and passion?

Mark: I should figure out what I do best and what is fun and find work that satisfies those needs. I grew up with the opposite attitude—work was toil and life was supposed to be tough. That was just what it was ... work was work, never pleasurable. Work should be a challenge. I sought the tough instead of pleasurable work. I must learn to identify with what feels good.

Astrologer: With Mars ruling your Aries Midheaven, your career and work environment needs cannot be separated. While you are deciding what you want to do next, would it be possible to deal with the security issue by leaving your present job and getting one that pays about $1200 a month? Don't answer right away now. Uranus is opposing its own position nearing the last conjunction to your Sun. Your restlessness is bound to increase, and without some kind of drastic change, so will your frustration level. Uranian solutions are often bizarre. For instance, working as a waiter could provide some financial security with little responsibility on your part, giving you time to explore other possibilities.

It is important to change your work environment because you are allowing Mars energy to keep you in a place where you don't want to be. You're using the staying power of Mars in Capricorn to maintain the status quo from fear.

Mark: That makes a lot of sense. It takes all my energy to survive. Right now, I am a city attorney and am involved in litigation every day. That's what I dislike about being a lawyer. I don't like the adversarial role.

Astrologer: You have Mars square Neptune in Libra. This explains your uncertainty, especially in areas that you view as combative. A job or career that combines Mars with Neptune must include passion, excitement and creative imagination. Faith in what you are doing is imperative. With Neptune in Libra, your working relationships with others are significant. Your 6th House stellium suggests that your health issues are directly related to your work environment.

Mark: There certainly is no passion in my work at this time. I feel thwarted, like I'm drowning. If I could ever find employment where I am comfortable with my coworkers, I would stay and never leave.

Astrologer: Have you ever considered starting your own business? You have an ability to help others and to provide service and information.

Mark: Right now, I am so confused that I don't see this as a way out. I don't know if there is any solution. My commitment is to redefine what work means to me and to find the courage to take the necessary steps to fulfill my needs.

Mars in Cancer

George has Mars and Pluto in Cancer straddling his Ascendant with Mars in the 12th House. He is in his mid-sixties and has had an opportunity to activate his Mars in many different circumstances. His close friends consider him much more assertive than he sees himself. George is quick to share his opinions and to help others solve what he sees as their assertiveness problems in the same way that he solves his.

George: There are two distinct styles of assertiveness. One is physical and one is mental. I am assertive in both areas. On the mental level, I am most assertive when I am

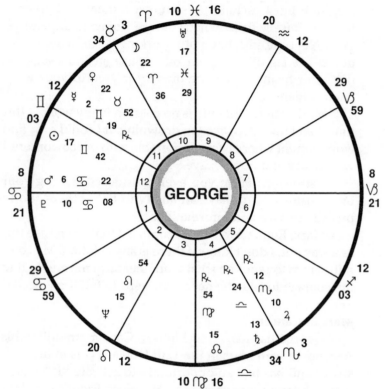

Natal Chart #5
Koch Houses

June 9, 1923 5:55:0 AM PST
22:47:07 ST
46N59'00"   123W53'00"
Hoquiam, Washington

dealing with people who have a tendency to tell me no.

Astrologer: Do you seek out these types of situations?

George: I don't avoid them. They have a tendency to seek me out. A good example is when I deal with bureaucracies. I've had to deal with them all my life, and people working in bureaucracies have a tendency to tell me no. Why? Because their job is over if I am weak enough to walk away. I won't give them that satisfaction. I want better answers.

Astrologer: Mars conjunct Pluto is rarely intimidated, and your determination to appear powerful is indicated by this combination. Do you become angry when you can't get the answers you want?

George: Yes. When I get annoyed, I might not finish the discussion at that time, but I will put it in the form of a letter. I document things, thus making my point, and it can't be ignored because a letter isn't something that can go in one ear and out the other like a telephone call, which is over when the phone is hung up.

Astrologer: With your Sun in Gemini, communication is a significant outlet for you. Mars square Saturn implies the need to give structure and form to any argument. Is it important for you to have the last word?

George: Good heavens, no. If somebody can show me where I'm wrong—it's difficult—but if somebody can show me where I'm wrong, I like to be intellectually challenged. I enjoy listening to a rebuttal once I have made a statement. If I can see anything in the opposing argument, we'll discuss it. Soon, there is no sense in further discussion because we have both made our points.

Astrologer: Mars trine Jupiter in Scorpio enjoys the openness and creativity of debate. What if the person keeps arguing? Do you ever blow up?

George: The other person would have to blow up first. Incidentally, my blowups are spontaneous and they're gone.

Astrologer: Your Moon in Aries expresses with emotional outbursts that are soon dissipated and forgotten. How do you express assertiveness physically?

George: I was a boxer because that was my natural inclination. I was also involved in track, and I knew I could be better at those two activities than any other. Boys always fight. I fought on the school grounds quite a bit. I wasn't an instigator, but I was one of the guys who got into the fights.

Astrologer: You didn't start the fights?

George: I don't think I have ever started one in my life, but I have finished a few.

Astrologer: Mars in the 12th House will wait for the action to start and then jump in; Mars conjunct Pluto on the Ascendant won't back down. Do you see a relationship between school yard fighting and boxing in the ring?

George: My opponent has a certain amount of skill and I have a certain amount of skill, and we're going to find out who is the most skillful. The purpose is to win the fight. If a guy gets knocked out in the course of that challenge, that is the way it is. He is challenging me the same way. If I don't do better than he does, he may knock me out. They didn't do that very often. If I knocked him down and he was bleeding, the first thing I wanted was to have him counted out and then I'd go over and pick him up.

Astrologer: Mars in Cancer has a sensitive and caring side that wants to nurture even after a fight. Others may not be as aware of your compassion, however, because Mars in the 12th House is more apparent to the individual than to the outside world. Do you think you could still win a fight?

George: Yeah. If someone challenged me on the street, I don't think they would want to do it a second time. I decided a long time ago that I would never be victimized.

Astrologer: Mars conjunct Pluto makes sure it stays in

control no matter what.

George: If my verbal ability can take care of a situation, I'm happy. If more people would handle their own problems and handle them instantly, there would be fewer problems in this world.

MARS IN ANGER

Anger is a reaction, an emotion that pushes back against someone or something. Some of us literally hit the object of our anger. We strike out at the person who said something we didn't like or hit the bedpost that "caused" the stubbed toe. Feeling anger isn't wrong. We can experience this emotion and channel the energy into productive and useful ways. When we don't find appropriate ways to express anger, we run the risk of Mars' energy taking over. Angry people and situations show up in our lives. We become victims. This is one of the reasons why someone who never gets angry can end up in physically and emotionally abusive relationships. The Mars energy is projected onto the "enemy"; we find others who will "do our Mars for us." Fire is warm and comforting in the fireplace; if a spark leaps onto the carpet, however, there's the potential for disaster. Learning to be alive does not mean burning the house down.

How we express anger is represented by our natal Mars through its sign, house and aspects. Our birth chart shows how we are apt to respond to certain circumstances. The planets are the tools that we have to integrate in order to actualize our potential. Our Mars tools can be cared for or left to rust. Astrologers can help people find ways to care for their Mars by discovering the attitudes and beliefs that bring about angry behavior. Anger is not to be feared but to be understood through an examination of Mars in the horoscope.

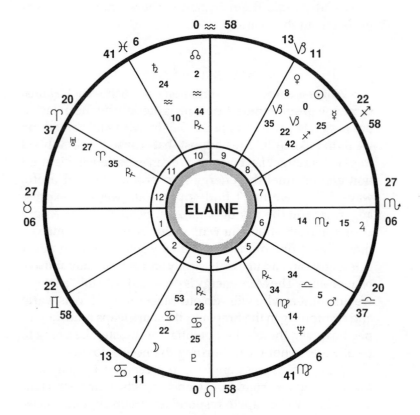

Natal Chart #6
Koch Houses

December 22, 1934   2:20:0 PM MST
20:12:44 ST
46N08'00"   107W33'00"
Custer, Montana

Mars in Libra

Elaine has Mars in Libra in the 5th House square her Sun and Venus conjunction in Capricorn in the 8th. She gives the impression that she is meek and mild. With Taurus rising, she can remain calm in crisis situations, so others tend to lean on her during difficult times.

Elaine: I use my Mars with intense force whenever I am blocked. I wait a long time to let my anger out, but when I do, everyone within earshot knows about it. I force others to take action and respond to me. I try to avoid the feeling of anger by seeing things in a spiritual light. If I am not capable of that, I still must be honest with my feelings. When I want something done about a particular situation, I'll try for a resolution. If there is none, I blow up. It is not for me to say whether it is good or bad, it just is.

Astrologer: How does your work as a massage therapist help you to understand the physical effects of anger?

Elaine: I use my hands to help people release tension and stored anger in their bodies. I am aware of the damage caused by repressing anger because I have seen the results. People with chronic pain often have difficulty getting mad.

Astrologer: Mars in Libra seeks balance, and your Capricorn Sun indicates the need for responsibility. The square between Mars and Venus often presents a crisis in personal relationships. Your occupation involves you in intimate physical relationships, responsible loving care and physical activity which is used for balance. Massage is the outlet you have developed to resolve your Mars dilemma.

Mars in Scorpio

Pearl is an intense, driven, professional woman who goes after what she wants. She is recognized as one of the leaders in her field. Her office walls are lined with degrees and awards which she has earned through her persistence and diligence. Mars is in Scorpio in the 10th House conjunct the Midheaven. It rules the intercepted 3rd House and sextiles her Sun in Capricorn and Neptune in Virgo.

Astrologer: Have you ever been emotionally volatile?

Pearl: I never have temper tantrums or fly off the handle; my anger builds up inside of me and I have to take action. As I have matured, I have tended to take more immediate action than when I was younger. I know that if I take care of this angry feeling it won't override me or override my decisions. I like to stay in balance. If I become angry on the job, I'll confront the person(s) involved and talk it out.

Astrologer: Mars in Scorpio in the 10th House denotes your need to confront issues immediately. The Moon in Libra mirrors your desire for balance. In what ways do you avoid destructive anger and express your emotions constructively?

Pearl: For example, I'm involved in a court case, and it makes me angry. I have been living with this aggravation for almost three years. Instead of being totally angry and picking on everyone around me, I realize it will take time for this to be resolved. Even though I feel anger, I try not to let circumstances get to me. I must live my life without becoming totally obsessed with this case.

Astrologer: Mars sextile Neptune typifies internal faith. The opposition to Uranus indicates directed and positive force when used properly. Have you faced many confrontational situations?

Pearl: Yes. I won't take on anyone else's anger. Just because someone else is angry in a situation, it is not necessary for me to respond in that way. I perceive confrontational situations differently than my professional peers. Circumstances that anger others to the point of nonperformance don't affect me in the same way. I work with the circumstance and get it resolved. That's how I've been all my life.

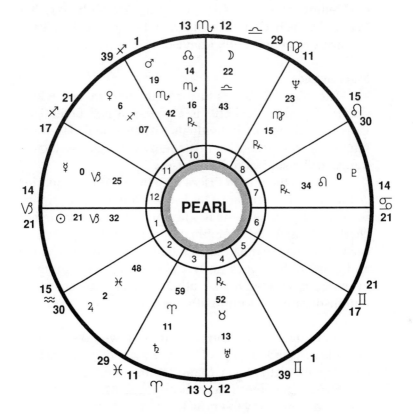

Natal Chart #7
Koch Houses

January 12, 1939   7:30:0 AM PST
14:42:58 ST
45N31'00"   122W59'00"
Hillsboro, Oregon

Astrologer: What is your philosophy concerning anger?

Pearl: I think that anger is a good, positive emotion. In my lifetime, it has evolved as strength. It strengthens rather than pulls me back. I have channeled anger into constructive achievement. I think I have done that very well.

Mars in Leo

The Mars, Saturn, Pluto conjunction in Leo which occurred in the late 1940s is a powerful and potentially violent combination. Individuals with this natal placement must find ways to utilize this energy through productive outlets or be subject to its misuse.

Sara has the Sun in Pisces with the Moon in Aquarius and a Gemini Ascendant. Her Leo stellium including Mars, Saturn and Pluto is at the IC (Imum Coeli), anchoring her chart. Although this combination can be interpreted as early childhood trauma, Sara remembers her youth as happy and content. She does not recall her parents arguing or even disagreeing with each other. Sara appears sensitive, optimistic and pleasant to others.

Astrologer: From your comments it would seem you never learned about anger from your family, which is surprising with a 4th House Mars. Tell me about this.

Sara: Sometimes I can't show anger. Most of my life I expected somebody to know what I needed and wanted, and when I didn't get it, it would frustrate and anger me. I don't get angry very often. I rechannel it. Sometimes I create scenarios in my mind to stimulate anger . . . events that never happen. I get angry internally, but I don't show it. I use hard physical exercise to vent hostility. I just punch it out; I even beat up people when I was a little kid.

Astrologer: Your Mars in Leo needs to find a creative

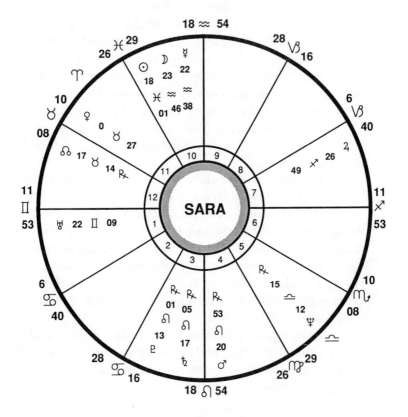

Natal Chart #8
Koch Houses

March 8, 1948 10:21:0 AM CST
21:25:19 ST
38N37'00"   90W12'00"
St. Louis, Missouri

or athletic outlet.

Sara: I always have been athletic. I learned martial arts strictly for self-defense and enjoyed the social aspects of training with others (Mars conjunct Saturn). As my skill improved, I got into competition and the artistic aspects of Akido. I found this to be a good way to channel energy, to channel frustration, to channel rage. Unfortunately, I became involved in a power struggle with my teacher (Mars conjunct Pluto opposing Mercury). He pushed me too far; he pushed me beyond my limits. I stopped enjoying myself. What I thought was a spiritual outlet turned into a war of wills. After 15 years, this part of my life is a completed chapter, a closed book.

Astrologer: So how do you channel your frustration without martial arts as an outlet?

Sara: I will always be athletic and will always seek a physical outlet. Currently, I am busy learning about myself, uncovering hidden things from my past (Moon opposing Mars), striving towards self-transformation and using astrology to help me find my way. By receiving counseling, the emotional fulfillment developed with my involvement in martial arts will be continued in a different way. I feel my Mars is an untapped powerful energy hiding behind a little door. I want to open it up and find out more about it. I am no longer afraid and am now ready to learn. I think I can find my personal power.

Mars in Gemini

With an Aries Midheaven, Duke used fighting as a way to gain a reputation and status in his peer group. Mars in Gemini in the 11th House squares Pluto in Virgo in the 2nd.

Duke: When I was a kid, I was always in trouble around the neighborhood (Mars in Gemini) ringing doorbells and running, things like that. I had two older brothers who picked on me because I was little, but they also taught me a lot. From grade school on, they would pick a guy out of the crowd and say, "Beat him up or we'll beat you up," and I used to enjoy that. It was fun, and I would get a lot of attention. It was better than getting beat up.

Astrologer: Mars in the 11th House is the hallmark of the social leader. For lack of another outlet, you chose fighting as a form of leadership. As you matured, did your behavior change?

Duke: I was a rebel, had longer hair, and wore different clothes while everyone else was pretty conservative.

Astrologer: Did you continue to fight?

Duke: I wouldn't just go up and bump somebody on the back of the head and start a fight. They had to do something first like call me a name or spread a rumor that wasn't true. I have never been afraid to stand up to anybody; I'm still not today.

Astrologer: Your Mars quincunx Neptune and Jupiter indicates the desire to assert power in a big way and gives a clue to your philosophical attitude concerning fighting. Gemini is an Air sign and Mars here responds to verbal cues. You didn't become hostile because people did something; you got angry because they *said* something. Have you stopped fighting?

Duke: The last time I remember having to defend myself was in the spring of 1982. This gentleman said I was the reason why parents used birth control. That's all it took. I smacked him. I objected to his saying things like that about me and others. I didn't think; I just got up from the table and hit him. It happened so fast. I didn't even realize I had done it until afterwards.

Astrologer: At that time, transiting Uranus opposed your natal Mars and squared your Pluto providing the impetus for a crisis to develop. This energy could have been channeled into creativity or athletic achievement. Why did

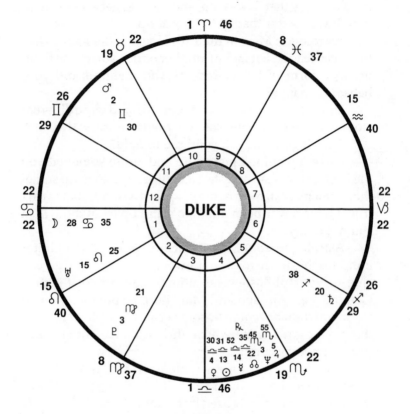

Natal Chart # 9
Koch Houses

October 6, 1958 11:17:0 PM PST
0:06:28 ST
44N05'00" 123W04'00"
Eugene, Oregon

this incident end your fighting?

Duke: When I fought before, I was uncontrollable and would lose sight of who I was hitting. I wouldn't realize I was hurting someone; it was like a dream until the fight was over. I would get to the point where I thought I had to fight for my life in a blind rage.

Astrologer: The negative outcome of Pluto square Mars can be a complete loss of control. It often represents the build-up of anger released violently. Has your attitude changed?

Duke: Being out of control and hitting someone without realizing it kind of got to me, kind of woke me up. I began to see that this was not intelligent behavior. Instead of leaving a mark as a bad guy, I would prefer to leave a mark as a somewhat controlled and intelligent person.

Astrologer: Mars trine Venus in Libra shows your desire to be liked. Pluto and Venus aspect Mars and are semi-sextile each other which brings together the issue of control and acceptance in a balanced and harmonious way. You should be able to achieve your desired results. How do you handle your anger now?

Duke: The best thing for me to do is to close up and walk away before I hurt myself or someone else. I don't have that need to swing and hit anymore, but I have to clam up and get away for a little while. That's hard for some people to understand. They think you have to talk about it, but that's the wrong thing for me.

Astrologer: By using Mars sextile the Moon in Cancer, you are able to think before acting. With Mars in Gemini sextiling the Midheaven, finding a proper business or career outlet focuses Mars' energy in a more acceptable way. Because you drive (Mars) a delivery truck and install (Gemini) appliances in people's homes (Cancer Ascendant), you have found an acceptable expression for your Mars.

MARS IN COMPETITION

The dichotomy present in competition centers around the theme of win-lose. Often winning implies one victor and a cast of losers. The concept of conflict resolution in a win-win situation is becoming more prevalent in our society. This philosophy allows competition to be an acceptable outlet for Mars.

The competitive aspect of Mars works on both an individual and team level. Setting personal goals to overcome limitations is a healthy way to achieve success, and each person can determine the context of his or her parameters. The joy of achieving brings a strong sense of self-worth and helps develop passion. It is through this competitive force of passion that Mars functions at its best. Individuals can soar to great heights physically, mentally, emotionally and spiritually by structuring competitive situations. The passion that results from the effort can be applied in daily endeavors such as business, education, recreation and relationships. *To compete is to win* because the victory is in the action of Mars and not in the gold medal.

Mars in Sagittarius

Court reporter Brenda shines as a triathlete. With Mars in Sagittarius in her 12th House, she competes for her own pleasure as well as to win. Many athletes have Mars in the 12th or Mars in Pisces if fancy footwork is required in their sport. Brenda also has the Sun and Moon in Sagittarius which adds to her athletic prowess.

Astrologer: When did you start to see yourself as an athlete?

Brenda: I have always been well coordinated and enjoyed doing physical things. When I started to ski, I realized I was skiing with people who were much better than I, and I wanted to ski as well as they did. In order to do this I had to develop my legs. I started running in 1972 but didn't get serious until 1980. My husband ran every day. I thought, "If he can do it, I can do it." It was a challenge to run every day, rain or snow.

Astrologer: Do you feel your commitment to running has benefits beyond the physical?

Brenda: Yes. When I first started running, I ran in the morning and that was my daily time for myself, to clear the cobwebs. It was fun to try to run a little faster each day. Running gives me a high; I feel good and at peace with myself. I have never looked at running as a chore; it is my time for me.

Astrologer: Because the 12th is such a private house, with Mars there you had to find a way to combine your need for solitude with any energetic endeavor. How did you become involved in triathlon events?

Brenda: Triathlons were just getting started on the West Coast in 1984. Since I enjoy swimming, I thought I would give it a try, and I loved it. I always got a high from running, but this tripled the high because of the three sports—swimming, bicycling and running.

Astrologer: I understand you did well in the Hawaiian Ironman. What made you decide to compete there?

Brenda: When I first watched the Ironman on TV, I said, "I will never do that. I couldn't put my body through that." By the spring of 1985, I had decided that someday I would.

Astrologer: Did you have to qualify?

Brenda: Yes. I entered the Cascade Lakes Half-Ironman in August 1986. I didn't go there thinking I would qualify, but I did. To qualify it was necessary to place in the top three in my age group. When they called my name, I couldn't believe it. That was August 16, 1986. On September 3, 1986, 45 days before the Ironman, I was hit by a truck. I had worked for three years to get to that point, and now it was

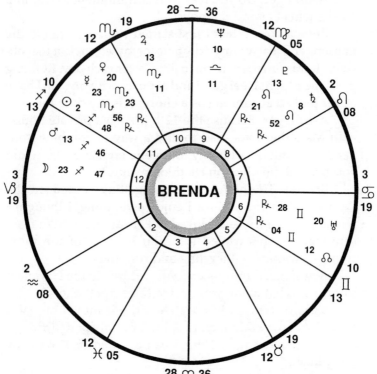

Natal Chart #10
Koch Houses

November 25, 1946 10:00:0 AM CST
13:46:19 ST
42N02'00" 97W25'00"
Norfolk, Nebraska

snatched away from me. I was bicycle training, riding by myself, when a 60-foot gravel truck struck me. I wound up in a ditch with a fractured back, a crushed left foot and a broken spirit. That December, my doctor told me that I would be in a great deal of pain for a minimum of three months and to forget the Ironman. I told him, "I'll be on the start line of the Hawaiian Ironman on October 6, 1987." He said, "I hope you are and you prove me wrong." I had made up my mind that my opportunity had been taken from me and I was going to get it back.

Astrologer: Optimism is a basic key word for Sagittarius, and the 12th House represents faith. You combined your faith and optimism with your competitive drive to set your athletic goals and to overcome the obstacles presented by your accident. At the time of your accident, transiting Uranus was at the midpoint of your Mars/Moon conjunction and approaching an opposition to its natal position. The impact of this sudden event activated your competitive nature (Mars in Sagittarius), your forceful zeal (Mars sextile Neptune) and your capacity to deal with unexpected events (Mars opposing Uranus). How did you regain your physical strength?

Brenda: I went to physical therapy daily; if I was told to do exercises at least once a day, I did them three times. I did what I could to heal myself. As soon as my back brace came off, I started swimming, then added walking and eased into running. I would train and cry. I couldn't work, I couldn't sit, but I couldn't give up. I did the Ironman one year, one month and one week after my accident. It was my dream come true, and I have never felt as good as that day.

Astrologer: How has your love of competition affected you?

Brenda: I am able to control my emotions now, except when I am under a lot stress. I have never been an angry person, except after the accident. Working through it was hard. I had a lot of anger about some driver that just didn't care what he did, wrecking my body, and it was a careless accident as most accidents are. He could have avoided it, but I was the one who had to pay the price.

I got some counseling, and I read books about confidence and overcoming obstacles to mentally prepare myself. I knew I would be physically weaker, but if I could get to where I needed to be mentally, I felt like I would have it made. This worked. I did visualizations and affirmations because I have learned you can do a lot with your mind. I'm the average person who enjoys life. You asked me about my love of competition. Without this to drive me, I may have been content to sit back and let life pass me by. I was fortunate. The greatest gift from my family was this quote which I think about every day, saying it to myself over and over, "Each day is a little life. Fill it with happiness if you can, with courage if you can't."

Note: Brenda went on to compete in the Canadian Ironman triathlon. She placed 2nd in her age group.

Mars in Aquarius

Lawrence is a divorced parent raising his seven-year-old daughter alone. He is a full-time student studying to become a registered nurse. His Mars is in Aquarius in the 5th House, totally unaspected. Mars rules his 8th House and co-rules his 3rd.

Astrologer: Lawrence, it sounds like you carry a heavy workload going to school, caring for your daughter, keeping the house and working part-time. Do you ever have time for fun?

Lawrence: Yes, I coach first and second grade girls in soccer and T-ball. I love to win.

Astrologer: Mars in Aquarius enjoys group activities. What does competition mean to you?

Lawrence: Winning. Competition means winning.

Astrologer: How do you motivate your team?

Lawrence: I motivate them by screaming a lot but in a positive sense. I'm constantly reinforcing what they need to be doing and encouraging them to strive and give 100 percent.

Astrologer: Do you really scream?

Lawrence: Yes, I do. I put on as good a show as the kids do. Some parents come out just to watch me.

Astrologer: From a Sun in Aries and an unaspected Mars, we can expect a one-man show. Would you rather coach or participate?

Lawrence: I don't feel I have the skills to be a great athlete. I couldn't measure up to my older brothers, so I chose coaching where I find more rewards. Interestingly, I wasn't competitive academically or athetically in high school.

Astrologer: How do you compete academically?

Lawrence: I have to have A's. I don't really compete against everyone else. I like to be at the top of the class, but that's not my primary goal. Competing with myself and the echo of being told "You can't do that" spur me on. As a child, I never tried to excel because I was convinced I couldn't.

Astrologer: What caused the change in your life?

Lawrence: I have finally stopped living my life for everyone else and have decided to live for myself. I am studying to become a registered nurse, and I'm harder on myself than anyone else. When I have an exam, I will go without sleep and forget to eat until I know I am prepared to get an A.

Astrologer: With Mars in Aquarius, intellectual competition appeals to you. Do you see your obsession for perfection as a way to express who you are?

Lawrence: Yes, I do. I have always had to prove it to myself that I could achieve. I got good grades at first, not

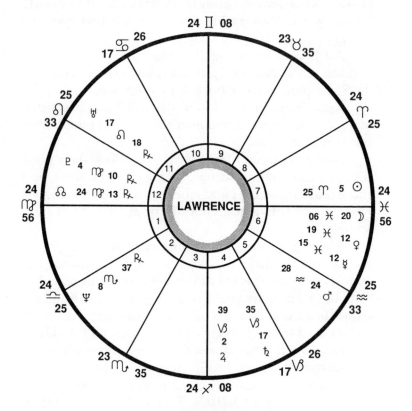

Natal Chart #11
Koch Houses

March 25, 1960   5:37:0 PM PST
5:34:25 ST
40N47'00"   124W09'00"
Eureka, California

straight A's, but good grades. If you are going to do something, you might as well be the best. I need to know that I have achieved. I feel a loss of self-esteem if I don't show other people what I can do. They probably don't give a damn, but I have to do it . . . there is no choice.

Astrologer: This addictive/obsessive pattern is due in great part to your Virgo Ascendant ruled by Mercury in Pisces in Virgo's 6th House. You do have an alternative way to use your Mars energy for service. Moderation is the key.

Mars in Leo

A firefighter and paramedic, Carolyn's Aquarian Sun rules and opposes her Mars, Saturn, Pluto and Midheaven conjunction in Leo. Scorpio rises and the Moon is in Pisces. Her 10th House Mars trines 2nd House Jupiter in Sagittarius and quincunxes the Moon in Pisces and Venus in Aries in the 5th House.

Astrologer: What made you decide to be a firefighter?

Carolyn: The competitive challenge. The fire department said no woman would ever pass the physical agility test. I have always been athletic and competitive, except for a short period when I considered it unladylike. Once I decided to be a firefighter, passing the physical agility test was my goal. Now the challenge is to see whether I can do what I have to do from moment to moment.

Astrologer: Your athletic ability is indicated by Mars in Leo trine Jupiter, and this can be used in your work because the 2nd and 10th Houses are involved. Your "I'll show them" attitude is represented by your Sun in Aquarius opposing Mars. Your Venus in Aries quincunx Mars in Leo shows your need as a woman to challenge a male-dominated occupation. How do you handle the dangerous aspects of your job?

Carolyn: I don't see it as danger so much; it's more the

challenge of doing something different, the variety, the physicality of it.

Astrologer: You went from firefighter to paramedic. What motivated that choice?

Carolyn: Being a paramedic has the advantage of being physical and versatile, being mobile and being out there, and it includes dealing with people rather than just structures and things. It satisfies my compassion.

Astrologer: This reflects your Moon in Pisces quincunx Mars in Leo. How do you express your anger?

Carolyn: I get frustrated once in awhile, but because I lead such an active life, I don't always have to blow up or let off steam when I get angry. When I get irritable and emotional, I withdraw. I find it hard to understand violent anger in others. I don't recognize that emotion within myself.

Astrologer: Moon in Pisces indicates that you withdraw rather than indulge in emotional outbursts. If your job did not require such demanding physical activity, you could find yourself repressing your Mars energy. How do you utilize your competitive nature away from work?

Carolyn: Not in organized sports. I compete with myself, trying to better my personal best record in running or weight lifting. This year I'm trying things I have never done before. Just the competition of me and my fear of doing something different, maybe not doing it very well, but doing it anyway, is pretty exciting.

Astrologer: What type of activities do you enjoy?

Carolyn: This year, physical ones. I did some vertical rock climbing for the first time. I raced my car in an auto cross on a small track at a slow speed through an obstacle course. I went skiing on a mountain glacier this summer, did some motorcycle racing and went scuba diving for the first time. It has become a year to "try something new."

Astrologer: Your Aquarius Sun has to be different.

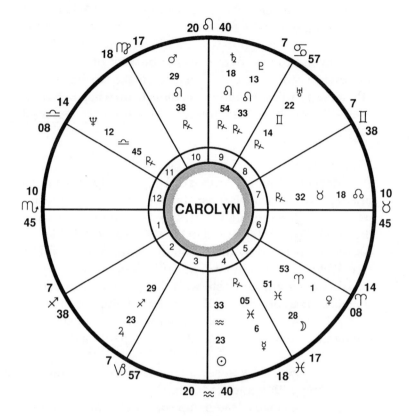

Natal Chart #12
Koch Houses

February 13, 1948 12:20:0 AM PST
9:32:14 ST
43N24'00"   124W14'00"
North Bend, Oregon

With Mars in Leo co-ruling your Scorpio Ascendant, you express the need for constant personal challenge. Your elevated Leo stellium signifies a need to be in the spotlight where you can motivate and inspire others. What does being a warrior mean to you?

Carolyn: A warrior is someone who does what s/he wants even though there may not be a lot of support or acceptance from society. I want to make an impact on others, supporting and allowing them to do what they want even if I may think they are not taking the best course of action.

Mars in Aries

Mars in the sign of Aries is direct, impulsive and enterprising. Its expression is most obvious in the horoscope of a person who has the Sun in Aries. Ted has Mars, Venus and the Sun in Aries intercepted in his 10th House. His Cancer Ascendant is ruled by the Moon in Pisces in the 9th. The Fire/Water combination can be difficult because the emotional Water signs compete with the Fire signs for center stage. Ted has solved this dilemma by developing an assertive yet compassionate role in his work. His business is organizing track meets and athletic competitions.

Astrologer: Do you see a correlation in your life between competition and leadership?

Ted: I will take a leadership role only when it's something I want to do or there is no one else to do it. I don't compete for the role. If there was someone else filling it, I could be happy in a supportive position.

Astrologer: Would you prefer that?

Ted: No, because I like being in the limelight, but I don't do it from a sense of competition. I don't say "I want to be in the limelight; I can compete and do a better job" and put someone out of business.

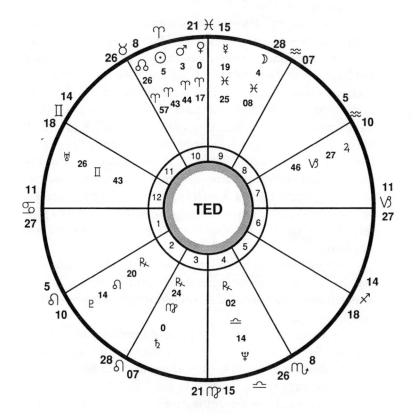

Natal Chart #13
Koch Houses

March 26, 1949   17:10 GMT
39N34'00"   89W21'00"

Astrologer: Spoken like a true Moon in Pisces with the Sun in the 10th. You are in a highly competitive field. A lot of cities are competing for the same track events. How do you feel about this?

Ted: I like to believe in win-win, and I observe a standard of fairness. To me, having the Olympic trials in Eugene, Oregon every time would not be fair, and it certainly would not be a win-win situation for track and field in this country. Neither should Indianapolis have it all the time. In fairness to the athletes, you don't just hand it off to a new city if they have no track background. One of the reasons I'm so bullish about having the trials here is because we have the expertise and it's our turn. I react strongly to people who are greedy. That's where my competitiveness comes out; if someone gets greedy, I say "Okay, let's take off the gloves and get to it. It comes down to who can do the best job and let's play fair." Life is not fair, but that doesn't mean you stop pursuing fairness.

Astrologer: Venus conjunct the Sun is almost like having the Sun in Libra, and this is why you are so concerned with fairness. Mars is also conjunct your Sun. Are you known as a tough guy?

Ted: Actually, I think I'm getting a reputation as a firebrand, which is ironic because I'm about the biggest conciliator there is as far as getting along and going along. My nickname among the Brazilians was "Vaselina" because I was so smooth. Now I'm getting national recognition as the guy who is stirring the pot. They quote me, not the other promoters who are older and more established, because they aren't saying what needs to be said.

Astrologer: Do you enjoy that distinction?

Ted: I enjoy the rush I get from it, but it could be counterproductive. If you get that reputation, people tend to discount what you say. I'd like to be the quiet one who says something pithy. I see myself evolving in that direction, but

I also think it's not the time to sit back and wait for the right moment. We're in crisis.

Mars in Taurus

A person with Mars in Taurus seeks security, safety, routine and organization. This type of competitive drive focuses on tangible results. Carmen is an astrologer with Mars in Taurus in and ruling the 3rd House. She is a published author who is also a pioneer in her field.

Astrologer: How do you most effectively express your competitive nature?

Carmen: I am intrigued by all kinds of head games: gambling, cards, word puzzles, anything that is mentally competitive. One of my favorite ways to relax is with a challenging solitaire game.

Astrologer: Your Mars squares Mercury in your 12th House. This often indicates intellectual curiosity. The 12th House influence is shown through solitary pursuits. How are you competitive with others? Do you enjoy debate, sports, or political activities?

Carmen: Though I am not particularly physically active, I am an avid sports fan and follow football and basketball with a vengeance. Politics bore me except on the local level. I consider myself a good lecturer and get my point across well, but debating is not really up my alley.

Astrologer: The Sun in the 1st House, although in Aquarius, has a strong Martian flavor. Since it rules your 7th House, have you had difficulty with relationships?

Carmen: As a youngster, I was extremely aggressive, came on much too strong and was handy with my fists. Marriage has been a challenge, and so have business partnerships, but with maturity I have been able to temper aggression with assertiveness.

Astrologer: That is your Mars square your Ascendant—

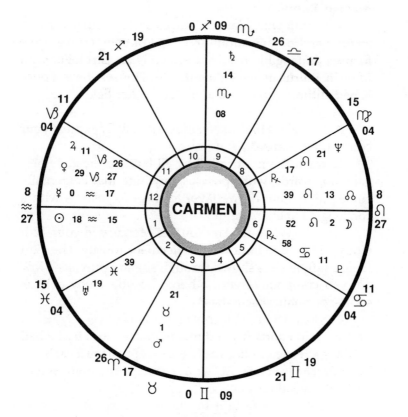

Natal Chart #14
Koch Houses

February 7, 1925 12:34 GMT
41N52'00"   87W39'00"

hot temper and physical force. With Mars square your Moon, what was your relationship with your mother?

Carmen: My mother and I shared a love/hate relationship, and yet I feel that everything I have accomplished is a reflection of her position as my role model. She was an achiever and was never afraid to tackle any chore. I am the eternal optimist and feel that nothing ventured is nothing gained.

The foregoing conversations indicate the various ways that the energy of Mars is utilized in the horoscope. When we first study the symbolism of the signs, planets and houses, we can forget that these components make up the life of a *person*. Astrologers have ideas about how Mars works, what its function is, where and when its force will manifest and why someone may or may not be attuned to its power. Talking with an individual about his or her life as it relates to the birth chart is an excellent way to begin to understand how the inner warrior truly manifests.

Don Borkowski

Don Borkowski holds a B.S. in Business with a major in statistics from Drake University and has done post-graduate work in Quantitative Methods at Ohio University. He also holds a diploma in data processing from the Computer Career Institute.

He has studied astrology since 1971 under Press Roberts and John Ray Galvin. In 1975 he joined Press and Ima Roberts in writing *Signs and Parts in Plain English*. Don is well known for his articles in *Mercury Hour* from 1979 to 1987, and he currently contributes to the *Heliogram*. He has lectured many times in the Portland area.

Don's wife Georgie is also an astrologer, and they and their 10-year-old son Ian reside in Salem, Oregon. Don works full-time as a computer programmer-analyst, and although this limits his astrological practice to part-time, he feels that not depending on astrological income keeps his astrology honest.

Born August 15, 1950, in Portland, Oregon at the rectified time of 4:17 p.m. PDT, Don belongs to FCA and AFAN and is a former member of AFA and ASC.

JUPITER

Two themes explain the fundamental essence of Jupiter—**expansion** and **preservation**. The key word approach to astrology offers, through semantic symbolism, a gradual attunement to astrological influences. A few typical words that express the concept of expansion are : *large, pervasive, excessive, magnanimous, growth* and *abundance*. Similarly, words that convey the principle of preservation include: *maintain, rescue, protect, perpetuate, status quo* and *synthesize.*

The theme of expansion is a direct analog of Jupiter's physical appearance in the solar system. As Jupiter is the largest planet and has more satellites than any other planet, it must serve as a symbol of largeness and expansion. Intrinsically, the concept of largeness, like any other astrological symbol, is neutral; yet society judges largeness to be either desirable or undesirable depending upon the situation. For example, think of body parts. What body parts are considered to be attractive if they are big? How do people judge others whose parts are not big enough? What body parts are considered to be unattractive if they are big?

Preservation is another equally broad, impartial concept associated with Jupiter. In one direction, preservation can mean the salvation from an unwanted alternative. What is now called a flotation device was once called a life preserver. Neutrally, preservation is associated with stability; negatively, preservation can be synonymous with stagnation. One may wonder how Jupiter can possibly link expansion to either stability or stagnation. The key to remember is that stability and stagnation are both marked by the lapse of a large amount of time between changes. While time taken by itself is a Saturnian factor, large amounts of anything are Jupiterian. Introductory astrology books almost always make the point that food is often preserved in tin cans and that tin is associated with Jupiter. Well, tin cans are out-of-date, but we should remember that the correct chemical name for the fluoride in toothpaste and drinking water is *stannous fluoride*. *Stannum* is Latin for "tin"; therefore, stannous fluoride is a compound of tin and fluorine. So for the last 30 years, Jupiter has been invoked to preserve our teeth in the same spirit that Jupiter's glyph has been placed on prescriptions since Roman times. In addition, Jupiter's position in a solar return chart often shows where the status quo will be maintained.

Historically, Jupiter has been assigned the rulership of **Sagittarius** and **Pisces**. Most astrologers, unless they use horary astrology in depth, tend to accept Neptune as the one true ruler of Pisces. This is a colossal mistake. At a recent Joan McEvers lecture, she asked the attendees for a show of hands to see how many people still used Mars as a co-ruler of Scorpio. Disappointingly, only about half the group did. The proportion of astrologers who accept Jupiter as the co-ruler of Pisces (and those who accept Saturn as a co-ruler of Aquarius) is most definitely much smaller. Frankly, of the three signs that gained higher-octave rulers, it is hardest to see Jupiter's association with Pisces at first glance. There seems to be such an overwhelming affinity between the planet and the sign of Sagittarius even if Sagittarius' preserving side is not obviously apparent. Pisces' component of expansion is not obviously apparent either. To accept Sagittarius as the only sign ruled by Jupiter is to deny Jupiter's attribute of preservation. Sagittarius is more expansive than sustaining. Pisces is more sustaining than expansive. Jupiter is both.

Two questions arise. First, how can we as astrologers evaluate the relative strengths within a chart of Jupiter and Neptune as co-rulers of Pisces? Practical experience shows that the earlier degrees of Pisces are more Jupiterian than Neptunian. The later degrees of Pisces are the other way around. This effect is proportional so that the middle of Pisces is just about equally Jupiterian and Neptunian.

Second, some astrologers attribute Chiron to be the true ruler of Sagittarius; how valid is this opinion? The logic of this is immediately suspect because if Chiron were to rule Sagittarius and Neptune to rule Pisces, then Jupiter would not have primary rulership of any sign, which is unnatural for such a large planet. This opinion was derived chiefly through a simplistic extrapolation of the mythological roots of astrology. Since Chiron was a centaur, the creature represented by Sagittarius, some people thought that Chiron must rule that sign. This specious logic is as defective as assuming that a man must be an excellent bowler because he has a Polish name.

To understand both sides of Jupiter, it helps to study both of Jupiter's signs in detail.

In Sagittarius, the principle of expansion is clearly more evident than the principle of preservation although they are both operative. Nearly every concept ruled by Gemini can be expanded into a concept that is ruled by Sagittarius. Whereas Gemini is attuned to the practical mind, Sagittarius rules religion and philosophy. Mere conversation and correspondence expand into mass communication. Sagittarius denotes voyages of the body and spirit, but Gemini only claims commuting and errand-running. Blood relatives are Geminian; in-laws are Sagittarian. Gemini is immediate and local. Sagittarius is global but lacks immediacy. Jupiter can often show how a person will function as a foreigner. Of course, this is not to say that Gemini is intrinsically shallow or that Sagittarius is intrinsically profound. It is merely that the Gemini/Sagittarius polarity is among the easiest in the zodiac to understand. The preservationist side of Sagittarius is far more obtuse. Sagittarius preserves cultural identity through higher education and religion. Evangelism, a truly Sagittarian process, combines the expansiveness of disseminating a set of beliefs to a broader circle of people with the preservationist intent of saving their souls.

Pisces is a sign that has acquired an undeserved bad reputation over the years. It could even be said that it was fated to have a bad reputation because it is the twelfth sign. Nonetheless, no sign is any better or any worse than the other 11 signs. Each can be upstanding, and each can be seamy. The same principle is true for planets as well. Wise metaphysicians have written that planets were not discovered until humanity could handle the addition of such planets to the collective unconscious. Sometimes, though, it seems that Neptune was discovered too soon. Too few people can relate to the spiritual heights that Neptune exemplifies. Instead Neptune brings escapism through substance abuse and lower astral phenomena, and Pisces is dragged along through the dirt with Neptune. Neptune has only been observed since 1846. Pisces shared Jupiter's rulership with Sagittarius for thousands of years. How can Pisces now be associated with a generally malefic planet that has only been known for 143 years? Pisces' role in preservation is easily seen through its association with institutions whose functions ostensibly include healing. Likewise, Pisces rules synthesis, the process in which lesser factors are preserved by becoming a part of the whole. Pisces' reputation as the "dustbin of the zodiac" actually relates to Pisces' capability to function as a catchall for anything that isn't particularly specified elsewhere in astrology. Externally, this leads to Pisces' advocacy for the most obscure minorities and forgotten underdogs. Expansion is also a

Piscean trait—most of the surface of the Earth is covered in oceans, an abundance of water ruled by Pisces. Likewise the aforementioned catchall attribute of Pisces is also keyed to the very large number of people, principles and things that are not represented elsewhere in the chart.

JUPITER RETROGRADE

The principle of retrogradation represents traits that must be grown into or grown out of over a period of time. Retrograde planets spell out lessons that may have to be repeated many times until they are learned. In an everyday sense, retrograde planets manifest both as delays and as attempts to do things after the fact. (Intercepted planets and planets at 29 degrees express their energies similarly to retrograde planets. The difference is that the Sun or Moon could very easily be intercepted or be at 29 degrees of a sign even though they cannot be retrograde.) So when Jupiter is retrograde, the principles of expansion and preservation tend to work after the fact. If a person with Jupiter retrograde wanted to have an antique car, s/he may purchase a junked hulk with many pieces missing. S/he would then expand it by adding the lost parts and preserve it by restoring lost functions and protecting it from further deterioration. If a person with Jupiter direct desired an antique car, s/he might purchase one that had never been allowed to deteriorate in the first place. The principle behind a retrograde Jupiter is very similar to the transformative power of Pluto because the effects are virtually identical. However, the motivation behind the processes could be entirely different.

JUPITER IN THE SIGNS AND HOUSES

In natal astrology, the most important factor is the

houses. The houses of the chart represent areas within a person's life, and whether a person ever chooses to have an astrological consultation or not, s/he will have a life to lead. In a lecture, Noel Tyl admonished his audience not to make the client's life fit the planets; he encouraged making the client's planets fit the life. Jupiter's house position shows where the life will be expanded and preserved. Of course, other areas may be expanded and/or preserved depending upon aspects and house rulerships. Jupiter's sign is secondary to the house position. Jupiter's sign will show the manner in which the expansion and preservation will function.

Jupiter in Aries With Jupiter here, the self-orientation of Aries is expanded, but the watery side of Jupiter tends to polish much of the Arian roughness. Aries goes its own way, usually instinctively. Jupiter in Aries goes its own way but only after a certain amount of thought and philosophizing is expended. Naturally, this can fluctuate widely depending on the rest of the chart and how the person has developed. Aries can be selfish and oblivious to others. Jupiter in Aries definitely seeks fairness between the self and other people. Unfortunately, Jupiter is not necessarily able to mitigate the obliviousness of this sign.

As Jupiter is inspirational, Jupiter in Aries often is inspired by the self, tending to seek more depth than any other Aries placement does. Yet the main caution here is that the philosophy of a Jupiter in Aries individual may be just too personalized for the rest of humanity.

Of course, the preservationist side of Jupiter operates here also. Since these people answer only to themselves, it is very difficult to change their attitudes. They resist and persevere. Any changes in their attitudes must be evolutionary, and they must be derived from within as well.

Jupiter in Aries almost always indicates self-confidence

and optimism. Usually the only impediment to this stems from Jupiter intercepted or challengingly aspected.

Jupiter in Taurus This placement is marked by two major recurring themes. First, there is often a strong link to music. How a person relates to music depends on which planets are found in Taurus and what their aspects are. The expansive principle of Jupiter invokes the urge to communicate on a higher level and to disseminate one's thoughts and feelings. This sign placement is naturally inclined to use music as a means to that end. Although such an interest in music is not guaranteed, it is almost always meaningful when present. With Jupiter in Taurus, you may even be a professional musician, or if not, a family member may be.

The second continuing theme is a tendency to eccentricity. Eccentricity can correlate with Jupiter because this planet is instrumental in formulating one's philosophy of life. Yes, it is hard to picture a sign as conservative as Taurus as being eccentric, but Taurus is marked by its resistance to outside stimulation. Consequently, if a Taurean Jupiter has developed its philosophy of life, whether it is mainstream or not, it won't change easily. So, if the path is unusual, the label of eccentricity will stick.

Jupiter in Taurus also tends to have an effect on the physical appearance. Venus and her signs Taurus and Libra affect physical beauty, the skin in particular. Many very attractive people have this placement, but the opposite is not rare. The beauty may be impeded by skin problems, or some body parts may be disproportionate in size.

Jupiter in Gemini Jupiter is in its detriment in Gemini. This sounds much worse than the actual situation. Although planets are reputed to have trouble functioning at their best in incompatible signs, the problems faced by Jupiter in Gemini are usually trivial. The expansiveness of Jupiter and the scattered state associated with Gemini tend to combine readily, giving an affinity for an abundance of little things. The best way to handle a lot of little things is to judge them as pieces of a whole. If a common ground is identified, then the pieces can be organized into a whole. For example, if you have Jupiter in Gemini and have insect problems in your home, you should hire a professional exterminator to eliminate all of them. If you get rid of only one or two at a time, they will keep coming back.

In a similar vein, Jupiter in Gemini tends to prefer quantity to quality. This placement may be found in people who buy multitudes of books only to skim through them. It may be found in people who run through a variety of shallow relationships in the hope of finding the right substantial one.

Jupiter in Gemini is a very useful placement for writers and speakers. It generally gives a wide vocabulary. Words become the little pieces that a communicator can build into a larger form for disseminating thoughts and knowledge.

When dealing with other cultures, the Jupiter in Gemini person will do what comes naturally—talk. S/he sees that learning about different societies can be greatly facilitated by communication.

Jupiter in Cancer The concept of exaltation allows for a planet to have a special affinity for a sign that it does not rule. Jupiter is exalted in Cancer. This exaltation makes a great deal of sense because both of Jupiter's major themes can function most efficiently in Cancer. Cancer is best described by the concepts of nurturing and motherhood. A mother nurtures by giving a child the wherewithal to grow, unharmed, until it can function as a fully independent person. Consequently, both sides of Jupiter work together at the same time in Cancer. The preservationist side will enable it to expand in an unmolested manner the traits of the house where it is posited. Likewise, Cancer is a very retentive sign, which can keep the Jupiterian expansion under control. Jupiter can be superficial when outward expansion favors quantity over quality of experience. Cancerian retentiveness forces depth onto Jupiter. For instance, if Jupiter were connected with the mind in a chart, it would show a major interest in places of learning and a great fascination with exposure to taught material. Yet if Jupiter in Cancer were connected with the mind, schools and colleges would be seen as merely a means to an end. Furthermore, a much greater portion of the taught material would be retained and learned.

The principles of expansion and preservation will also be applied to the home and/or family. There is a resourcefulness to make a home even if circumstances seem against it. One interesting case is that of a man who had Jupiter in Cancer in the 4th House. This man lived in a storage locker so that he could save enough money to own an expensive imported sports car. As other factors in his chart showed, he was able to make extreme self-sacrifices in order to support other self-indulgences. He could have easily parked his car in a parking lot and slept in it there. Jupiter in Cancer provided a "home" for him even though housing was not an issue. (Fairness dictates that I mention that his Jupiter was also conjunct Uranus in Cancer in the 5th House.)

Jupiter in Cancer also colors the function of Cancer working as a sign. Cancer's zoological symbolism of shelled creatures is reinforced by Jupiter's presence. Jupiter tends to diminish Cancerian vulnerability, either positively through added optimism and self-confidence or negatively through excessive weight gain.

Jupiter in Leo Of the four elements, the Fire signs are the most primal in their nature. From the time of birth, traits attributed to fiery planets and the Fire signs are among the first to develop. It follows that habitual behavior of a fiery nature is the hardest kind to alter. Of the three Fire signs, Aries and Leo are most easily linked because of the Sun's rulership of Leo and its exaltation in Aries. Since Jupiter rules Pisces as well as Sagittarius and since it is exalted in Cancer, Jupiter tends to be labeled as a bit of a misfit here when compared to Mars and the Sun.

A Leo Jupiter tends to overcompensate for its watery side as if Jupiter was in competition with the Sun. If you have Jupiter in Leo, you can be every last bit as generous, magnanimous and noble as a Leo Sun or Ascendant. In Leo though, Jupiterian expansion can easily slip into being much too much of a good thing. Leo as a sign and the Sun as a planet are both fairly expansive in their own right. The traits of both Jupiter and Leo reinforce each other without the necessary checks and balances.

There is a clear and present danger for people with Jupiter in Leo. They can easily be overly impressed with the magnitude of their imagined importance. It stands to reason on the positive side that the same influences that can summon up a prodigious ego can also produce a bounty of creative talent. If a leonine Jupiter manifests as a gigantic ego, it may be fruitless to attempt to suppress it. Instead, such an ego should be given a reason to exist. Any and all latent talents should be identified and developed.

The talent found with Jupiter in Leo is no fluke. There are well-known cases in which a philosopher or astrologer becomes so identified with his or her life's work that the mere mention of the name invokes discussion of the philosophy.

Jupiter in Leo also symbolizes very clearly the ability to make a powerful political statement, either positively or negatively, outside of the country or state of birth.

Jupiter in Virgo Jupiter is in its detriment in Virgo as well as in Gemini. Whether Jupiter in Virgo is an easy or difficult placement is truly the choice of whomever is dealing with it. The common thread that links the vast majority of people with this placement is that the influence of Virgo is exceptionally pronounced. Jupiter will take any attribute or personality trait of Virgo and develop it on a grand scale. Naturally, if you relate well to Virgo's influence, Jupiter in Virgo people will be very refreshing for you. Yet on the other hand, if the sign exasperates you, these people could be the last straw. Where Virgo is analytical, this placement is highly analytical. Where Virgo is picky, Jupiter evokes extreme pickiness. Where Virgo on its own is intelligent, Jupiter in Virgo adds depth and often giftedness. The most problematic case is that Virgo is a shy sign that often lacks confidence. Here the joy and exuberance of Jupiter can be stymied and a person may be excessively shy or timid.

A recurrent theme that we can't readily explain is the difficulty in relating to the father. Either the father is physically absent for significant periods of time, or there may be some cultural or societal barriers that function to keep the father and the child in totally different worlds.

To a much lesser degree, we have seen where the boisterous side of Jupiter clashes with Virgo in the area of health. Sometimes these people have cavalier attitudes toward health practices or they may take inordinate risks.

Jupiter in Libra Jupiter in Libra fits its key words well as people with this placement seek balance on a multitude of levels. They might attempt to gain maximum knowledge by exposing themselves to as many different experiences or cultures as they can. Or they can espouse contradictory philosophies at different times—even at the same time. This is a credible position for a politician who doesn't accept everything his or her party stands for, such as a liberal Republican or a conservative Democrat. However, a person does not have to seek office to maintain a philo-sophical balance. It should also be stressed that although this placement heightens independence of thought, it does not lead a person to a solitary existence. Any planet in Libra is going to have some effect on one's attitude toward others, and Jupiter in Libra expands the need for others.

Libra symbolizes a balancing of opposites; Jupiter rep-resents the expanded higher consciousness. So Jupiter in Libra is often found in the charts of people who have experienced a religious conversion. In such a case, the two sides of Libra represent the times before and after the con-version. One of these time periods may involve an extreme in the nature of the religion. The yin-yang nature of Libra does not readily symbolize transferring membership from one mainstream denomination to another.

The key words also suggest that Jupiter in Libra can disseminate information through manipulation. This place-ment has proven to be an effective one for teachers.

Jupiter in Scorpio As a rule, this sign placement is suc-cessfully described by key words without much glaring contradiction. One interesting combination that appears more than just occasionally associates Jupiter with abun-dance and Scorpio with getting even. Scorpio can easily invoke the water side of Jupiter even though it is the only Water sign not directly involved with the planet. Some-times, these people appear to receive more than their share of punishment. In some cases, they will receive a formal form of punishment such as losing a job over a trivial mat-ter. In other cases, they may be maligned for just being themselves. (They often can't understand it even if others can.) Yet in still other instances, there may be feelings of cosmic retribution. The person may be victimized either personally or by grief over another.

All signs can evoke both sides of Jupiter. Inappropriate behavior falls in the domain of Sagittarian boisterousness. As sexuality is usually an issue for those with Scorpio placements, Jupiter in Scorpio can symbolize inappropriate sexual behavior. Actually, if you have this placement, you may never do anything wrong sexually in your life. Yet if you ever did, the repercussions could be intense.

Jupiter in Scorpio gives the desire to learn about topics in depth. There is a willingness to do thankless research for the sake of knowledge. But Scorpio tends to manifest extremes in every direction, and some shallow people with this placement merely believe that they have profundity.

Jupiter in Sagittarius Since Jupiter rules Sagittarius, there is little conflict inherent in this sign position. People with this placement usually have an interest in Sagittarian matters, such as travel, education, religion, etc., and they often do well for themselves in such pursuits. This placement tends to feel that more success can be found away from the birthplace. A smaller proportion of those who stay close to home have reached success. Generally, this placement inclines people to travel and to enjoy it. When away from home, they are appreciative guests and gracefully accept unfamiliar customs.

As a rule, Jupiter in Sagittarius is also inclined toward education. There is a preference for formal, structured direction, and many people acquire education for its own sake, garnering more than they could possibly need or use. Others will be pragmatic in their educational goals and seek only what they need; they are inclined to be "street smart." They keep their eyes and ears open for bits of knowledge to expand.

Religion is approached much like education by Jupiter

in Sagittarius people. A certain proportion will follow a religion or philosophy in an orthodox or formal manner. They may adopt a new religion during their lives, but the new one will also be followed formally. Others will display some pragmatism in their choices. Some who are known in other fields may become unintentional religious leaders.

Jupiter in Capricorn When a planet is in its fall, it has to contend with a sign that it doesn't relate to especially well. Sometimes the planet seems to have mastery over the sign, but other times the sign seems to have the upper hand. Jupiter in Capricorn is no exception. It is very easy to visualize the workings of a Capricorn Jupiter. Picture trying to inflate a balloon (Jupiter) inside a closed container (Capricorn). Remember that Capricorn is concerned with the themes of structure and decorum. Jupiter's expansion can only progress so far. Then either all further expansion is stifled, or the structure itself has to expand. Neither alternative is particularly natural or fulfilling. Likewise, the natural boisterousness of Jupiter clashes with the Capricornian decorum. Jupiterian expansiveness can function best when Capricorn needs it. Capricorn decorum insists that appearances be maintained at all times, and Jupiter can give that extra little push when maintaining certain appearances goes against Capricorn's main nature. Jupiter can also fortify Capricornian ambition.

Fortunately, the Jupiterian principle of preservation is able to function compatibly within Capricorn's standards. Jupiter can support, strengthen and preserve unstable structures, but this sign placement also has the greatest danger of preservation turning to stagnation.

When the nature of Capricorn has mastery over the function of Jupiter, there will often be rigidity, orthodoxy, or at least a need for structure in a person's philosophy, religion, or educational pursuits. This position is also likely to submit to authority and to accept data as truth without questioning it.

It is not uncommon for a person with Jupiter in Capricorn to acquire an enterprise in which its structure and its reputation are inextricably linked. The enterprise may have a good reputation because it has a good structure. At any rate, the new owner, usually to assert his presence and influence, will attempt to change the structure of the enterprise. It doesn't matter whether these changes are sound commercial practice or merely an exercise in egotism. The reputation of the enterprise must then be rebuilt under the new structure, and the new owner is left puzzled.

Jupiter in Aquarius Aquarius is a fixed Air sign, but Jupiter is not associated with any fixed signs. Nonetheless, the astrological influences seem to readily find a common ground. The nature of Aquarius embraces broad, scientific, objective thought. Yet Aquarius is also associated with big business. Regarding personality, an Aquarian influence can be erratic, contrary, or stubborn as well as original. Next to Pisces, Aquarius is the most humanitarian sign of the zodiac.

Jupiter in its own right can replicate most of these traits under the proper circumstances. Jupiter in Aquarius is the missing link. The expansiveness of thought as offered by colleges and universities is an attribute of the Sagittarian side of Jupiter. Big business, like any large endeavor, must also relate to Jupiter in some form. A Jupiterian weakness in personality, especially tied to the Sagittarian side, is inappropriateness. The major difference between Aquarian and Piscean benevolence is that the Aquarian side is more intellectual and the Piscean side more emotional.

If you have Jupiter in Aquarius, whether you are a

philosopher or not, you will have an outlook on life that could be described as philosophy. This outlook appears to be reached through some sort of mental rationale even if the logic behind it appears to be faulty. It is also evident that the outlook is derived from mental rather than emotional experience. Furthermore, this outlook is not held lightly, nor is it easy to change. If you have Jupiter in Aquarius and are actually involved in the practical application of philosophy as a clergyman or astrologer, you will strive to leave your mark. Your philosophy will show originality and uniqueness, which may actually be more important to you than its acceptance by others. Any bit of brilliance and revelation is often lost among the parts that are different for the sake of being different.

Contrary to the conventional interpretation of astrological key words, Jupiter in Aquarius does not make a person more detached. The warmth of Jupiter is much stronger than the coldness of Aquarius. Hence this position is actually symbolic of less detachment than would be indicated, other factors being equal.

Jupiter in Pisces Like Sagittarius, Pisces is ruled by Jupiter. When Jupiter is in Pisces, it is very strong, especially the sustaining, preserving side. It is easy for astrologers to make mistakes in delineating this sign placement because accepting Jupiter's rulership of Pisces has fallen into disfavor. Consequently, half of the nuances of Jupiter's meanings are overlooked. This problem is workable when Jupiter is in other signs, but it is a serious error here. Not only is the Sagittarian side secondary, but the house or houses with Pisces on the cusp should be read with Neptune as the subordinate ruler.

The greatest strength of Pisces is the ability to synthesize—to create a new whole from an assortment of unrelated parts. Pisces also learns from the absorption of external stimuli. Jupiter in Pisces expands these processes on a grand scale. On the positive side, these people are extremely eclectic possessing a vast wealth of references from which to draw. Negatively, the osmosis that characterizes this sign placement can be overwhelming. As Pisces is the polarity of Virgo, experience can be soaked up indiscriminately. At one extreme, this could cause disorganization and muddled thinking. On a lesser level, one can merely assume, usually incorrectly, that other people can follow one's unique thought patterns.

In unfamiliar surroundings, Jupiter in Pisces people usually mind their own business until they feel comfortable. Then the ability to adapt to a new environment becomes active. Much of the inappropriateness of Jupiter in other signs is absent when it is in Pisces.

JUPITER IN THE HOUSES

Jupiter in the First House Traditional interpretations of Jupiter in the 1st House state consistently that this placement is a significant indicator of a weight problem. Very few people fit this outdated aphorism. While the key words suggest expansiveness in the physical body, experience shows expansion in the total ambience or persona. These people will definitely expand, usually in a classically Jupiterian manner, to present more than just what they were given at birth. A religious conversion is a fairly common manifestation of this placement. Although some individuals may have had a lifelong religious persuasion, Jupiter generally broadens through expansion of experience. Religion, particularly faith, also fulfills the preservationist side of Jupiter as it helps these people to sustain efforts in the face of discouragement.

Similarly, Jupiter in the 1st House can be inspirational,

even when not tied to a religion. This position is not uncommon for lecturers. Here again, the Piscean and Sagittarian sides of Jupiter are evenly stressed. Jupiterian inspiration tends to take the form of "I've been there; I conquered it; you can too." This position often leads the person into feelings of superiority. There is never any guarantee that s/he will learn in proportion to the quantity of experiences that s/he faces.

Sometimes, the Jupiterian expansion is totally unsubstantiated. In this situation, the individual may merely be overly impressed with the self. The outright phoniness that Jupiter in the 1st House can engender is a first cousin to the air of superiority just mentioned. This air of superiority is based upon overvalued experience. Insincerity is more of a reaction to the hurt felt by a person who lacks, but dearly craves, real experience.

The association of foreignness with Jupiter may manifest in this house by giving the individual a foreign ambience. S/he may truly be from a foreign land, may just have a highly ethnic name or appearance, or may easily overidentify with a culture other than the culture of birth. This trait may also function by allowing the person's works to be well received in international circles.

Jupiter in the Second House Jupiter in the 2nd House does not guarantee wealth or other financial success though it certainly is a contributing factor. Under most circumstances, it comes as no surprise that money and possessions, in all their ramifications, are issues for people with this position.

Generally, earnings from one's profession are more accurately a manifestation of the 11th House, but if a person's salary gives cause for him or her to be noticed, then money is an issue. If one's earnings are too large or too inappropriate for the nature of one's work, then one's finances may cause trouble with other people. For example, they might have strong reactions about a millionaire musician who was once part of just another tavern band, a word processor who was paid a middle manager's salary, or even a prostitute who could not legally charge for her services.

On the other hand, if one's earnings are too small for the nature of one's work, then one's finances become an issue to the earner. Sometimes, this facet of Jupiter in the 2nd House illustrates the "If you're so smart, why aren't you rich?" syndrome. In that instance, the 2nd House would represent the 12th House from the 3rd. And Jupiter's position there symbolizes vast, but underutilized, mental resources. Consistent with the principles involved, a man's mental illness manifested in a belief that his imagined grandiose financial schemes were true.

Most astrologers realize that the 8th House is other people's money, but it must be remembered that the 2nd House represents money in general. The derived houses are used to specify details regarding money. Jupiter in the 2nd House is not an uncommon position for bank employees and officers. Although they handle other people's money, there is still an element of cash transactions involved. (Insurance companies are almost exclusively in the domain of the 8th House.) Some people with this 2nd House position may choose to live near financial centers because the monetary environment invigorates them. This house deals with movable property, and Jupiter here can represent a need to collect either physical possessions like records and books or nonphysical possessions like astrological birth data.

The mental and inspirational side of Jupiter can manifest as an interest in mathematics as the 2nd House is akin to Taurus in this regard. This placement is often found in charts of therapists who help inspire self-worth in others.

Jupiter in the Third House The 3rd House relates to the sign Gemini. Just as it does in Gemini, Jupiter functions rather well here. The 3rd House is associated with the conscious, practical mind and with oral and written communication. Jupiter, which connotes expansion and profundity, does not cause many problems here. However, some difficulties may arise via Jupiter's preserving quality.

When the conscious mind is expanded, there may be some difficulty in discerning between an accumulation of knowledge and genuine wisdom. So this position can lead a person to have an inquiring mind. Whether one becomes truly wise, or merely a collector of information, s/he will have the satisfaction of having bettered the mind.

The word *practical* is the adjective form of *practice*. Therefore the *practical mind* refers to mental processes put to use. Jupiter in the 3rd House often depicts writers whose works have limited circulation. Although this seems to contradict the expansiveness of Jupiter, the 3rd House is not normally associated with publications. Each influence mitigates the other. Such writers may include newspaper columnists and even computer programmers. In cases where Jupiter outweighs the effects of the 3rd House, we can find philosophers who avoid theory and concentrate on words to live by.

Since the 3rd House equates to the sign of Jupiter's detriment (Gemini), most difficulties can be attributed to the polarity of the two influences. In some instances, Jupiter in this house brings unearned credit. In one case a person accepted recognition for extensive ghost-written material. In another a publisher who controlled submitted material with an iron hand did not fulfill promises to pay royalties. The expansiveness of Jupiter here can also accentuate any mental eccentricities a person may have.

The problem with Jupiter's sustaining side is that some people with this position will quit expanding their conscious minds when they decide that they know everything. They can become the typical know-it-alls with dogmatic opinions on everything. Others cannot be told anything because they want to preserve their knowledge intact.

Jupiter in the Fourth House The 4th is Cancer's house and represents Jupiter's sign of exaltation. Jupiter in the 4th is similar to Jupiter in Cancer but does not always have weight problems. Oddly enough, Jupiter in the 4th tends to evoke more classically Cancerian attitudes than Jupiter in Cancer. The traditional definitions of liberalism and conservatism state that liberals are fond of change and that conservatives are fond of staying the same. Cancer, though cardinal, tends to dislike change and has a tendency to support traditional values. Yet, the angular houses impart both activism and ambition. Jupiter in the 4th House tends to be motivated by positive traditional values. However, this motivation can lead either to conservatism *or* liberalism. It depends on whether the person with this placement fears the loss of values for society as a whole or whether s/he perceives some part of society as being deprived of traditional rights.

Jupiter in this house often suggests a person who moves to a foreign country, but this is not nearly as strong as when Jupiter is in the 7th. The 4th House's equivalence to Cancer stresses the watery side of Jupiter. Consequently, the home, the family and the native country serve as sources of inspiration. This is a common house position for politicians. Astrological indicators of political interest are fairly easy to spot, but the direction the politics take is much more challenging to ascertain.

The 4th is a parental house and is most associated with the parent who provides nurturing. Nonetheless, all parental influences are going to affect the home and everyone within it. Jupiter in the 4th is often found in charts of people who have a parent who is well educated, a professional person, or eminent in some other way. Usually parental support is available. This support is often of an emotional nature whereas Jupiter in the 10th House indicates support of a material nature.

Jupiter in the Fifth House The 5th House relates to the sign Leo, but there are some major differences in the function of Jupiter here. Jupiter in Leo can tend to manifest as an almost uncontrolled pride; however, Jupiter in the 5th House functions on a largely exterior level.

Jupiter in Leo can be directed toward creativity with some amount of success, but it requires astrological guidance or other counseling. For those with Jupiter in the 5th House, the creativity seems to flow more easily and naturally. An old astrological rule of thumb is that success in writing is shown by linkages between the 3rd, 5th and 9th Houses and their rulers. Although this combination can be fulfilled in several ways, it is especially dynamic to have Jupiter, the natural ruler of the 9th, in the 5th.

Jupiter in the 5th House is not without pride. The pride is there, but it is controlled and/or justified. The pride expressed by this house position is to some extent comparable to Jupiter in the 1st House. Here it is the direction of the pride that makes all the difference. Jupiter in the 1st expresses itself as *personal* pride of accomplishment. Jupiter in the 5th takes pride in the *task* done, especially if the accomplishment is of a tangible, physical nature, such as written work or sports achievement.

Success in creative self-expression is not necessarily guaranteed by this house position. Jupiter's greatest fault, complacency, is all too often found here. Inertia is exacerbated by the 5th House's association with fun, pleasure and self-indulgence. There is a very strong inclination to party too much and lose sight of one's ambitions.

Surprisingly, Jupiter in the 5th does not seem to be any more fertile than average. If anything, Jupiter's presence might actually decrease the number of children a person has. Jupiter in this house often indicates intelligent children. Whether their intelligence is garnered from heredity or from beneficial time spent with the parents is still a matter of conjecture.

Jupiter in the Sixth House Approaching a project with the intent of finding a new perspective is often illuminating. Jupiter in the 6th House gives some surprises. Of all the 12 house positions for Jupiter, the 6th seems to have the greatest proportion of intelligent people. Traditional application of key words suggests that the 3rd or 9th Houses would be the most logical places to find Jupiter in an intellectual person's chart.

Jupiter in the 3rd House tends to accumulate information; Jupiter in the 6th House tends to process it. The 6th corresponds to Virgo, which is the lesser-known sign of Jupiter's detriment. Like Virgo, the 6th House gives a tendency to analyze. Consequently, information for information's sake is not necessarily sought here. By the same token, the mental orientation of people with this Jupiter placement tends to favor the use of knowledge over theory. Naturally, the ability to philosophize is determined by the 9th House, but Jupiter in the 6th tends to translate philosophy into practical terms.

The major problem with Jupiter here is underemployment. Rarely do these people find occupations that fit their abilities. Once again, a superficial interpretation of traditional key words spells out "a good job." But this house position usually offers the opportunity to pursue career rather than just a job. The preserving side of Jupiter can manifest as stagnation which in the 6th pertains to employment. It is true that this house position suggests a good worker. However, it is not necessarily true that good workers always get the promotions. If an employee is a good worker, management often keeps the good worker trapped in a subordinate position. This is especially true if the person is doing more than his or her share of work or if the position is especially hard to fill. On the other hand, a person could learn a job so well that s/he becomes complacent about it. With Jupiter in the 6th House, it is up to you to make the most of your abilities.

Jupiter in the Seventh House The 7th House rules how we see the world. It represents both the people we draw to us and how we project our needs onto others. Prevalent astrological theories suggest that our environment is a manifestation of the 4th House, but Jupiter in the 7th contradicts this observation. A logical extrapolation of key words suggests that Jupiter in the 4th represents living in a foreign land. In fact, it is more common for those with Jupiter in the 7th to live in a foreign country. This observation is consistent with the correct knowledge of what the 7th House means.

Jupiter in the 7th tends to seek out the exotic in culture or relationships. Although it is common to move to a foreign country, this position can lead you to seek out and get to know visiting foreigners. In this instance, the expansionist principle of Jupiter is invoked; such pursuits are motivated by the prospect of personal growth. As the 7th House relates to Libra, the sign of balance, the examination of foreign cultures can be seen as an attempt to gain knowledge of the self from a reflection of the not-self.

Interestingly, Jupiter in the 7th House is not a strong

indicator of interpersonal relationships with people of different cultures. (Jupiter in the 8th is much stronger in this regard.) The preservationist Piscean side of Jupiter manifests strongly in the relationship facet of the 7th House. This position does not guarantee a happy, long-lasting marriage, but people who have it often judge the quality of their relationships to be better than they are in actuality. If the partnership ends involuntarily, it is often the partner who will initiate its conclusion. Without studying an individual birth chart, this position is hard to evaluate. Does Jupiter sustain the relationship, or does Jupiter protect the individual from the relationship? Both choices are viable and realistic.

Jupiter in the Eighth House A number of years ago, we were asked to help a client with a problem. She was a white woman who felt a pronounced attraction to black men. Her parents, despite being well-educated and liberal, could not readily accept this part of her being. Whenever she dated white men to please her parents, she felt as if she were being untrue to herself. We were asked if interracial attraction showed in a chart. Unfortunately, all we could answer then was that we did not know how to tell. This led to a serious study, and we concluded that a primary, but not exclusive, factor was that Jupiter was often associated with the 8th House in similar cases. If Jupiter were not in the 8th itself, it ruled the 8th or was strongly aspected to a planet there. This preliminary result made us uncomfortable in that the old junior high school locker room rumors—black sexual prowess was the the only reason for interracial attraction—might be true. Fortunately, the full symbolism of Jupiter made the issue much clearer.

Since Jupiter represents expansion, it transcends the issue of physical size. As shown by Sagittarius, Jupiter offers broad horizons, geographically, culturally and spiritually. In a birth chart, the placement of Jupiter will often show where foreign or multicultural influences are experienced. Jupiter in the 8th reflects a magnetic, sexual attraction to a person who is somehow different in a cultural sense. If there is no difference in race, there might be a difference in religion or ethnic heritage.

Regarding sexuality, Jupiter in the 8th House does not necessarily mean an uncontrollably expansive sex drive. Although that interpretation is not unknown, Jupiterian expansiveness usually manifests as a philosophy or an outlook on life that is colored by one's sexuality.

Although Jupiter in the 8th is a position that is consistent with inheritance, it is by no means a guarantee of such. Jupiter's preservationist side comes to the forefront here. Usually, resources are managed with a consistency that smooths out the peaks and valleys. Windfalls are disbursed slowly, and pitfalls are cushioned.

Jupiter in the Ninth House Here Jupiter is in its strongest house position. This house represents Sagittarius, one of the signs that Jupiter rules. When the concepts associated with this house are listed and analyzed, it is clear that Jupiter here can overcome any difficult sign placement.

With Jupiter in the 9th House, the individual may travel extensively at some point in life—and enjoy it. The travel may be associated with employment, parents' employment or just pleasure. Regarding employment, this may include some form of military service. In the United States, the Navy and the Air Force are ruled by the 9th House as well as the 6th. (The Army, Marine Corps and Coast Guard are strictly 6th House entities.)

When in this house, both sides of Jupiter are actively involved in one's religious outlook. Many people with

Jupiter here have been exposed to religion at either an early or very critical age. They benefit from the growth and support that religion can give and are able to live their lives without encumbering religious entanglements. Others approach their religion from a philosophical perspective that allows them to feel untroubled by various and sundry prohibitions, while others may change their religious affiliations freely.

Higher education is another concept linking Jupiter and the 9th House. People with this house position often encounter interruptions in the classical lock step progression of high school, college and graduate school. These people are natural learners, observers and philosophers and sometimes find that education gets in the way of actual learning. Occasionally, the interruptions are for financial reasons. Nonetheless, academic types with Jupiter in the 9th are rarely stuffy and usually retain a joy in learning.

Jupiter in the Tenth House Just as Jupiter is in its fall in Capricorn, this house position is equally incompatible. On the surface, Jupiter in the 10th House is a position that offers more potential than many other house/planet combinations, yet it is all too often a potential that remains unfulfilled. The influences of various aspects can be compared to planetary energies so that astrologers can gain insight through analogy. The converse is valid as well. Jupiter is very similar to a Grand Trine. Few people have them, but Jupiter exists in every chart. Like a Grand Trine, Jupiter can be utilized for a great deal of accomplishment, but just as a Grand Trine gives a tendency to coast, so the preservationist side of Jupiter can elicit a wave of inertia when its function is impaired. This is the danger of the 10th House placement.

Many people with Jupiter here simply want something

for nothing, believing that success is owed to them. Some of these people really do get something for nothing. This house/planet combination has been found in charts of people who have succeeded through the support of their parents or grandparents. This support can be purely financial or it may rest upon a parent's reputation. Furthermore, this position may even lead one to marry to gain reflected glory.

Working with Jupiter to achieve success is like working with a Grand Trine with the same goal in mind. A sustained effort will pay good dividends and may help to perpetuate itself. Jupiter's co-rulership of Pisces does give the planet a little-known psychic side. Many successful people with Jupiter in the 10th display a knack for knowing what other people need. One instance was a man who owned a combination variety and grocery store when this was rare. Yet another was a professional wrestler who the fans loved to hate. As obvious as it seems, this position is facilitated by having a Jupiterian career, such as those involving academia, long-distance communications, law and travel. We have seen cases of people who have made great sacrifices in their personal lives for the sake of their professional lives.

Jupiter in the Eleventh House The 11th House is probably the least understood house of all. The 12th is clearly the hardest house to understand, but so many astrologers have delved into the workings of the 12th House that much written material exists on the topic. The 11th House is traditionally defined as the house of friends, hopes and wishes. In recent times, it has been associated with the concept of love received with the 5th House representing love given. Furthermore, love is not sex and sex is not love. Sex is categorized with the 8th House. These are definitions;

problems occur when people live their lives outside the definitions.

The major recurring theme among persons with Jupiter in the 11th is that there is a deep need to receive love. The issue of love that is received correlates strongly with the concept of hopes and wishes. With Jupiter in the 11th House, these hopes and wishes are often inflated to extremes. There is nothing in life that guarantees that a person will receive love, so it is perfectly normal to hope for love and wish for love. In fact, a friend is someone who accepts you unconditionally, expecting only the same in return. The 11th House does not necessarily show friendliness unless it is a means to an end.

In many cases, Jupiter in the 11th shows a crying thirst for love that may create problems. This often manifests in leading a person to give sexual favors in an attempt to receive love. Unfortunately, this pitfall usually victimizes women. In the case of men, the desire to receive sexual favors is often a goal in and of itself.

In other cases, the desire for love manifests as a need for an audience, and Jupiter here requires that it be substantial. There is a tendency to pander to such an audience, and sincerity may be sacrificed along the way. Jupiter in the 11th may be found in the charts of those who find they have a lot of people who claim to be their friends. Often they have some renown and they desire privacy, which reflects Jupiter's Piscean side.

On a positive note, Jupiter in the 11th House is not an uncommon position for healers. They give of themselves unemotionally for the betterment of others. They know that they will be rewarded in their hearts and thus can feel good about themselves.

Jupiter in the Twelfth House On first glance, the concept of unbridled expansion running rampant in the house of self-undoing is a bit frightening. Fortunately, key words can only go so far. Certainly, the negative side of the 12th House is the most famous, but it functions quite well as a significator of solitude, healing and self-improvement. The 12th House's energy is similar to that of the sign Pisces. Pisces is ruled by Jupiter and Neptune, so it stands to reason that Jupiter should function in an unimpaired manner in the 12th House. Yet, it must be remembered that Jupiter operates in the 12th with a Sagittarian side as well.

The Sagittarian side seeks self-improvement through breadth of experience. These people are inclined to take physical risks that other people could label as tempting the Lord. Among our charts of people with 12th House Jupiters are a soldier who went to Viet Nam without facing combat, a professional motorcycle racer, a professional skydiver, an amateur chemist who specialized in explosives, and a man who, besides surviving several automobile accidents, even used a club to survive an attack by a bear. Traditional wisdom sees this position accurately. The Piscean side of Jupiter offers a substantial amount of protection so that this house position gives the necessary leeway for experience seekers to test their dreams.

Nevertheless, the 12th House should not be judged too lightly. Jupiter is associated with the principle of higher education, but the 12th House can symbolize deficiencies, blockages and other dysfunctions. Although Jupiter in the 12th can present an abundance of experience, people with this position often miss the point of just what it is they are supposed to learn from the physical peril.

Even when the element of physical risk taking is mitigated by other factors, astrological or not, Jupiter in the 12th offers protection and preservation, if not prevention. The circumstances of such protection are loosely, but not exclusively, related to Jupiter's sign. For instance, before the advent of civil rights legislation, foreign-born American citizens often found various avenues of employment closed to them. We know one such person, however, who with Jupiter in Virgo in the 12th spent over 40 years in civil service where employment rights were preserved.

To understand Jupiter, one must be aware of its two major principles, expansion and preservation. Jupiter's house shows the areas which are expanded and preserved. How these principles manifest is shown by Jupiter's sign. The principle of expansion is most closely aligned with Jupiter's rulership of Sagittarius. The principle of preservation relates to Jupiter's co-rulership of Pisces. As astrologers, we must never forget that Jupiter rules Pisces along with Neptune. We can capture the essence of Jupiter only if we experience both sides of this important planet and not take it for granted.

Gina Ceaglio

Gina Ceaglio is a professional astrologer, counselor, teacher, writer and lecturer with more than 25 years of experience. She has been a leader in the movement away from event-oriented astrology to a psychologically aligned astrology of personal responsibility since 1970 when she established the Academy of Astrological Studies to teach such principles.

A dynamic speaker, she is in great demand nationally and internationally to lecture at seminars, symposia and conferences. She has taught hundreds of students and has an extensive private counseling practice. Her company, Pegasus Tapes, distributes educational cassettes on astrological, psychological and mythological themes by some of astrology's most renowned speakers.

Her background includes training in drama, public speaking, psychology and counseling. Before becoming a full-time astrologer, she had successful careers in direct sales, business management, sales motivational training and personnel management.

SATURN

"A man of genius makes no mistakes. His errors are volitional and are the portals of discovery."

—James Joyce

Astrology recognizes and identifies the inherent genius within us all. Each sign and planet describes an archetype and function of unique and exceptional qualities. The chart of a life cycle graphically reveals that there are no mistakes, only experience. Errors are merely inaccurate outcome predictions and are, on some level, always volitional.

Experience is the living of a life and an end in itself. When we attach judgmental labels that categorize experience as good or bad, success or failure, pleasant or burdensome, we have dismissed its value without investigating its meaning. Every experience opens a door to self-discovery, and while some may be painful, all experience is good.

Saturn is the planet that most clearly symbolizes a life experience. It describes by its transits through the natal chart how we are trained and seasoned to function productively in our world. Saturn also differentiates the human organism from the animal kingdom. It rules our skeletal structure which allows us to stand upright instead of moving on all fours and represents our ability to distinguish right from wrong as conscience dictates.

I call Saturn the planet of *freedom* because self-discipline supplants the need for external control. When we take personal responsibility for our actions, respect the rights of others and operate within the prescribed parameters of societal dictates, we are totally free to exercise our options without interference, coercion or restraint.

When the ancients looked up at the heavens, the outer-most planet they could see was Saturn. It was their delimiter, the boundary of their universe. As they observed the celestial tableau and kept records of the planets' positions, they discovered that their movement was orderly, regulated and totally predictable. In contrast to their day-to-day existence on Earth, which was unpredictable, confused and disturbingly chaotic, it was a miraculous discovery.

Through the years, they noted that certain planets in given proximities to one another or in certain configurations meant floods, famine, war or the birth of a terrestrial king. Believing the planets were causal in nature with powers far superior to their own, they endowed them with superhuman, godlike capabilities appropriate to the role they appeared to play in earthly affairs.

Since Saturn circumscribed the entire celestial field, it was reasonable to equate it with the outer limits of experience and expression. It was assigned attributes like *definition, confinement, impediment, barrier, constraint* and *restriction.* Since it "contained" the other planets, it was also believed to rule such concepts as *regulation, structure, preservation, supervision, order* and *control.*

The connotation of Saturn as a malefic causing lack, loss, tragedy and denial was a natural outgrowth of humankind's proclivity to associate limits and the restriction of personal desire, pleasure, will and well-being with evil intent from an outside source. The ancients believed the angry god was visiting his wrath upon them, and modern man continues the process of projection by blaming parents, teachers, the government, bosses, bullies or other hostile beings intent on his destruction. The correlations are obvious. The common denominator is an authority outside oneself and beyond one's control against whom the individual is impotent and powerless.

The Greeks assigned dominion over each planet to one of the gods in their pantheon. In the Greek myths, each god displays characteristics that are synonymous with capacities astrology attributes to that planet and the sign it rules.

According to myth, genesis occurred in this manner. Gaea (the Earth) bore Uranus (the sky), and they were equal in grandeur. Together they created the universe, the gods and the human race. Gaea and Uranus gave birth to the Titans, the first divine race, two of whom were Cronus and Rhea. Cronus (Kronos) is the counterpart of our Saturn. At his mother's request, Cronus mutilated his father Uranus and cast his genitals into the sea. With Uranus reduced to impotence, Cronus then became king of the dynasty and married his sister Rhea.

When it was foretold that he would have a son who would challenge his power and overthrow him, Cronus devoured each child as it was born to escape fulfillment of the prophecy. However, Zeus, the last of their six children, was spared when Rhea fled to Crete and gave birth to him there. She wrapped a stone in swaddling clothes and gave it to Cronus who swallowed it, believing it was the child. Cronus was ultimately banished when Zeus reached manhood and gave his father a liquid causing him to vomit up his children.

Thus, absolute authority, dictatorship, control, power, shrewdness and defensive paranoic fear of loss or diplacement are some of the qualities associated with Saturn. The message of the myth is very clear. Drastic consequences are inevitable if one seeks to preserve one's position of undisputed autocratic rulership by cold, cruel and calculating design.

Other attitudes and principles we identify with Saturn are described in this myth including the superior authority of the male, his innate fear of castration, and anxiety over being surpassed or replaced by a grown son.

SATURN AS THE FATHER OR MALE MODEL IN THE NATAL CHART

In my opinion, Saturn and the Sun both represent the male model in a native's life. Saturn refers to the early life conceptualization of authority, control, restraint, limits, discipline, responsibility, work, conditional (earned) love and acceptance. These concepts derive as the child perceives those qualities embodied in the father or male model and experiences a relationship with him. The child's perception is totally subjective, and the father is seen as an omnipotent god. Therefore, any discomfort in the relationship will be attributed by the child to some fault or lack on his part, not an inadequacy of the parent. Our guilts and low self-worth quotients can often be traced to a painful or discomforting relationship with the father (Saturn) or the mother (Moon).

The Sun, on the other hand, indicates the adult view of authority, autocracy, vitality, effort, leadership, assertion and husbandry. How we accept or reject, translate and integrate our early impressions of these principles into our personal beliefs and expectations helps formulate our individuated ego, our essential self.

In adult life, Saturn becomes our *identity* in the world, our *internalized father* and *social conscience,* which must conform to gain approval. The natal relationship between Saturn and the Sun by sign, house placement and aspect often helps describe the dichotomy and attendant angst we may feel about the person we truly *are* (Sun) and the person we believe we *should be* (Saturn).

Consider, for example, Saturn in Leo and the Sun in Aquarius. Early experience and conditioning certify to this child that father is king, his authority unquestioned by divine decree. Unless Saturn is configured in stressful relationships with other planets, he likely will be viewed as a generous, warm and beneficent king who rules in a caring, loving way—a father who uses his power and inflicts his constraints in a life-giving, not life-limiting, fashion. On the other hand, if Saturn holds hard aspects to other planets, the child will experience him and the principles he represents as autocratic, demanding, dictatorial, unbending and extremely controlling.

The Sun in Aquarius describes an adult view of royalty or anyone endowed with absolute dominion and control over other people as diametrically opposed to his innate ethic of equality for all. The adult in this scenario must adjust and apply the kingly qualities he observed in his father to the philosophy of leadership by example rather than by force. He may feel it is inappropriate to give orders to employees and service personnel but feel a sense of guilt that he is not as forceful and commanding as he should be. He may fear rejection and loss of respect because of his reticence to dominate situations and take charge in a powerful way.

If Saturn in the natal chart is in Virgo and the Sun is in Gemini, the adult may have difficulty applying the Virgoan principles of perfect function, focused attention to detail, careful analysis and hard work to his innate need for change, variety and multiplicity of interests. His self-worth will suffer when he settles for anything less than perfect craftsmanship in any endeavor.

Natal Saturn in Sagittarius and the Sun in Aries will accommodate quite easily to adult integration of assertive action in acquiring knowledge, an academic education, and a personal philosophy and ethic that was modeled to the child. Here we have a natural flow of energy to live up to the internalized father's expectation, assuring a positive sense of identity and self-worth.

NATAL SATURN IN THE SIGNS AND HOUSES

To interpret Saturn in the signs, we must add the functions of order, control, form, structure, organization, discipline, longevity, fear of loss or lack, confinement, impediment, barrier, caution, constraint, restriction, economy, preservation, defense, supervision, autocracy, effort, definition, boundaries, management, regulation and authority to the needs each sign archetypically represents.

We will select those faculties associated with Saturn which can appropriately be applied to the needs of each sign. Likewise with houses, we will choose the Saturn attributes which are pertinent to the circumstances of life each house rules.

Always consider the planet that rules the sign in question. By mentally assuming a conjunction of Saturn with that ruling planet, you will be able to flesh out more complete interpretations. For example, Saturn in Aries is mentally viewed as if Saturn were conjunct Mars. Aspects link planets together so they can dialogue. As we take Saturn through the signs and houses, listen to the conversation between the archetypal needs of the sign, the functions symbolized by its ruling planet and the functions of Saturn.

Saturn in Aries or the First House Here we have two energies, Mars and Saturn, that are contradictory in purpose and design. Aries and Mars symbolize the need to act assertively in pursuit of one's personal desires. When combined with Saturn, the effect is a conflict of needs. Go versus stop; impulse versus caution; risk versus security; motion versus crystallization; challenge versus fear, etc.

If Saturn in Aries or the 1st House holds stressful aspects to other planets in the chart, a kind of "action paralysis" may result. The fear of rejection, error or failure can overpower the need for personal initiative. These individuals require a guarantee of a successful outcome before daring to act on their own behalf. They can forestall, delay, and procrastinate awaiting assurance of positive results. Since life gives no guarantees, their wait can be endless, and personal initiative is effectively immobilized.

Saturn in Aries people will resist personal regulation and may overcompensate by assuming a defensive dictator posture or otherwise abusing their authoritative role. Most likely they will project the blame for frustrations or failures onto other people and circumstances, but a stressful Saturn in Aries really describes a self-blocking mechanism.

If Saturn in Aries or the 1st House is harmoniously aspected, the interplanetary dialogue will produce careful, well-planned, responsible, self-disciplined action and an economical conservation of personal energy. Authority and control will not be abused; leadership, organizational and management skills will be abundant.

Saturn in Taurus or the Second House Archetypically Taurus and Venus represent the five senses of touch, taste, sight, smell and sound with the need for sensory gratification, affection, artistry, personal values, and innate and accrued resources and assets. Effective function in the material world is the mandate for fulfilling these needs. The Taurean Venus has to do with practical matters and a fond appreciation for "the good life," i.e., the touch of velvet . . . the taste of fine wine. The Libran Venus, described later on, refers to people and human interrelationships.

Saturn in Taurus or the 2nd House adds qualities of conservatism, economy and control to affectionate display and personal values, and the accumulation and use of assets. There is a fear of lack or loss in these matters, and the natives will exercise extraordinary care in their disbursement. Cost conscious and shrewd, they expect full value for their money, and others who are more cavalier in attitude may consider them tight-fisted.

Their identity and self-worth are directly connected to the quantity and quality of possessions they acquire. Although their resources may be adequate or even extensive, they never have quite enough to feel successful. Emotionally and materially, there may be a "deprived child" self-perception arising from their early conditioning and relationship with the father model. A poverty consciousness or pervasive feeling of hardship can result from a stressed Saturn in Taurus or the 2nd House, while harmonious aspects keynote an excellent money manager, shrewd bargainer and long-range investment planner.

All Saturn in Taurus people feel they should closely monitor their sensory needs. If Saturn is stressed, they may adopt a hair shirt existence with few creature comforts to boost their self-worth, and guilt follows fast on the heels of self-indulgence. A harmonious Saturn will not ameliorate the cautious regulation of sensual pleasures they feel permitted to enjoy, and even those will be paid out in a frugal, economic way.

Saturn in Gemini or the Third House Gemini, Mercury and the 3rd House are all symbolic of the thinking process. Logic, basic learning and communication are the province of Gemini; function of the mind and how it works refer to Mercury; the 3rd House specifically relates to early or elementary education in addition to siblings, neighbors and the immediate environment.

When Saturn is introduced, self-worth and identity are intimately tied to educational and mental accomplishments. Fears of intellectual inadequacy can create the perpetual student who feels he never knows enough to risk testing himself against others and the world. As with all Saturn positions, it is a self-blocking mechanism which goes back to early childhood and can be removed once the native understands its source.

Saturn in Gemini indicates an organized mind that thinks carefully, logically and perhaps slowly. When compared to quick-study types, these natives may feel they are slow learners who must study harder than their peers to grasp the material. However, once learned it is theirs forever.

These people think before they speak; their speech is measured, carefully articulated, and precise. Depending on aspects, there may be a speech impediment. If so, it can probably be traced to a subconscious fear of mental and linguistic ineptitude associated with early conditioning.

The skills identified with Saturn in Gemini include mental discipline and focus, orderly thought, concentration, mind control and intellectual dedication. There is a strong sense of responsibility toward achievement in all communicative and educational pursuits. Management proficiency will be apparent in community concerns. A need/ability to supervise and care for siblings or neighbors, teaching in a structured environment, i.e., the elementary grades, and regulating the flow of commerce or information are all emphasized with this placement.

Saturn in Cancer or the Fourth House When Saturn is in Cancer or the 4th House, it combines with the Moon, and there is a possibility of parental role reversal in childhood. It may denote a circumstance where, in the native's perception, one parent played both roles or the father was viewed as the nurturing parent. For an accurate analysis of the parental experience, much will depend on the Moon's position in the individual's natal chart. Most certainly, however, with Saturn in Cancer or the 4th House, the person's conception of nurturing is authoritative, strict, disciplined and emotionally controlled.

Cancer, the Moon and the 4th House are all symbols of the need to be needed, the need for unconditional love, emotional security, responsiveness, nurturing and protection. They also describe the early (and later) domestic environment. When Saturn links with these needs and abilities, we have an unlikely equation. Cancer/Moon = emotional need-response, vulnerability and unconditional love. Saturn = control, restriction and reward commensurate with performance. Therefore, Moon + Saturn = the belief that emotional needs or displays are childish and weak while controlling or denying one's feelings signifies strength.

The child with Saturn in Cancer or the 4th House feels emotionally deprived, rejected and somehow unloved. Again, because even a serious, strict and somewhat joyless parent is viewed as an unerring god, the child feels the fault must lie with him or her and perceives him- or herself as unworthy and unlovable. This is the child's perception only. It is the way s/he processed experience with that parental model, and it may not coincide with the views of other family members.

All that matters is that it was real for him or her because s/he carries to adulthood an unworthy, unlovable identity. Once s/he understands the parent's characteristics and philosophy, s/he will recognize s/he was not singled out as the target of the father's emotional repression. That realization allows a conscious transformation of the unworthy self-concept. At this point, s/he can also decide whether his or her personal view of the nurturing process agrees with the mode being dictated by the internalized father. If it does not, s/he can now follow his or her own precepts without feelings of guilt or betrayal.

Domestic life (past and present) for individuals with Saturn in Cancer or the 4th House follows conservative, strict rules and regulations. A sense of hardship, duty and responsibility early in life and a serious, disciplined home environment are fundamental to this placement.

Among the innate skills and abilities identified with Saturn in Cancer or the 4th House are proficiency in managing property, real estate and domestic concerns, food and beverage control and the conservation of basic resources. Emotionally steadfast and faithful, these people are capable of making and maintaining long-term commitments. Practical nurturing is their *modus operandi*, and by reliably providing the necessities of life (food and shelter), they demonstrate their love. Male or female, they will rule the roost and run a home with authority and dispatch.

Saturn in Leo or the Fifth House Can a king and a dictator cohabit or even converse? Yes, indeed, though both are father/authority symbols with totally different modes and accommodation will be required to avoid conflict.

Leo, the Sun and the 5th House are symbols of vivacity, warmth, generosity, leadership, vitality, self-expression, recreation, progeny, creativity, romance and sexual activity. Saturn in Leo or the 5th House introduces qualities of law, order, control, fear of displacement or inadequacy, caution and economy.

These individuals will automatically dominate and may overreact when their authority or opinions are questioned. In one circumstance, they will be generous and giving, but in another they will withhold warmth and demand strict obedience. This apparent vacillation can be unnerving to their followers and an enigma to themselves.

Heavy-handed control will be evident in the areas of life where they feel most threatened, where they have a need to prove their worth, where their *identity* and reputation are on the line. The high dynamic (hard) aspects to other planets in the natal chart will provide detailed descriptions of these fears and self-doubts.

Saturn in the 5th House people view with trepidation the prospect of having children. They feel it is a serious responsibility and may opt to have none. But if they do, total submission and unquestioned obedience will be expected. Since their identity is somehow dependent on their children's performance, a child may be required to replicate their efforts (follow in their footsteps) or realize their unfulfilled ambitions.

These people also have inhibitions and fears of rejection connected with their sexual prowess. They have the need to perform well and prove themselves in bed to bolster their self-worth. They will be traditional and faithful lovers, though not sexually inventive or experimental. They will seek and maintain long-term, committed relationships.

Saturn in Leo clearly exemplifies the Greek myth of Cronus. Is the subconscious fear of displacement by a powerful child the basis for the need to control offspring? It may well be since, contrary to the conscious intent, dominating treatment often creates dependency and ineffectuality. That same subconscious dynamic could be the origin of sexual performance anxiety since the act produces a child.

As with all Saturn placements, inherent skills become conscious and available when self-blocking mechanisms are removed. A harmoniously aspected Saturn in Leo or the 5th House denotes a responsible, fair and dedicated parent, a self-disciplined, organized leader or teacher who structures, defines and demonstrates by example, and a charismatic, expressive, reliable pacesetter who is an advocate for his followers.

Saturn in Virgo or the Sixth House The genius inherent in the Virgo/Mercury archetype combines productively for the most part with the functions that Saturn contributes. Virgo's Mercury, unlike Gemini's Mercury, describes an analytical, problem-solving, efficient mind with meticulous attention to detail. Saturn's attributes of control, caution, order, concentration and discipline emphasize and further refine those innate capacities. Both have a natural dedication to work, so application, analysis, research and development, methodical compilation of data, trouble-shooting, finding economical solutions, and efficient use of time are some of the abilities this combination will produce.

Saturn and Virgo have similar psychological hang-ups, however, and the combined emphasis can result in exaggerated self-doubt, depression and low self-esteem. Virgo requires perfect function with tangible results from the effort, so its people suffer from a fear of inadequacy. Saturn, on the other hand, must live up to the expectations of a critical parent whose standards were so high s/he could never be entirely pleased with the person's performance.

With these requirements for excellence in both mind and deed, Saturn in Virgo individuals feel extremely inadequate if they make the slightest error in judgment or conduct. They can be very hard on themselves, and their inner anxiety level becomes self-destructive. Once they realize that perfection is a process and not a static state or *fait accompli*, they can accept themselves or their work as perfect in its current stage of development.

Sixth House activities are subject to the same efficient function requirements. Saturn contributes steadiness, strict discipline, control and tested methods to employment endeavors, to routine chores, and to health, diet and physical fitness regimens. Saturn in the 6th House will engender demanding managers or employees, but since their identity and reputation depend on worthy accomplishments, they will be dedicated, hard workers.

Saturn in Libra or the Seventh House Libra/Venus/ the 7th House is the archetype/function/setting symbolizing the need for completion by a significant other who is not related by blood, love given and received, gentleness, consideration, egalitarianism, moderation, social grace and acceptance, partnerships of all kinds and the need for approval. The Saturn functions most compatible with these needs are steadfastness, commitment, faithfulness and reliability. Attributes contrary in intent to this essence are domination, control, emotional restraint and authoritative attitudes.

This position of Saturn can be self-defeating. These people seek loving, equal partnerships that will validate their worthiness to the world, but the fear of relinquishing control and losing their identity compels them to dominate.

Libra is the sign of the tactician, and Saturn in Libra or the 7th House individuals will employ shrewd methods to gain control. They are adept at being silent, withholding love and affection, being cold and implacable, or telling others what they want to hear. If the partner submits to domination, the native assumes a paternal role, egalitarianism is gone and it becomes an unsatisfying parent-child relationship with attendant loss of respect. If the partner resists, a power struggle ensues, and the conflict of wills negates the harmonious, loving ideal that was envisioned.

There may be a subconscious search for the father model in a partner. In this case the person must be willing to play the child role in a relationship, assigning personal control, responsibility and discipline to another. The natal chart will show other evidence of a need for dependency.

Saturn in Libra or the 7th House requires authoritative control in situations involving other people in general. There are many circumstances where this is not only appropriate but highly recommended, and the individual has the skill as well as the need. Counseling, teaching, interviewing, arbitrating, negotiating, presiding, coordinating are some of the endeavors where command of the operation is a must for the project to be successful.

Coupled with the Libran abilities for cooperation and fair judgment, these uses of the Saturn energy bring approval, self-esteem and respect. The constant challenge will be to direct Saturn's controlling potential away from personal one-on-one relationships and into other more suitable arenas.

Saturn in Scorpio or the Eighth House Scorpio's potentials are a fascination with the underworld and the death/rebirth process, personal power, mastery, possessiveness, intensity, depth search and investigation, resourcefulness, thoroughness, relentlessness, manipulation, sexual reproduction, salvage and metamorphosis. The sign is the archetype for these needs and abilities; Pluto, its ruler, symbolizes the function that activates and manifests them.

The Saturn identity in Scorpio or the 8th House must actualize these capacities in a responsible, controlled, cautious and lawful manner to feel valuable and worthy. This child may have experienced violence or abuse in the parental relationship or had a psychologically "devouring" parent *à la* the Cronus myth. Surely, the early impression of authority figures is power so formidable that one is impotent against it.

Scorpio and Pluto need power over themselves, other people and their environment to feel safe, while the Saturn aspect in our natures requires authoritative control for the survival of identity. When these two highly charged dynamics combine, a fight-for-your-life sensation is created. Cold, calculating cruelty and ruthlessness may be employed to protect oneself or one's possessions, especially if there are stressful aspects involving the Ascendant, Mars, the Sun or the Moon. Scorpio finds it difficult to forgive and forget an inflicted wrong, and when Saturn is in this tenacious sign, the response may be shrewdly vengeful and vindictive.

Saturn in Scorpio individuals innately comprehend the continuum of energy through reconversion, have a respect for tradition, history and the past, and possess outstanding aptitudes for reclamation and restoration. Their natural resourcefulness and love for depth investigation complements their ability to translate precepts into form, and they are highly qualified for research and development enterprises. When they apply their talents to investigating the human psyche, they are gifted psychologists with a special ability to motivate the self-search process.

In a practical sense, Saturn in Scorpio or the 8th House indicates proficiency in managing other people's resources, assets or investments; acting as an agent; involvement in insurance and designing long-term security plans; salvage, waste and renewal engineering; law enforcement and debt collection.

These persons have the tools at their command for self-mastery and self-discipline once they stop projecting their fears on others. Harshness, extreme control, power struggles and peril result when their volatile dynamics are directed toward people. Their challenge is to find avenues of application where these same dynamics are highly prized and rewarded.

Saturn in Sagittarius or the Ninth House With this placement, we have two energies. Jupiter symbolizing abstract thought and intellectualized ideals is coupled with Saturn's practical method and applied reality. The interface of Sagittarius/Jupiter/the 9th House and Saturn can be extremely productive. Bringing ideals and theory down from ivory tower clouds and manifesting them firmly on Earth in a pragmatic way results in a useful, serviceable doctrine.

Saturn's requirement of utilitarian conservatism and status quo in regard to philosophy, religion and personal ethic will place some boundaries on free thought ideology, abstraction and theory. What it contributes in method, structure and practical application, however, will usually compensate for the limits imposed.

These individuals evaluate their self-worth in direct proportion to the extent of their higher education and intellectual accomplishments. The fear of testing their knowledge and failing in the real world can create perpetual students who hide in academia and continue to collect college degrees, never feeling they know enough. Perhaps the fear that they are not intellectually equipped to achieve on a university level can prevent them from trying, but they continue to feel inferior without an advanced degree.

On the other hand, Saturn in Sagittarius or the 9th House people can be somewhat narrow-minded and appear to have an inflated identity. They overcompensate for their fears of mental inadequacy with a strong need to be right and are extremely defensive. To be proven incorrect is processed as a personal rejection. It is such a blow to their self-esteem that they will continue to defend their position even when demonstrable facts refute it.

These disturbing behaviors derive from subconscious guilts and fears surrounding intellectual accomplishment brought from childhood. The parental model who puts down the child's intelligence, who demonstrates by word or deed that "you're nobody without an education," and "you are what you know," or who is intellectually deficient will be the internalized conscience of the adult.

Saturn in Sagittarius or the 9th House people exhibit outstanding ability to define, structure and organize thought. These are essential ingredients for effective teaching, lecturing, writing and all manner of communications. Their defensive, debative skills can be profitably used in business or corporate law and in any circumstance where espousing a principle or ethic is vital.

Saturn in Capricorn or the Tenth House Capricorn, Saturn, and 10th House principles are identical and can manifest purely according to the need, function and context. Additional nuances, harmonious contributions and stressful conflicts will be found by examining the natal chart.

For help in delineating Saturn in Capricorn in a specific natal chart, refer to the section in this chapter which applies to the house where Saturn is posited. In other words, for Saturn in the 2nd, look at Saturn in Taurus or the 2nd House. Refer to the appropriate section for planets in aspect, too. For example, if Mars is in opposition to Saturn, look at Saturn in Aries or the 1st House.

The need to prove our worth and the fear of not measuring up to others' expectations and suffering rejection are the underlying Saturn motivations for achieving, gaining status and establishing a positive identity in the world, regardless of the sign or house the planet occupies. When it falls in Capricorn, its process is unadulterated, and the native's possibilities of attaining his or her goals are greatly increased.

Harmoniously aspected, it describes a father model who positively exemplified the realities of life. Hard work brings just rewards (conditional love); application, self-discipline and responsibility are gratifying, not onerous; order, structure, and organization prevent chaos; rules and authority supply safety and security; impediments are self-created and can be overcome; accepting personal responsibility for our lives promotes self-actualization. The child will accept these tenets as his or her own and internalize them comfortably as an adult.

High dynamic aspects indicate an overemphasis on any of these principles which can color, distort, project, repress or deny the concept itself. These contorted views will have to be reevaluated by adult natives at some time in their lives to either discard or adjust them to coincide with their conscious concepts.

Saturn in Capricorn or the 10th House individuals have an innate understanding of the work ethic, are high achievers and perform in an organized, well-planned, methodical manner to accomplish their goals. They have the need/ability to be the boss and to manage and direct others. They can run their own business or, if working for others, can supervise and take autonomous control over an arena of operations.

Identity and self-worth are synonymous with their career role, so when they retire or for any reason cease to be active in their chosen field, they can have a severe identity crisis. Ennui and depression may follow, so it is imperative that these people set new goals of accomplishment and then work toward them.

Saturn in Aquarius or the Eleventh House At first glance, the two planets that co-rule Aquarius seem contradictory in nature. Uranus with its progressive, unorthodox function and Saturn's affinity with rules and the status quo do not appear compatible. On deeper examination, however, we get a more comprehensive picture of the consummate Aquarius archetype by combining their functions.

The ideal prototype is respect for authority and structure (Saturn) with individual freedom and rights (Uranus). Control is *self-control*, and individual freedoms are exercised with *responsibility*.

Saturn in Aquarius or the 11th House emphasizes the management, organization, control and authority needs within the context of equal rights and individual freedoms. The philosophy of this placement may be "Let all men be free, and then do as I say." Conservatism is accented, and there will be greater adherence to tradition than avant-garde concepts.

Without stressful aspects, the parental model was probably experienced as a strict but fair disciplinarian who encouraged independent thought and self-determination in the child—someone who was a free spirit but followed the rules and functioned in a reliable, responsible manner. The child would feel that this parent was also a friend and a "buddy," growing into adulthood with the conscious desire to emulate him.

If Saturn in Aquarius has stressful aspects, the parental model would be viewed as more demanding and controlling of others but also personally irresponsible or unreliable. The child could get a mixed message like "Do as I say, but not as I do," with the impression that the father model was somehow a law unto himself. He also might be off doing his own thing and unavailable to the child when needed. Other planets and signs involved will describe how the scenario played.

If the father was absent or undependable, the child feels it is because s/he is unworthy of concern. As an adult, this person has a fear of rejection and may seek attention or try to prove his or her independence by eccentric, noncaring or rebellious behavior. This irresponsibility then creates the very thing feared.

Saturn in Aquarius people have leadership, management and directorial skills and are drawn to groups or organizations with humanitarian motives. The ability to translate inventive, original ideas into concrete, practical, usable form is an outstanding talent of this placement. Hard workers for common good projects that elevate the disadvantaged, these individuals are naturals for the Peace Corps or similar enterprises.

Saturn in Pisces or the Twelfth House When Saturn is posited in Pisces or the 12th House, we must combine fantasy with reality, illusion with actuality, intangible with concrete, faith with fact—a striking array of opposites! The Neptune function and Pisces archetype refer to emotional beliefs for which there is no tangible evidence, while Saturn requires physical testimony, empirical examination and practical application.

The human organism instinctively feels there are forces at work which cannot be seen or verified. Our inspirational flashes and experiences with déjà vu and the paranormal result in an almost universal belief in God or a higher intelligence.

Traditional religious doctrines which prescribe moral behavior that will please "our Father in heaven" will be most acceptable to Saturn in Pisces people. They can be the proof seekers and debunkers of illusionists, psychics, metaphysicians, yogis and mystics.

Artistry that translates into physical form is their province. For example, writing poetry or inspirational text, sculpting, painting and any type of handiwork will be more attractive than music, which is ephemeral and transitory. Compassion for suffering humankind will be demonstrated through practical service rather than relying on divine intervention.

Psychologically, this placement when stressed indicates an identity connected with martyrdom, anguish and a fear of ineffectuality. These individuals can either have a messiah self-concept or feel that they were born to lose, depending on other factors in the natal chart. By interpreting the characteristics of the father model as the child perceived him, we can determine how the adult self-worth factor will most likely be played out.

With a stressful Saturn in Pisces or the 12th House, the father is most often seen as disappearing, weak or somehow ineffectual to the needs of the child. Consequently, in adult life these people will subconsciously view themselves and all men as potentially weak, unreliable, deceptive and impotent.

Their resistance to face the reality of painful circumstances or their fear of inadequacy to deal with them can encourage the use of various escape mechanisms such as excessive sleep or TV, alcohol or other drugs. Severe depression, feelings of worthlessness and considerations of suicide may be encountered. When these people recognize that it is not imperative that they live up to the model that was presented and their own subconscious self-expectation, they are free to exercise conscious options and choose fulfilling ways to manifest their potentials.

The harmoniously supported Saturn in Pisces or the 12th House will tell quite a different story. These children perceived the father model as reliable, compassionate, gentle, gifted, inspired and sensitive. Consequently, their adult identities will be defined by benevolent service, imaginative use of practical methods to alleviate misery and pain, inspirational work and management roles in hospitals, prisons and the backgrounds of life. Their self-worth will directly equate with the measure of sensitive care they extend to those who suffer.

SATURN IN TRANSIT

Transiting Saturn eloquently describes the natural cycles of life and provides astrologers with perhaps the most valuable tool of their craft. Its returns to the position it occupied at birth and the intervening angles it forms to the natal Saturn clearly define the stages of *identity unfoldment.*

Saturn's complete revolution through the zodiac can vary from 28 to 30 years in an individual chart, which you can check by reference to an ephemeris, but for purposes of this discussion, we will assume a 30-year cycle. Based on an average life expectancy of approximately 75 years, we can anticipate at least 2½ Saturn returns.

Saturn forms sextiles to its natal position at age five, 25, 35, 55, 65 and possibly 85. It forms trines to its natal place at age 10, 20, 40, 50, 70 and possibly 80. The sextiles and trines refer to successful periods during each complete cycle when opportunities are present for creative input and profitable feedback.

Transiting Saturn forms a waxing square to its natal place at age 7½, 37½ and 67½. It opposes its natal place at age 15, 45 and 75. It forms a waning square at age 22½, 52½ and possibly 82½. It conjuncts natal Saturn at age 30, 60 and possibly 90.

As each cycle concludes with the conjunction, we are required to reach a critical decision based on all our experience during its circling process. The squares correspond to major adjustment decisions, and the oppositions signal recapitulation, review and summary.

In the drama of identity unfoldment, transiting Saturn is the principle player, and the high dynamic aspects it forms (squares, oppositions and conjunctions) are of the greater significance. At these times, we are required to make serious decisions, choices and changes which direct our lifetime process of self-understanding. This investigation focuses on such important periods.

THE FIRST SATURN CYCLE

The first cycle signifies our *search for an identity*, and at its completion, we must decide for the first time what we want to be when we "grow up." During our first 30 years, we are literally experimenting with ourselves in the world. We are defining where and how we fit in, identifying our comfort and anxiety zones, attempting various ways and means to achieve individuality, getting feedback on our significance and evaluating our self-worth. It is not possible, nor should it be required, to reach a final judgment on who we are and our ultimate goal in life until this experimental cycle is completed.

The Waxing Square From birth to age 7½ (the first square to natal Saturn), we are learning how to operate our bodies and minds in the physical world and are building a self-image based on relationships. We acquire an initial concept of who we are from the way we are treated by parents, siblings and other blood relatives. In this protected environment, we are at the center of our own universe where we can be vulnerable without fear and receive unconditional love.

When we move out of this reassuring nest of emotional protection and into the world of others, our first identity crisis occurs. The love we received from family was unconditional. The love (acceptance) we receive from peers and teachers depends upon performance and must be earned.

Our universe has expanded, and we must learn consideration, respect for authority and others' rights, fair play and cooperation. It is a shock to discover the world does not revolve around us, and our response is critical. This is our first opportunity to accept *personal responsibility* for discomfort in our lives instead of projecting the blame on others. If we do not reassess our self-centered narcissism and begin to develop a social consciousness, we will experience profound rejection and a loss of self-worth.

The Opposition At age 15 and the first Saturn opposition, circumstances in our lives will facilitate the review and digestion of our progress in social relationships since the square. We will be challenged to form a new identity within a significant other context. For most of us, it coincides with our first serious, committed love affair, and the cycle that began with "*I* am all that matters" culminates with "*You* are all that matters."

At this point in our lives, we must expand our self-concept to include a significant other and learn to relate as an equal, cooperative partner. We must define what we are willing to *invest* in this type of relationship and what we *expect* in return.

If in the past 7½ years, we have developed effective social skills and are comfortable playing the co-star role in life, this opposition phase will not be critical. We will continue to create variations on the same theme and positively verify our self-worth.

If, on the other hand, we have been loathe to relinquish our egocentric attitudes, another identity crisis that assaults our self-worth will likely occur. But regardless of the result, our experiment is a success. We have answered the question "How adept am I at social relationships?"

The Waning Square From the opposition to the waning square, we become involved in a much broader world than we have heretofore experienced. These are the years, from 15 to 22½, when we go out on our own for the first time. We move away from home, the immediate neighborhood or the community to take our first job, go away to college or get married.

Our self-discipline, sense of responsibility and independence are mightily tested. How we function in the world of disinterested others reflects immediately on our self-esteem, and we are trying to live up to the expectations of our actual and internalized parent. The results of our performance will come home to roost at the waning square, and we will be forced by circumstances to assess our progress.

Now we must evaluate our *public identity*, our status and reputation. If self-defeating attitudes have blocked our advancement, they must now be released or our efforts thus far will not succeed. This is another grand opportunity to accept personal responsibility for our actions and not project the blame onto others.

The Conjunction From age 22½ to 30, when Saturn returns to its natal place, we get feedback on our experiments and accomplishments during the entire 30-year cycle, particularly from the last 15 years. This is a digestive period when the results are in and we reap the rewards of our endeavors. We seriously evaluate our total identity, feel satisfaction or disappointment, and reflect on changes we need to make.

The Saturn conjunction at age 30 is not only a major identity crisis, but a crisis in consciousness. It marks the end of the tentative, experimental cycle and the beginning of a more confident, self-assured presentation of ourselves in the world. We must leave childhood behind and become mature, responsible adults. Having decided what we want to be when we grow up, we must integrate into our personality and efforts the valuable lessons we have learned about ourselves in the world, and begin again.

THE SECOND SATURN CYCLE

We are at any time of life the totality of our cumulative experience. Armed with the self-knowledge acquired during the last 30 years, we now begin the cycle of substantial achievement. The years between the waxing square, opposition, waning square and second conjunction are utilized in the same context as in the first 30 years, but we're operating on an elevated plane of comprehension. Crises in our inner and outer environments will occur at the squares, oppositions and conjunctions of the second and subsequent Saturn cycles, providing new opportunities for course corrections.

Our self-definition from age 30 to 37½ (and age 60 to 67½) will be based on our need, ability and mature determination to set new personal goals. We will develop and establish a new personal identity, expand on talents and knowledge and gain a more stable sense of self.

The following 7½-year cycle from age 37½ to 45 (and age 67½ to 75) will refer to our adult associations. We will redefine and develop an expanded social identity through romantic and business alliances as well as relationships with our children. Decisions about marital and all significant other unions will be required at the culmination of this 15-year cycle which began at age 30 (and age 60).

The next cycle from age 45 to 52½ (and 75 to 82½ for the stimulated oldsters) will be the years of solidifying our achievement in the world. With its conclusion at the waning square, we must again review our progress, define our public identity, status and reputation, discard whatever attitudes or efforts are blocking fulfillment, and reassess our worth.

In the final 7½ years before the second conjunction of transiting Saturn to its natal place at age 60 (third at age 90), we reap the rewards of dedication our accumulated efforts have earned. We evaluate and digest our life's experiences, do some serious searching of the self, then ask the question "What do I want to be when I grow up?" once again.

At the conjunction, we set new goals based on our recent discoveries and determine what personal changes are necessary to support their accomplishment. Then with a fresh perspective, we resume our process of unfoldment on a higher level of consciousness than before.

TRANSITING SATURN TO THE NATAL ANGLES AND QUADRANTS

There is another identity-actualizing cycle which is based on the angles and quadrants of the natal chart without reference to the position of natal Saturn. Both cycles are from 28 to 30 years duration, but unless Saturn is conjunct the Ascendant at birth, their timing will be different.

Since Saturn can fall in any of the 12 houses at birth, the pivotal points in the return cycle (squares, oppositions and conjunctions) will occur in different houses for each native. In the Saturn-to-angles transits, however, the points of significant change are always the Ascendant, the IC, the Descendant and the Midheaven. Although these placements are the same for all of us, the *times of contact* during the life will vary for each individual.

The complete cycle begins at the Ascendant, the waxing square occurs at the Imum Coeli, the opposition takes place at the Descendant, the waning square forms at the Midheaven and the conjunction is back at the Ascendant once more. Dane Rudhyar's overall characterization of the four quadrants is extremely useful and reliable. He describes the first quadrant as a time to WITHDRAW, the second as a time to EMERGE, the third as a time to TAKE ACTION, and the fourth as a time to REAP THE REWARDS.

The message of all Saturn transits is to concentrate, define and apply energy in a realistic, practical way. The concerns of whatever quadrant, angle, house or planet Saturn transits are "up for review," and the opportunity is present to make whatever changes we deem necessary.

SATURN IN THE FIRST QUADRANT
(Ascendant to IC)

When Saturn conjuncts the Ascendant, it marks the start of a new cycle of new beginnings to establish a new identity in the world. During its 7½-year transit of the first quadrant, we withdraw from the active arena to concentrate on ourselves. This is the time to set new goals, shore up our inner resources, lay the groundwork and prepare for the challenges ahead.

First House While Saturn is in the 1st House, we concentrate on our appearance and personality and how we present ourselves to others, defining what character traits we want to discard or incorporate into our personal expression. We have self-discipline at our command and can follow through on self-improvement regimens.

Second House In the 2½ years Saturn transits the 2nd House, we define and realistically appraise our assets, both materially and philosophically.

We will concentrate on budgets, savings, plans for long-term financial increase and methods to fund the goal we identified at the Saturn/Ascendant conjunction. We have the chance to make changes and adjustments and to manage these affairs more productively than in the past. By evaluating our skills, we will probably recognize areas where additional training is needed.

Third House During Saturn's transit of the 3rd House, it is appropriate to acquire education and develop mental abilities that support our goals. We should concentrate on making contacts, developing communications networks, refining our writing skills and putting preparations in place to begin testing our plan in the next cycle.

Interactional involvement within our immediate community will help solidify the groundwork we have laid during this first cycle.

SATURN IN THE SECOND QUADRANT
(IC to Descendant)

At the waxing square and Saturn's conjunction with the 4th House cusp (Imum Coeli), our personal preparations should be complete. It is another end and new beginning, an identity crisis when we appraise the capabilities we have acquired and our readiness to prove our competence. If our review uncovers lacks, we can make adjustments to fill them.

In the Emerge Cycle of 7½ years, we are obliged to apply what we have learned. We must shift gears and come out from the shadows to test our progress within a semi-protected environment. It is similar to a shakedown cruise which checks the integrity of a vessel. We will be testing our plan, getting feedback on its merit and ironing out the "bugs."

Fourth House During Saturn's transit of the 4th House, we may encounter environmental limitations, delays or circumstances beyond our control that prevent us from getting our project off the ground. These provide positive opportunities to establish a firm foundation for our base of operations. We should review our life style and domestic surroundings with an eye to creating a more constructive atmosphere.

Fifth House At this point, we openly declare our intentions and put our plans into operation. We express our creative ideas, increase our social contacts and evaluate our popularity quotient. We inventory our talents and can bring into play those that were dormant or latent.

Relationships with youths and children, our ability to teach and share, our capacity for romantic commitment and the joy we derive from life are all up for review.

Sixth House Here we analyze, repair, refine and concentrate on the nuts and bolts of ourselves and our projects. We review our methodology and upgrade our efficiency in health regimens as well as work habits.

We recruit and evaluate coworkers who assist in our tasks and get a sense of our ability to supervise and cooperate. We may seek employment where our ideas are welcome and we can fully utilize our skills.

SATURN IN THE THIRD QUADRANT
(Descendant to Midheaven)

At this point, we end the Emerge period and begin the 7½-year Action phase. Saturn opposing the Ascendant and conjunct the Descendant also marks the close of a 15-year cycle. If we have utilized the time responsibly, we will have a sense of positive culmination. Preparations and testing are over, our self-confidence is in place and all signals are "Go."

We can proceed with the same objective, developing and expanding our initial concepts, or begin something entirely new at this point. Whatever option we choose, it will include other people intimately and the public universally.

Seventh House Saturn transiting the 7th House is a time to concentrate on relationships. When we define our identity in the context of an equal other, we may end a partnership or form a new one, depending on our findings.

With regard to our goals, during this 2½-year transit we can actively promote, publicize, reach out and gather others in towards us. We will deal with legal issues and make contracts and deals of all kinds. We have the chance to evaluate our cooperative potentials, our sense of fair play and our capacities for negotiating win-win agreements.

Eighth House Now is the time to review and define our attitude toward sex and our concept of life, death and the continuum of energy. We are motivated to dig deep for answers to these questions, and circumstances in the environment often facilitate the process. We have the opportunity to recognize and accept that there are things over which we have no control and to discover the true meaning of self-mastery.

We should look to reclaiming ideas and things that have outlived productivity in one context and transforming them or their application to a new or different use. By defining our security needs, obtaining financing, insurance and licenses, and utilizing other people's assets or resources, we further our goals.

Ninth House By realistically appraising our philosophical and religious beliefs, our personal ethic and morality, we can discard what is not truly our own and solidify what is valuable to us.

Once again we must review our educational deficiencies but on a more advanced level of training. If an academic degree will bolster our self-esteem and increase our chances for success, now is the appropriate time to obtain it. We will be mentally concentrative for the next 2½ years and especially adept at studying.

All background preparations for ultimate goal achievement should be completed during this transit. If publishing, writing, teaching, distant contacts, imports or exports are part of our project, we should work on them now.

SATURN IN THE FOURTH QUADRANT
(Midheaven to Ascendant)

At the waning square when transiting Saturn conjuncts the Midheaven, we begin the Reap cycle and all that we have invested during the past 22½ years is revealed to the world. Our reputation is on the line for public acceptance or rejection, and we experience a critical identity crisis.

If our efforts have been productive, the payoff is recognition, acclaim, triumph and victory. If we have resisted self-discipline, projected blame and refused to accept personal responsibility for our lives, the payoff will reflect the result of those actions.

Whichever occurs, this is our opportunity to reassess our worth, release attitudes and expectations that are self-blocking, adopt those that promote fulfilling accomplishment and move into the next phase of experience.

Tenth House For the next 2½ years, we concentrate on parental and authority matters, our status, career, reputation and position in the world. We will define our ambitions, feel gratified with our attainments or end one career and begin in another direction.

For many, this is a period of crowning achievement when their efforts are amply rewarded with elevated status and increased authority and responsibilities. For others who encounter disappointment, loss, demotion, diminished authority or status, a realistic review of the circumstances which led to these results is in order.

Eleventh House During this phase of Saturn's transit, we reap the financial rewards of a successful career effort. We concentrate on establishing stable friendships and getting seriously involved with groups or organizations. We identify our long-range hopes and wishes and review and clarify relationships with our children.

Delineating our position on equality, humanitarian principles and work for the disadvantaged is part of the 11th House process, as well as teaching and sharing the experiential wisdom we have gained. We can also learn to define and identify with agape (spiritual or universal) love during this transit.

Twelfth House During this last 2½ years of Saturn's 30-year cycle, we reflect, review and digest everything we have encountered. It is a period of inner search when we literally take our own inventory and decide how we measure up to the person we had hoped to actualize 30 (or 15, if we began anew at the opposition) years before.

In the process of dredging up subconscious psychological garbage brought from childhood, enumerating our failures and assessing our identity on the basis of accomplishment, we may discover much about ourselves we want to change. Often we uncover character traits that are appalling, and we run the risk of falling into depression. But once we realize it is impossible to change something until we've recognized it, we can begin the process of replacing that trait with one more desirable.

By the time Saturn conjuncts the Ascendant, we are poignantly aware that a significant phase of our life is over, and it is a major identity crisis. We must decide once again what we want to be when we grow up and begin to incorporate our 12th House discoveries into the new identity that embarks on another cycle of *becoming*.

Bil Tierney

At the age of 23, Bil Tierney became a certified, licensed astrologer in Atlanta, Georgia after passing that city's annual eight-hour qualifying exam. A professional astrologer for 16 years, he has been a student of this discipline for more than two decades.

Bil has always been intrigued by the psychological, character-shaping potential of natal astrology, rather than its popular forecasting techniques. He has dedicated himself to a better understanding of astrology's basic principles operating through the planets, signs, houses and aspects.

With a B.A. in English, Bil has always known that writing would be part of his career. Author of *Basic Astrology for a New Age* and the highly popular *Dynamics of Aspect Analysis*, which has been translated into three foreign languages, he is also the author of many articles in journals and newsletters. Bil is a frequent speaker at national and Canadian astrological conferences.

A Scorpio with a Taurus Moon and Ascendant, Bil has Uranus (ruler of the 11th) in the 3rd House sextile his 3rd House ruler (Moon) and trine Mercury. No wonder he has chosen to write about this planet.

UNDERSTANDING
THE URANUS PRINCIPLE

Primarily centering upon fine-tuning this exhilarating yet offbeat planet, I will attempt to present Uranus from many innovative points of view. Some readers might easily find these perspectives provocative, controversial, and debatable.

If this article excites within some of you a strong sense of recognition, then perhaps I've done my job in helping you experience the Uranian "eureka" concept of instantaneous wisdom. Uranus represents an intellectual revving up in the pursuit of pure truth.

Uranus the planet is as unique as Uranus the archetype. It is the oddball member of our solar system in many ways and is the astrological symbol of original patterning. Uranus' equatorial plane is at a right angle (97+ degrees) with its orbital plane. With its axis practically in the field of its orbit, Uranus appears to roll on its side as it moves around the Sun. Every 48 years, one of its poles reverses and faces the Sun (currently its South Pole), emphasizing Uranus' changeable and sometimes extreme nature. With its backward rotation, Uranus, while orbiting in normal counterclockwise fashion, rotates clockwise. This rotational motion symbolizes an observed Uranian tendency in human personality to go in a different direction from the norm, to act in a nontraditional manner, to literally march to a different drummer.

Since many of Uranus' moons appear to make right-angle formations with its orbit, symbolizing square aspects which denote sharpness and acuteness, it seems fitting that its action is often considered abrupt, separative and unsettling. These moons appear to be spinning in retrograde motion. With at least a dozen rings surrounding it, Uranus is the most visually eccentric member of our solar system.

In myth, Uranus was the original sky god who mated with his mother Gaea (Earth) to sire, much to his surprise and dismay, the Titans. Some of his offspring, such as the Cyclops, were freakish and frightening. Others represented Nature's more tumultuous forces. What Uranus created was not serene nor composed in its essence. Uranus suggests mutation as a force necessary for evolutionary change and growth.

Though Cronus (Saturn), the last child, was apparently one of the more normal children fathered by Uranus, he and his siblings were imprisoned in Tartarus, the lower bowels of the Earth, as punishment for being so monstrous at birth. In order to free the Titans, Cronus took it upon himself to avenge his mother who had suffered because of Uranus' uncompromising action. He castrated his father with a sickle.

This myth has set into motion a painful psychological dilemma that today seems to have much power within the collective unconscious. The dilemma revolves around the father archetype. Uranus represents the role of *father rejection* due to standards of perfectionism that cannot realistically be met. The god Uranus created as much distance as possible from his disappointing offspring.

Cronus/Saturn plays out the role of father killer in standing up and opposing the harsh and unloving authority figure. Saturn today is still sensitive to being overpowered by others who would seek to control. The other side of Saturn is an often unrecognized need for father love and father acceptance.

The battle against the paternal image can create inner guilt and sadness. A neglect/reject syndrome may occur. A needy child is hungry for a father's love; a father is unable or unwilling to respond. Resentment and hatred replace love and need, and the urge to make the troubling father image impotent (castration motif) becomes a central goal.

Saturn also fears his own inadequacy as a father and protects his vulnerability from his offspring by swallowing all his children except Jupiter. It is appropriate to inspect Saturn/Uranus aspects with this ancient dilemma in mind.

On a more esoteric level, Saturn castrates Uranus in order to rob the cosmos of its fundamental timelessness and spacelessness. Saturn attempts to make chaos powerless. Time and form thus reign supreme at humanity's conscious, waking level.

In my experience, signs and their ruling planets have a lot in common but are not identical in their essential natures. Fundamental themes of any planet and its associate sign/house share significant similarities, yet variations always exist. Planets describe basic drives and subjective motivations of the individual; zodiac signs give information about broader cultural programming. Signs depict social phenomena. Planets describe the workings of human experience, and may be expected to operate more overtly.

I view the outer planets, even watery Neptune, as collectively representing **spiritual fire**. Neptune can be quite charismatic, full of high drama, and fervent when emotionally aroused.

All three outer planets share a potential for exceptional willfulness and an unbending (even fated) sense of certainty about reality, possibly becoming distorted in their functions. All have tremendous power. All can also offer us vast insights, broad perspectives, and boundless vistas.

The outer planets work best when operating beyond

the ego-structure of Saturn. When they aspect the ego-bound inner planets in a natal chart, these planets may be imbalanced or extreme in expression, producing chaos rather than transcendence.

But our main concern is **Uranus**—planet of the unexpected, earthquakes, explosions, oddities, aviation, intellectual brilliance, and the sociological end result of randomly distributed "deviance/perversion" questionnaires.

URANUS AND AQUARIUS

Currently Uranus is accepted as the ruler of **Aquarius**, but Saturn as the medieval ruler of this sign also makes a lot of sense. While it is hard to think of Aquarius today in Saturnian terms, society used to be more structured and limited to the dictates of an existing elite such as the clergy, the royal family, or academia at large.

Aquarius used to depict nondemocratic group efforts like the pyramid builders, the serfdom system and children toiling away in unhealthy industrial factories. Radical changes for the better started taking place many decades *after* Uranus was discovered and could be better assimilated by humanity.

Similar themes involving both Uranus and Aquarius are altruism, a live-and-let-live attitude, a fascination with futurism and ongoing social progress, and an overall appreciation of high-tech. Both planet and sign tend to be quick in response, but Uranus is much quicker. Uranus and Aquarius look forward to what is new and fresh.

Aquarius, with some degree of Saturnian reservation, believes there is ample room in society for all the oddballs, eccentrics, outer fringers and other colorful but fascinating types. Uranus also has an appreciation for off-the-wall self-expression, experimentation, and anything smacking of the bizarre. The social surprise factor does not unnerve Uranus.

Another common denominator between planet and sign which may prove problematic is the difficulty in being intimate, expressing warmth, and feeling emotionally connected to significant others. Thus, commitment can become a dilemma. Both Uranus and Aquarius are known for their varying degrees of aloofness and detachment. Their orientation is cerebral and intuitive—not of the heart. That's more a matter of their polar opposites, the Sun and Leo. Thus, expect a pulling away from many levels of one-on-one closeness as a standard reflex response.

Uranus can act/react in an extreme manner according to a wide variety of situational stimuli. This display may not be in the emotionally smoldering and eventually eruptive style of Pluto but more like a highly charged, unexpected bolt of lightning!

However, there are facets of Uranus that do not align themselves well with Aquarius. Uranus is mentally restless in ways Aquarius wouldn't or can't consider. Uranus is also more jumpy and nervy. Aquarius, a fixed Air sign, is apt to be more objective and capable of sustained mental focus.

Uranus is also fiery and volatile in temperament compared to the more sociable and mental Aquarius. Uranus is potentially disruptive, often displaying a sudden unexpectedness that we typically do not associate with Air sign dynamics. Very much aware of its individualistic nature, Uranus does not recognize itself as "just another one of the gang."

Uranians sense early in life how **different** they are from others. Seldom fitting into the expected structure of group consciousness, Uranus is typically out of synch with current social standards. However, a Uranian can be catalystic, helping any collective unit progress and advance.

Uranians demand the freedom to explore on their own exclusive terms their need for space. This planet can behave much like Mars with a broader perspective and sporadic detachment (Mars is not detached at all). Seldom are Uranians dedicated to social causes or crusades for long periods of time, however, unless given leeway to radically alter their approach at will should they so choose.

When situations start becoming less exciting and more routine, a Uranian feels the urge to bolt out the door and seek new interests. Aquarians would sooner stick around and work at reforming the group ideal. Fixed signs seldom abandon ship; they endure. Expect Uranus to be more impatient, restless, and impulsive than Aquarius.

A true Aquarian feels societally linked to others and willing to network in a more equilateral and democratic fashion. This explains why Aquarius better represents the social joiner than does Uranus. While Uranians attend group functions in an on again-off again fashion, seldom do they volunteer to be on any committee where predictable, reliable involvement is a must. Much depends upon how bored they were the last time they attended their once-a-month club, society, or association. Uranus abhors boredom!

Stephen Arroyo (*Relationships & Life Cycles: Modern Dimensions of Astrology*, CRCS, 1984) astutely points out how self-centered most Uranus-dominated people can be, especially in intimate relationships. It is a paradox that this planet of humane social concern is also a key to our unique expression of separative, uncooperative individualism.

Self-will is indeed an issue for true Uranians to address. This partially explains why they tend to pull away from close emotional contact. Jupiterians also have to deal with this problem to some degree. Both planets represent "distancing" themes in the chart, but Jupiter is a fire planet capable of great warmth and givingness. Jupiter just doesn't want to hang around and give to the same person all the time when the world is so big and time so short!

A real Uranian is one who believes in exclusive privilege

for him- or herself, unlike the Aquarian who champions inclusive civil rights for all. Uranians are less agreeable when they *know* they are right in principle, especially about any self-involved issue. They probably do not care how inflexible they sound or behave when they are caught up in such a state of "knowingness."

Aquarians, mentally firm regarding their inner principles, are more willing to work out a negotiable resolution accommodating the diverse needs of all parties involved with a greater measure of fairness and equality. Perhaps the Saturn connection keeps Aquarius from acting too self-centeredly. Uranus, however, is less willing to surrender its individuality for the greater good. Uranus is more a brash nose-thumber regarding society's expectations!

Before going any further with this planet/sign comparative analysis, I should make it clear that an Aquarian type is not necessarily one with just the Sun in Aquarius. An Aquarian stellium or much 11th House emphasis qualifies in most cases. My concepts in this article are actually more descriptive of Aquarius*ness* and Uranus*ness*, which may be too abstract for some to appreciate. Let's face it. Nobody fits pure Uranusness anyway, except possibly E.T. and Robin Williams!

Defining a true Uranian is tricky. Astrologers typically seek to devise formulae they can always count on regarding the birth chart, but I'm realizing how unrealistic this is the more astrologically experienced I become. A Uranian is NOT just someone with this planet aspecting the Sun, Moon, ASC, or MC. Uranus may even be unaspected in the chart, and still the individual may express Uranian traits quite vividly.

While I may not be able to profile a Uranian easily through a listing of unmistakable natal factors, I know one when I see one! The vibe, for me, is quite evident. The same goes for Neptunians and Plutonians. After sufficient years of study, astrology teaches us how to recognize such living and breathing archetypes.

While Aquarius resists intimacy because it can't figure out how to emotionally bond on a one-on-one level, it can mentally merge with others in terms of intellectuality. Aquarius *shares* easily with strangers and seeks to become part of a larger body of humanity. Granted, it does not merge itself with others like Pisces. Retaining individuality is a prerequisite, but Aquarius is willing to incorporate (at least intellectually) into the whole. For the *betterment* and the *enlightenment* of the whole.

In contrast, Uranus views itself as an unduplicated one-of-a-kind maverick. It's definitely more a symbol of the **unique** than is Aquarius. Do not forget that Aquarius belongs to the realm of the fourth quadrant. Capricorn, Aquarius, and Pisces all represent how we relate to the larger world around us. These signs evoke a sense of social responsibility within our otherwise egocentric framework. The fourth quadrant pushes for community consciousness and societal obligation, helping us to rise above egotism for the sake of universal collectiveness. Self-willfulness has no place here. Standing out like a sore thumb is not a basic Aquarian theme.

Uranus is another story, often being a rebel without a cause. This planet defies rules and regulations in favor of creating its own policies at will. While Uranus may not lead, it rarely follows. Most times, it just simply ignores whatever it doesn't agree with.

Aquarians often feel part of a group, for better or worse. Uranians have less trouble being and feeling alone. Indeed, *ego* is not such a "dirty word" for Uranus. Even evolved Uranians are still ego-active. The danger with Uranus can be the development of a superiority complex along with an increasing impatience for slower minds unless the Neptune factor of empathy is well developed to offset this unattractive quality.

Uranians often have a need to be outstanding in some fashion and have little trouble straightforwardly projecting special abilities and uncommon talents, whether the world is ready or not. Note how often Aquarius feels uneasy owning up to the fact of its potentially big ego and need for attention. It would rather keep Leo at a 180-degree distance. As a result, Aquarius can behave awkwardly when it comes to flaunting anything about itself, except on occasion its specialized brainpower.

Even then, the urge to show off isn't in Aquarius' genetic make-up. While Uranus is quick to dazzle its audience with its awesome brilliance and colorful audaciousness, Aquarius is less attention-grabbing regarding solo performances. It shies away from center stage but may come alive when supported by a talented ensemble. Aquarius needs a backup. Uranus more easily wings it alone.

While flip-flopping is not usually an Aquarian issue, **yo-yoing** is definitely Uranian. Uranus will change both direction and intent quickly and easily in midstream without feeling any sense of illogic or interruption. True Uranians apparently live in a state of NOW, NOW, and even more NOW! With additional Mars patterns in the picture, we may end up with a truly spontaneous soul whose inner reality is faster than the speed of sound.

Uranus denotes a rapid mental state that Aquarius often fails to comprehend. Uranian energy is seldom reasonable although amazingly on target!

Regarding Uranus' inbred love of the strange and novel, I doubt if fixed Aquarius can handle unpredictable unusualness for long. Even looking bizarre is a cultural statement about the freedom of selfness as opposed to agreed upon dictates of social unity. Expect Aquarius, a sign of group cohesion, to collectively ventilate in more conservative ways. Aquarius networks while Uranus tends to individualize lone wolf style.

While both planet and sign tend to impersonalize, appearing somewhat open yet aloof, Aquarius is much more strategic when it comes to mass social improvement. Compared to impetuous and urgent Uranus, Aquarius is more deliberate in its intent. Uranus is anything but thorough and methodical. However, Uranians, when passionately aroused, respond to conditions more emphatically than do Aquarians.

Uranians flirt with fitful passions and high-strung volatility. While Aquarians seek an intellectual overview, Uranians would rather get to the same point intuitively. Uranus lives very much for the moment, no matter how unstable or erratic. Aquarius indeed has a conservative streak; it values *organized* teamwork spirit. But don't expect airy Aquarius to be passionate.

Uranians are apt to behave impetuously when aroused, often acting/reacting without rhyme or reason. Erratic activity goes against the grain of Aquarius, a sign that first composes master plans with an ingenious sense of a gestalt before implementing action.

Yet Uranus acts confidently when driven by clarity of vision and flashes of insight. That "flashes" factor is exclusively Uranian; no other planet or sign of the zodiac can match it. This goes beyond mere brightness; it is more akin to the sudden, vivid illumination of lightning bolts out of the blue combined with the intensity of laser beams.

Therefore, expect Uranus to respond to anything and everything in a more dramatic manner than would Aquarius. Uranus does not depend upon logical continuity for its security. It has no trouble zigzagging, thrives upon the unknown and the unfamiliar, and is a guiding force to an enlightening future. Uranians often live a more ideal life style that Saturnians can only dream about, especially in terms of giving themselves permission to be free.

Aquarius represents the scientific establishment at large. Uranus is more depictive of the inspired yet often misunderstood genius coming out of left field. A Uranian is the "odd" one who daringly brainstorms the "impossible"— to later win the Nobel Prize. The august committee that presents the prize is, of course, Aquarian. The point is that Aquarius is not a sign of single-minded trailblazing. It is less filled with Uranus' individualistic and inventive spiritedness.

Obviously, there are some Aquarians who are notable exceptions. Inventor Thomas Edison did not seem to have Uranus in high focus as far as aspects are concerned, but he was an Aquarian with Mercury also in that sign. If anything, Aquarius is inspired to create a new wave of brilliant techno-evolvement based upon the initial impetus of Uranus' seed concepts.

I have a hard time seeing excitability as an innately Aquarian characteristic. Aquarius is really not that high-wired. Yet, in contrast, Uranus can be quite buzzed out and capable of contradictory behavior. Freedom of self-expression, no matter how senseless or inappropriate, is a stronger issue within the Uranian make-up. This planet can be truly electrifying!

Cool-headed Aquarius is sane, nonemotive and less prone to overreact. While Aquarian hostility is more low-key, it can still be deadly. Aquarius is prone to mentally calculate its violence. If anything, Aquarius denotes the cold-blooded terrorist who quietly plants a plastic bomb in a crowded airport and slips away unnoticed.

On the other hand, Uranus represents the wildly out-of-control soccer enthusiast who willfully and defiantly throws a rock or beer bottle at fans of the opposing team only to unexpectedly spark a full-fledged riot! Uranus is an initiator of sudden chaos. Aquarius is better at plotting that which results in civil disorder. The Uranian typically acts alone. Bold and sometimes shocking, Uranus would rather rebel against social convention, shaking up the world around him. As *the* planet of earthquakes, Uranus is more turbulent in disposition than Aquarius.

Aquarius is more timely about its social revolts. A Uranian, seldom feeling on equal footing with anyone, is driven to bust up and/or break out of existing confinements with unexpected energy. While Aquarius is aware of the power of democratic social involvement, Uranus embraces an immediate style of personal rebellion, a somewhat romantic concept of freedom not ordinarily understood or shared by others. Expect Uranus to demand elbow room Aquarius doesn't even recognize as necessary.

Uranus and Aquarius arouse within our psyche an urge to reach out and touch the unknown, no matter how strange and unfamiliar. Aquarius is into the grand social schema while Uranus demands instant self-gratification. Uranus readily ignores rules and/or simply does not care about karmic consequences and other sensible end results. At least it validates the assumption that the hand of God works in strange ways.

Uranus and Aquarius have something different to offer us in terms of erotica, romance and sexuality. Uranus deals with the pure excitement factor; Aquarius throws in the mixed message known as platonic love. Uranian sexual energy is more intense than that of Aquarius (oddly a sign of many Hollywood sex symbols). Both planet and sign lean toward an androgynous/ambiguous identity.

Sex for Uranus is often open, experimental, and freely experienced but devoid of true intimacy. Emotional depth can be lacking. Novelty and the search for unusual physical sensations may unfortunately override closeness and caringness. Cool-headed Aquarius *is* responsive to its opposite sign Leo. Leo loves love. Leo loves to be loved. Leo loves to radiate itself onto others. But Uranus does not. This planet frequently has problems with warmth and givingness and tends to be aloof and remote in this regard.

Liz Greene, one of our few truly genius astrologers, has stated that "Uranus is not concerned with feeling values ... Uranus must trample on the heart because otherwise it gets in the way of general principles." (*The Outer Planets & Their Cycles: The Astrology of the Collective,* CRCS, 1983, p. 148.)

While Uranus can push for civil and human rights on a grand scale and advocate liberty for all, it seldom becomes vulnerable on the heart level, rarely surrendering to mushiness or sentimentality. Its tendency to clearly and somewhat quickly see the less attractive or less ideal facets of romantic relationships discourages it from fuller commitment. Once the negative elements of a relationship become evident, Uranus rapidly loses interest and begins to detach and dissociate. It often safely distances itself by turning romance into a casual degree of friendship much like Aquarius.

Thrill seeking motivates Uranus to pursue the unknown. Uranus-dominated individuals will often break society's rules when it comes to developing relationships. Unconventional unions are common. Uranus is very much the planet of infatuation and "love-at-first-sight" attacks!

You know you are dealing with a Uranian lover when s/he responds to you very strongly early in the relationship. Much initial enthusiasm is common along with an above average amount of shared mental stimulation. This individual appears to you as sparkling and effervescent. You find yourselves easily discussing exciting travel plans. Your daily routines and activities have been put on hold, and friends have a hard time reaching you. This is an example of Uranian magnetism.

Everything seems to be happily speeding along in a lively fashion, and you are convinced that this relationship is something you want to last. Why not, it's all so ideal, right? WRONG! Once the superintuitive Uranus lover picks up on the fact that you are starting to become serious about a lasting commitment, there is a good chance that s/he immediately will begin to pull away, becoming less available or accessible.

If you are not prepared for potentially increasing indifference, this kind of love connection can leave you dazed and emotionally shell-shocked. You cannot hate this person because you've never had a fight or any unpleasantness, but you are left feeling wounded in a strange way.

The Uranian may disappear for a while only to pop up again when you least expect it. Once you arrive at such a point in this weird relationship, you must tread very carefully psychologically since your feelings may be going on yet another roller coaster ride.

Uranus **suddenly** angers, flares up and surprisingly bursts forth without warning. Uranus rules explosions, and when mixed with Fire (especially Mars), this energy vigorously seeks a target. Uranus does not seethe and simmer. It does not build up a slow but steady level of resentment in the manner of Pluto, Saturn, Taurus and Scorpio.

Aquarian anger is less easily aroused. Typical of all fixed signs, Aquarius assumes itself to be too logical and reasonable to get emotionally uptight. It closets its anger/rage for long periods of time before finally reaching the boiling point. When it does blow like the other Air signs, it tends to be highly irrational and prone to random targets like a tornado. Uranus, however, rarely pushes anger down and back into the subconscious. Indeed, it can unexpectedly get ticked off at the drop of a micro chip!

After covering various expressions of Uranus and Aquarius on the more vulnerable human levels, a discussion of the spiritual facet of the planet is at hand. Uranus was the first of the invisible higher octave planets to be discovered, symbolizing a level of transcendence over form/matter (Saturn).

Astrologers speculate that Uranus represents the operation of the **Universal Mind** with its awesome, pure truth-revealing clarity. Unlike Neptune (Universal Heart), Uranus does not work to unify diverse and unequal elements; it cannot easily lose itself in a nebulous blending of connective Oneness. It wouldn't recognize itself in such a state. At least, this is my assumption.

I believe there are **three primary spiritual paths** available to us, according to our current evolutionary stream. A heavily aspected and/or otherwise prominent natal Uranus, Neptune, or Pluto will show which path is most significant in one's chart.

The Neptunian person is the mystic. Neptune's spiritual path is one of an almost unquestioned surrender to delicate and/or indefinable altered states. Some are induced by ritualistic self-denial; others come from a heightening of the senses as in the repetitive gong of heavy and ancient Tibetan bells in a deep echoing cavern. The same effect may be produced by hallucinogenic mushrooms.

Neptunians may feel very sensitized to invisible pathways regarding higher communication. This path often involves spirit guides, channeling/mediumship, automatic writing, and other forms demanding full ego-harnessed receptivity. Those with a talent for "ghostbusting" may be Neptunian, but heavy-duty exorcism is usually Plutonian.

Imaginative visualization is a strong Neptunian technique. Spiritual symbols and ritual are both beautiful and appealing to their subtle senses. Awareness of color and sensual intensity are also evident. Many Neptunians obviously seek and find God through the visual arts—painting, sculpture, dancing, acting and Tarot. The Neptunian path is typically quiet, gentle and very subjective.

Pluto's path is typically more driven and severe. Plutonians are intense, relentless, and given to extremes. They struggle with stark duality. Awakening the kundalini (the latent serpentine energy force at the base of the spine) is a Plutonian quest. Alchemy and all other branches working with the powers of Nature and the life force, including voodoo, witchcraft, and tantric yoga, are under this planet's influence.

Plutonian spirituality involves deep and absorbing personal experiences of an empowering kind. The power usually has to be earned through trial by fire or by awesome feats of endurance. A conscious commitment is involved.

Pluto's path is typically experienced alone, but sometimes Pluto shares Neptune's merging motif as an ultimate goal. Plutonians take a serious, no-nonsense approach toward their God-search needs yet are often inscrutable. Pluto never surrenders to anything but a superior form of itself.

Unlike Neptune or Pluto, Uranus describes the quasi-scientific, practical occultist who wants to learn spiritual "facts." On every level, Uranus offers objective detachment. Driven by both a powerful curiosity and an urgent need for insight, Uranus needs to explore all facets of the unknown without fear. Whether you agree with them or not, Uranians are articulate about their beliefs and theories. If possible, Uranus would be eager to videotape God! Uranians rarely get knotted up regarding what others consider irreverent or blasphemous. They are unshockable.

If you are on the Uranian path, you experiment and seek truth from a variety of avenues. Ecclecticism and off-beat slants are a part of your make-up. A Uranian could conceivably believe Christ will make his second coming in a

UFO. While the extremely orthodox Saturnian types find such speculation abhorrent, Uranians just accept it all as another interesting theory that could prove true.

If anything, Uranus makes sacred the uncommon mixture of gut-level belief and exploratory surgery regarding Deity. Uranus wants to know WHY universal creative intelligence does what S/He does! Here is where Uranus is very much like Aquarius. Both planet and sign want answers to phenomena.

Aquarius is not a naive sign. It does not favor simplistic explanations based upon emotionalism, especially regarding the ultimate realities concerning the cosmos. It cannot believe in the attainment of world peace by mere chanting and meditating in solitude. Aquarius would more easily find miracles through a computer and political networking of a progressive nature. Religion/spirituality for Aquarius must have social impact.

However, spiritual passion is more Uranian than Aquarian. A burning desire for truth, even if only for oneself, is a Uranus concern. Aquarius de-emphasizes the individual in favor of the greater good, and here is where planet and sign spiritually take different courses.

Uranian spirituality is more clean-cut than either the Neptunian or Plutonian routes. It seems to gravitate towards systems and methodologies that can be freely shared with open-minded others. Neptune wants to save souls, Pluto attempts to reform the weak, but Uranus basically *intuits* and then seeks to *educate*. Faith is not such an issue for a planet that is confident in its ability to know what the God/ Mind wants.

When God speaks through a Neptunian, s/he wants to heal/save the world. When God speaks through a Plutonian, s/he wants to control/transform the world. When God speaks through a Uranian, s/he often grins and shrugs, realizing its just another flashing revelation coming down the pike! It may or may not end up as some big, burning social mission.

If Uranus grants us clear and unbiased spiritual vision, then it should also enable us to get a better grasp of the personality roadblocks we run into regarding the remaining planets in our charts.

URANUS IN THE SIGNS

Uranus stays in a sign for about seven years, so its zodiacal position is more sensibly read as a generational influence. Astrologers should not minimize the importance of natal Uranus. It plays a role in character development, even if only on a subliminal level. From a societal viewpoint, the sign Uranus is in reveals how that generation attempts to make sudden and unpredictable changes within the group structure.

Personally, Uranus by sign reveals how we rebel within our societal time/space. While not all souls awaken to the pressing cause, those who do cannot help but feel ripe and ready to take on a new, experimental vantage point. The Uranians are those who feel uptight about collective slavery. They choose to burst forth and implement new options.

Uranus was transiting through a cardinal Water sign, Cancer, when I was born, suggesting that my generation may attempt to alter and reform the nuclear family concept. This generation unexpectedly and dramatically broke away from what their sacrifical Neptune in Leo parents attempted to glorify. Uranus in Cancer people learned communality. Private space was comfortably shared with strangers and/or interesting friends.

Natal Uranus points out how we might reach a limit in terms of mediocrity, eventually striking out against the established norm. It does this in sudden spurts and spasms, often in a colorful way, while occasionally taking unique detours.

URANUS IN THE HOUSES

Uranus' house placements denote where we are challenged to devise new solutions to otherwise mundane, ordinary problems. This is not the place to mindlessly go with the mass flow. Expect waves to be stirred up and sparks to fly.

Uranus by house is where we may have paradoxical, contrary urges regarding issues of that life sector. Consistency may be lacking in our approach to this department. Freedom of action is very important if we are to enjoy the enlightening, eye-opening experiences we need for optimum growth. In likening the natal houses to a pack of 12 cards, the Uranus sector becomes our "wild card!"

This is where we are allowed to go against the flow in favor of brainstorming and originality. Since we live within a greater and powerful Saturnian framework, we need to know what our limits are and where responsible action is imperative. Lawlessness, Uranian-style, is not condoned by the social structure. Uranus out of control could result in anarchy which always proves devastating.

Our Uranus house is where instability can serve a higher purpose. While we are not grounded here in the manner we are in our Saturn house, neither are we rut-bound nor stagnant. Should we allow ourselves to resist change and block progress, Uranus imposes its energy in forceful, surprising ways. We thus are jolted in matters that insist we undergo quick and sometimes radical attitude adjustments!

I am not sure that an angular Uranus is more potent and important to consider than Uranus in the cadent houses. Perhaps its influence is more noticeable. A true Uranian can have this planet in any house at birth.

For those of us less willing to be put in touch with Uranian energy due to fear of the unknown, addiction to habits left unchallenged, narrow-mindedness, etc., Uranus' house is subject to external surprises involving the breakup of the status quo. Here we feel subject to earthquakes on many circumstantial levels.

If we allow ourselves to stagnate for too long a time, Uranus will shake things up by force. The results, although often refreshingly beneficial, can be shattering to us while they are happening. It is only when years later we look back and review such critical phases of our lives that we appreciate how the fickle finger of fate provided us a better game plan than we thought possible.

ASPECTS TO URANUS

The difference between the challenging aspects (conjunction, square, opposition and quincunx) and the flowing aspects (trine and sextile) deals with intensity and control. Hard contacts with Uranus tend to express in extreme, demanding ways. Quick reactions to restraining conditions are apt to be premature, inappropriate, and conflict-producing. The urge to act freely and openly is strong, but common sense and sensible planning often are weak. Outbursts are typical, especially when squares are activated. Perhaps we protest too loudly against authority, rules and regulations, or we stir up difficulties for ourselves with our own thoughtlessness and rash responses. With hard aspects, Uranus needs to learn a lot about the limitations of immature, selfish behavior.

If the stressful squares to Uranus operate through the self-blocking mode, pent-up tension develops, needing periodic release. Accidents and bodily malfunctions are frequently manifestations of Uranian energy applied in frustrated, indirect ways. Not enough individualism has been allowed to surface and develop, so chaos is often internalized or directed back to the self, creating disruptive crises.

The more Uranus aspects you have, the more elbow

room you need to find proper self-expression. Aspects to the Sun and the Moon seem to be the most potent, while aspects to Neptune and Pluto are least effective in most cases. A T-square with Uranus at the fulcrum may be a powerful signature of a Uranian with all the potential unsettling elements.

Uranus aspects, whether challenging or flowing, tell us what areas need to be reformed internally in such a manner that enables us to deviate from society's established patterns. We have few, if any, outer role models to draw from in this regard, so we must be willing to listen to the voice within us. Uranus aspects push for the development of intuition as our best guiding principle.

TIPS ABOUT TRANSITING URANUS

I refer to Uranus as the "fickle finger of fate" planet, especially when it transits natal placements. Uranus makes us shake, rattle and roll! As humans, we view Uranus as representative of something we should not necessarily encourage in our accustomed life styles due to its unpredictability. Uranus ushers in the unfamiliar, provoking uneasiness, anxiety, even fear, if we are rather inflexible. This safety factor versus unpredictability is yet another Saturn/Uranus dilemma gathering within the collective unconscious.

If given complete cosmic license, Uranus would swiftly and eagerly attack mindless, highly repetitive life patterns that we passively allow to go unchallenged and unmodified. Wherever we behave like automatons, going through typical robot-like moves, we leave ourselves wide open for a Uranian sweep. Such periods can be drastic at times, or at least punctuated with surprise twists in our life plots.

With all this in mind, it is important to remember that Uranus presents us with meaningful and timely instability. Try not to hang on to anything in a heartfelt manner during a major Uranus transit. Instead, let loose and create a degree of sensible distance, sitting back and watching the action.

Do not allow emotional defensiveness or frustration to cause detachment. You could end up becoming psychologically bent out of shape in ways you never thought possible, especially if you have a change of heart and desire to reclaim what is no longer and can no longer be possessed. Where Uranus transits, we must expect shake-ups.

While Uranian activity goes against our immediate expectations, we fail to see any benefits. Observe with eyes wide open and mouth shut. Things will fall into place. No matter what we think we want or really need, we must realize that Uranus will do its thing. That's typical of all the outer planets; they are not here to do our ego-absorbed bidding nor act in ways that support our limited goals or selfish behavior without providing pitfalls.

When your affairs become topsy-turvy during Uranian transits, do not fret because the cosmos is devising a more brilliant timetable than those of mere mortals. This is why it is not wise to become uptight about Uranian interruptions and sudden detours.

Uranus can touch our lives in ways that make us feel fresh and awakened to a different, more invigorating level of reality. Being open to Uranus means being open to life, observing its variety within Nature and the human disposition and making space for that which is different or uncommon. Uranus will never be creatively assimilated by those of us filled with hate, bigotry, religiosity, intellectual arrogance, and stubborn attachment to the past.

Tolerance is of utmost importance; Uranus urges us to accept the unknown and embrace without fear the unfamiliar. Strangeness should not be viewed as threatening (a lesson even mythological Uranus needed but failed to learn). Stereotyping based upon ignorance is definitely non-Uranian.

Uranus shows us the beauty of being free from mental/
emotional cages we unwittingly create when we refuse to
recognize the power of our inner spirit. A gift of Uranus is a
life that is truly ALIVE!

Karma Welch

Born October 15, 1931, at 8:36 p.m. PST in Sacramento, California, Karma Jean Reese is the seventh of 10 children. While serving the California State Education Department for 10 years, she came to the realization that her education should include knowledge of the "inner person" as well as the "outer person." Her pursuit since 1950 has been to discover the total person through the study of astrology, numerology, I Ching, graphology, palmistry, color, dream interpretation, symbolism, reincarnation, runes, hypnosis and regression and every mystical subject she has ever heard mentioned.

Karma's many credits include certification by the American Federation of Astrologers and the First Temple of Astrology in Los Angeles, where she taught from 1970-74, numerous TV and radio appearances, articles on astrology, I Ching and numerology, and video astrology lessons. She is also the founder of "Seeds of Wisdom" and lectures and gives seminars at colleges, universities and major astrology and metaphysical conferences from coast to coast.

Karma has two daughters, Michelle and Lisa, and resides on the coast of central California.

NEPTUNE

NEPTUNE . . . illusive, mystic, romantic loner of the solar system associated with "out of this world" influences. Its energy is highly sensitive. Receptive, indefinite, unfathomable, elusive yet magnetic, it veils with illusion all that it contacts, creating mystery and unsureness, even confusion, in mundane matters.

It can represent the irrational, the unreal, hidden and deceitful intrigues and secret conspiracies.

Inspiration
Ideals
Imagination
Devotion
Magic
Myths
Music
Fine Arts
Mission
Faith
Hope
Charity
Miracles

All are represented by Neptune, the planet which also governs sleep, dreams and grace. It rules all that is vague, nebulous, secret and unseen. It has to do with universal laws that operate on dimensions unknown to us as well as the astral plane and its mysteries.

Because of its otherworldly influences, it has been described as fearful, underhanded, insidious, and treacherous. Even the highly evolved have a difficult time determining Neptune's true identity. Its elusiveness is like a dream you attempt to capture upon awakening; the harder you try, the more elusive it becomes. Nervousness, anxiety and an inability to move forward may be the result of trying to view this planet in a practical way.

Neptune rules the dreams that without which there would be no reality. Most people have been taught that strength and courage are associated with Mars and Pluto. Neptune's strength is silent. When noticed, it is often looked upon as bizarre, odd, strange, curious and ridiculous. The truth is Neptune's strength can move mountains through meditation, prayer and faith, that spiritual energy that creates a tidal wave of higher consciousness.

Sensitives, psychics, metaphysicians, astrologers, actors, artists, musicians and those in the helping professions are well aware of Neptune's encompassing silent energy that can be sensed, felt and sometimes heard through the voice within or in a dream or alpha state. A "let go, let God" attitude is the best way to use Neptune energy in the horoscope. Wait and see, take one day at a time, trust and have faith.

During the Piscean Age, having faith and trusting was *de rigueur* when you could not answer questions about religion and the mysteries of life and death. As the Age of Aquarius begins, more people are using independent individualistic ways to seek answers to these questions. They realize that Neptune is the planet of spiritual light and is the promise of what will be.

Premonition, psychic energy, prophecy, forecasting, divination and omens all come under the jurisdiction of

Neptune. Many unspoken dreams are often not realized without tears, sorrow and pain, all Neptune ruled. There is always an earthly struggle to accomplish the Neptunian dream.

Anything worth achieving takes the struggle of effort, stress and strain which is represented by the squares and oppositions in the horoscope. Neptune's strength is expressed as depth of vision, upliftment of mankind, meditation, prayer and faith. While Venus radiates warmth and affection, and Jupiter expansion of consciousness, Neptune radiates silent powers of spiritual perception . . . the at-one-ment (atonement) that most of us seek.

NEPTUNE AND VENUS

Neptune is the higher octave of Venus. Venus is earthly. Neptune is heavenly. Venus is concerned with fairness, equality and justice. "I will love you if you love me in return." "I will love you if I get my money's worth." "I will love you if you give me enough of your time and energy so it is worthwhile for me." "I will love you if it is fair and equal." Venus rules values of time, energy, love and money. It rules reciprocity, sharing, give and take, and equality through its connection with Libra and the 7th House. Through its association with the 2nd House and Taurus, it is connected with money and values. We question love through Venus' value system. We have learned to shop for a mate, to get the most value for the love we give, to not be foolish and allow our hearts to guide us in mate selection. We should find a partner who fits snugly into our set of values.

Neptune is another story . . . love on a higher octave. It *feels* more deeply than Venus; it *sacrifices* more willingly; it *devotes* its energy more freely. Far beyond the earthly form of love, it says very simply, "I love you." It represents an innocent and highly evolved form of love with no strings attached and nothing desired in return. "I want you for yourself." Neptune rules soul mates, that beautiful expression of love rarely glimpsed. This love is so pure and right there is no room for jealousy, competition, greed or envy. The worldly plane of existence has very little true Neptunian love, yet it is exactly this that most of us spend a lifetime trying to find.

As the Age of Aquarius progresses, Neptunian ideals will be easier realized. As authority is questioned and people think for themselves, becoming more knowledgeable and intuitive, the understanding of love will rise to the higher Neptunian level. At the dawning of the Aquarian Age, heralded by the "flower children" of the '60s, many crystallized stereotyped relationships disintegrated. It will take many generations of new attitudes to fully realize that love may be better expressed selflessly (Neptune) than for what one can derive from it (Venus).

The love expressed through Venus is that of beauty, riches, pleasures and the joys of the physical; the love of Neptune expresses like a country meadow, a newborn child, a quiet sanctuary or the mysterious depths of the sea. Neptune is not concerned with riches but seeks pleasure through inspiration, music, art and any artifical means that uplifts the ordinary and mundane. Neptunians may go to extremes to camouflage their animal natures with ritual, candles and other paraphernalia that in their estimation bring a heavenly connection. By comparison, Venus is far more practical. If a choice was given between a loaf of bread and a violet, Venus would admire the flower and desire it but would choose the bread for its sustenance. Neptune would choose the violet to feed its soul.

THE NEGATIVE NEPTUNE

Neptune is not all ethereal and spiritual light; it is not always compassionate, understanding and sympathetic. As with all the other planets, there is another side to Neptune.

Neptune represents the highest of the highs and the lowest of the lows. Just as it can express love, light and beauty, it can also depict hate, darkness and distortion. Its doubleness of nature is well marked like the sign Pisces which it rules, defining the greatest spiritual insights while concealing important issues. Neptune in its negative expression rules deception, intrigue, hidden motives, negative entities, the irrational, the unreal or fake, the artificial and bizarre. Hallucination, delirium, unconsciousness, nightmares and spirit possession come under its jurisdiction.

Neptunians can be saintly on one hand and sinful on the other. Often in religion, we see the clergy playing both roles. When a person is taking a giant step toward heavenly enlightenment, there is often a karmic condition of devastating experiences, even perversions, that must be worked through. Both sides of Neptune must be experienced in order to advance in a spiritual way. The last dregs of earthliness can hold some very dark influences.

Astrologers choose Neptune as the planet responsible for addiction, alcoholism, neurosis, multiple personalities, phobias and other mental disorders. With Neptune prominent in the horoscope, it is often as though everyday existence is too boring, too false, too mundane to deal with, so we escape by whatever means possible. Often the Neptunian personality is covering an inconceivable facet of the self that is concealed and locked away, invisible but lurking in the background, waiting for the right aspects to energize and expose it. Often loners, Neptune people long for love, sympathy and understanding, but find it difficult to establish down-to-Earth relationships. Marilyn Monroe is a good example of a prominent (1st House) Neptune. Her charismatic aura, her lack of touch with reality, her need for glamour, beauty and adulation were all part of her Neptunian personality.

NEPTUNE AND THE HOUSES

Anything stored deeply in the subconscious is difficult to bring to the surface and analyze and is often related to the 12th House, which in the flat chart is ruled by Neptune. A person with many planets in the 12th may be one who needs help or who is involved in a helping profession. The need to save and protect the underdog is very deeply marked in these personalities. They are often wonderful nurses, doctors, psychiatrists, psychologists, metaphysicians, astrologers, reformers or employees in hospitals, prisons, social welfare and mental institutions.

If you have an active 12th House and do not engage in helping others, you may become the needy one, enduring illness, mental problems and, in extreme cases, imprisonment. This house seems to represent the "cobwebs of the past," fears, frustration, inadequacies, the "what ifs" and unanswered "whys" of yesterday that can often contribute to self-imprisonment. It is imperative that the astrologer lead these individuals into a useful way of aiding others.

Neptune's placement in the birth chart, as well as the house it rules, are havens where one can retreat, pretend, build fantasies, have blind faith, and camouflage conditions too frightening or too sensitive to face. So when the world seems harsh and cruel, take advantage of the quiet strength of Neptune. These houses can be a source of beauty, love and devotion. They are places where you can recoup energy, get a spiritual fix and go on with life. Neptune rules *past lives* (through its connection with the 12th House) and *karma*. Most of your karma is connected with people within your close environment: mother, father, siblings, husband, wife, children . . . those to whom you feel bound. The planets signifying these people and the signs and houses they are in describe the lessons you learn and the help you receive through them. You are bound to these people through family links, and by learning to relate to them, you can step out into the world and get along with anyone.

When Neptune is connected with the love and sex planets, Venus and Mars, the sexual nature may be expressed in an unusual or different way, especially if either Venus or Mars is retrograde. Wherever Neptune is, the principles of receptivity, sympathy, devotion, impressionability and imagined obligations will be apparent. Neptune wants to harmonize with all circumstances, trying to get rid of boundaries, differences in background, such as race, color, or creed; it needs to feel, sense and romanticize ordinary situations and make them in some way what they are not.

Neptune in the First House

You often have a delicate and highly sensitive outlook on life and yourself. The 1st House signifies the window through which you view the world, set the stage, and direct your energy through physical movement—your personality. With Neptune here, you often feel an unsureness, a need for approval and appreciation. You may try one personality after another until you feel acceptance for your image of yourself. Your world of make-believe may be closely entwined with the world of reality, and you can switch from one to the other with ease. Dreaming big dreams, you can lie to yourself and others in order to create your world of fantasy.

Easily influenced by other people, you may find it difficult staying with any single idea. Restless, you long for far distant places visible in your imagination. Vagueness, fanciful notions, self-deception and a lack of planning are often noticeable with this placement. Like Pisces Sun people, you can readily build a case against yourself, becoming your own worst enemy. Your imagination is highlighted, and you need time alone for contemplation and fantasy. Serenity, music, art and spiritual outlets are necessary for you to use your continuous flow of visualization.

Tenderly caring of your fellow person, animals, children and the world of Nature, you feel the need to help the underdog. Because of your highly sensitive nature, you can psychically pick up the needs and frailties of others, suffering with their suffering, often helping them anonymously.

Your longing for faraway places can take you on jaunts to unknown worlds, but these trips may be unplanned, even unrealistic, and you may be unable to find what you seek.

You often express a child-like quality which is reflected in your need for fun and entertainment. You will take the time to smell the roses and follow your dreams, especially if you limit your intake of alcohol and drugs. If you use Neptune energy positively, creativity and a saintly demeanor is evident. Negative use may indicate bizarre behavior and a lack of clarity in your life's goals.

Neptune in the Second House

The 2nd House has to do with values of time, energy, love and money, and you may find it difficult to get in touch with these values with Neptune here. Creative talents are often strong, but you may have trouble focusing them. With well-directed Mars energy and strong Saturn staying power, you can achieve financial success by following an artistic or spiritual profession. Often you have unrealistic ideas about finances, spending money on mindless projects.

The values of pleasure, time for yourself and "spacing out" can get mixed up with your ability to earn a living. You dream about "get rich quick" schemes so you can live a life of ease, following your dreams, so it is easy for you to be taken financially. Neptune's influence here can bring the opportunity to earn from some off-the-wall or strange business.

Neptune in the Third House

Since the 3rd House represents the conscious mind, Neptune here brings out your imagination. Similar to Neptune in the 1st and 2nd, impressionability is pronounced in your make-up. Inspiration is highly marked, and you may experience strong psychic vibrations. This position is often found in the charts of writers, speakers, teachers (especially music and art), ministers—anyone in a position to inspire others.

This house describes siblings and relatives, and with Neptune here, you may encounter unusual circumstances in dealing with these people. Step or half siblings may complicate your family tree, for instance.

Because of restlessness, you may travel for travel's sake to experience new places, new faces, new things to do. Travel by water may be fun for you. Your thinking and communication is often tied to your emotions, and absent-mindedness may be a concern.

Neptune in the Fourth House

The 4th House signifies your roots, your early home life and the circumstances in your later years. Neptune's affinity with Cancer, the natural sign here, suggests qualities of caring, kindness, affection for those you feel close to, sensitivity and romance. Usually you are tied to family members and feel a need to care for and nurture them if you are using your Neptune energy positively. Your home is a sanctuary, and peace and quiet are essential to your well-being.

Family problems, financial hardship, quarreling, and loud noises or personalities are unnerving to you, and you may sense an obligation to make things ideally suitable for those around you. Nature, flowers and plant life, and a place in the mountains or near water (ideally the sea) is your preferred home life setting. You like colorful but sub-dued interior decoration and often deck your surroundings with keepsakes or objects of sentimental value.

You may choose to live alone so you can retreat and revitalize your psychic vibrations. If you do not have some sanctuary, you can get tangled up in the vibrations of others, confused about your needs and identity. It is important to consciously separate yourself from others by constantly analyzing feelings, thoughts and motives and taking action to rid yourself of vibrations that do not belong to you. Sac-rificing and unselfish giving to family are characteristics of this Neptune position.

Since the 4th House is connected to both your early training and the end of life, the spiritual ideals you were nurtured with return in later years, no matter how far you may have strayed in your lifetime. Those in-between years could be muddled or lack clarity. If Neptune has challeng-ing aspects, there may be a mystery or something nebulous in your background. Secrets may surround one of the parents; s/he could be religiously fanatic or alcoholic, and these traits may be accentuated in your life in some way. Confusion may be evident in your home life because wherever Neptune is found the extremes of heaven and Earth are well marked.

If other chart factors so indicate, Neptune in the 4th House can bring out the hermit side of your nature. You may hunger for beauty and peace but could also practice some strange belief or have rather peculiar tastes which appear foolish, even insane, to the average person. When using Neptune negatively, your home lacks order and form, and you may see drugs or alcohol as a means to escape to the utopia your soul craves.

Neptune in the Fifth House

Your devotion to your family is well marked and your creative ability is strong. You may have acting, artistic or musical ability for you have a colorful and imaginative way of expressing yourself. You feel your children can do no wrong as your tendency to idolize them often prevents you from seeing them realistically. Challenging aspects to Neptune and no clarification of these attitudes could lead to neurotic problems as your children grow up.

You exhibit a lot of enthusiasm for your projects and you view everything you are involved in as a "big deal," often exaggerating and bragging about your activities. Neptune energy in the 5th House can bring strange experiences that affect your feelings and sexual attitudes. Because of your active imagination and ability to fantasize, your love nature can be hard to satisfy. Even though you may travel the world over, your naiveté is here to stay.

Neptune in the Sixth House

The 6th is the house of service and work, and with Neptune here, you are often devoted and dedicated to service, asking nothing in return. You are more than willing to serve family and children (the preceding houses of the quadrant), especially where routine and habitual duties are concerned. While this is an excellent placement as far as nursing or other medical fields are concerned, you often experience sensitivity to drugs or anesthesia, and health problems are difficult to detect or diagnose. Often the etheric body or auric field is disturbed. Faith healing and metaphysical cures may work for you, but many people are not aware of this and can go from doctor to doctor and treatment to treatment with very little relief. This Neptune placement can suggest psychosomatic illnesses or addictive problems to prescribed medication, street drugs or alcohol.

Since this house relates to your working habits, if Neptune is not properly applied, you may have difficulty holding a job or getting along well with coworkers. Perhaps you prefer to work alone or on jobs where you can be your own boss. Many times this is the indication of someone who works at sea or around water.

Neptune in the Seventh House

Wherever Neptune is placed in the horoscope, the nature of the house is receptive, sensing and receiving information and signals that others may miss. In the 7th House, Neptune enables you to pick up the pulse of the public thereby becoming an integral part of the community. You may become socially involved in "do good" projects. Caring about others and their spiritual evolution may be your "thing." Many of the reforms and initiatives you occupy yourself with may be "impossible dreams," but you are pulled in with your eyes wide open because of your compassion for others and your need to make the world a better and more loving place.

Always searching for the perfect, the ideal, not just in public and community matters but also in a mate, you try to attract one who fills your ideal in some respect. You can fall madly and helplessly in love, sometimes as though all reason has vanished. If you're lucky, the feeling will last a lifetime.

Sometimes when reality sets in, your mate may slip from the pedestal and a bitter disappointment confronts you. With Neptune here, you may be attracted to musicians, artists, medical professionals, drinkers, neurotics, drug addicts or those who are just very gentle or dependent. Because Neptune's nature is willing to blend and be adaptable, it is easy for you to be attracted to subterfuge, con games, illegal activity or to others guilty of this type of behavior. Business partnerships are not recommended unless Neptune has positive aspects.

Neptune in the Eighth House

A keen awareness of people is well marked, and you are able to pick up clues and information about others through your highly developed perception. You can key in to their secrets, especially in life and death situations, even though the other person may not be able to put his or her needs into words. You lend spiritual support and will find other ways to be helpful. With challenging aspects to Neptune in the 8th House, you may experience strange dreams, nightmares, even astral projection.

Because this is the house of secrets, it is often simple for you to zero in on many of the universal principles veiled to others. Neptune is cosmically comfortable here, and you may intuit unique or unusual ways to gain financially. You can inherit material worth but find strings attached. Financial difficulties could arise from nebulous or deceitful practices of a marriage or business partner. You often express your sexual needs through fantasy on one level, through celibacy on another, and possibly through perversion on a third.

Neptune in the Ninth House

Neptune here still reflects the interest in other people coincident with the third quadrant, but here you key in to their thoughts. You enjoy delving into the philosophy and beliefs of others . . . religion, law, metaphysics and philosophy attract you. Travel intrigues you, especially to mysterious places such as the great pyramids or Stonehenge. Your imagination and flights of fancy could even lead to out-of-body experiences.

If you choose to use Neptune's energy negatively, there may be misunderstanding and a lack of communication with your in-laws. Legal affairs are confused, complicated or deliberately misrepresented. Caution should be employed when you travel in foreign areas or on long trips.

Neptune in the 9th suggests impressionability and susceptibility to the persuasion of other people. You may find it easy to believe what others wish you to believe. Religious ceremony and spiritual seeking often attract you, and opportunities to change your spiritual and philosophical outlook abound.

Neptune in the Tenth House

This can be a rather awkward position for Neptune since it is placed in Saturn's house and this combination of influences is not easy to express comfortably. Nebulous and impracticable, Neptune does not lend itself well to a practical pursuit of goals. Success may come through art, acting, singing, writing or composing; many politicians have this placement. Neptune on any angle (1st, 4th, 7th, 10th) suggests charisma and an inspirational nature, and with it here you can bring your imagination into play in connection with your career.

Because of Neptune's impressionable qualities, you may be changeable when it comes to career and goals. A born investigator, you prefer to leave no stone unturned. Improper use of Neptune's energy may attract disgrace, notoriety or humiliation. You may have illusions about your worth, but bosses and those in higher positions may overlook your capabilities, forcing you to play an uncomfortable role. You need to develop humility and a more modest presentation of self.

Neptune in the Eleventh House

You tend to choose your friends more for their ideals than for their position in life. Immediate attractions connect and bond more on a soul than a mundane level. You may opt to make friends among artists, musicians, poets, mystics, astrologers, psychics and those who have to do with the sea and the arts. Your preference is for people who are odd, nonconforming, the underdog or the minority. It is easy for you to become involved in groups that talk about what needs to be done but do not always take action to accomplish. When you are expressing Neptune positively, your humanitarian ideas and ideals are easily carried out.

Negative expression of Neptune in the 11th can bring unfavorable attachments and unsatisfactory relationships. You could even be the victim of treachery, seduction and unreliable advice. Often your hopes and wishes are vague, undefined and difficult to put into motion; this is the house of goals, and fairy tale-like Neptune here can make it difficult to center in on what you really desire.

Neptune in the Twelfth House

This is Neptune's natural house, and you are able to express its qualities quite simply and give compassionate service. Sensitive to the needs of others, you work well with the sick and disabled and are very societally caring. Through quiet, secluded and often secret methods, you can accomplish goals in such fields as laboratory research, occult investigation, and detective work as well as religious and philosophical pursuits.

You need time alone each day to meditate, pray and get in touch with your ethereal energies. Your natural understanding of ancient wisdom and teachings may not always be easy to articulate, but you feel a need to care for and protect small children and animals.

Strange, subconscious feelings and weird or peculiar dreams may result from the misuse of Neptune in the 12th House. Long illnesses resulting in hospitalization, scandal and sorrow are some of the negative manifestations. Much depends on the rest of the chart and whether you are outgoing or a loner. Remember, patient waiting is a way of serving the masters.

THE ASPECTS OF NEPTUNE

Neptune/Sun Aspects—"The Great Pretender"

This planetary combination focuses on a full expression of soul-life. You have enthusiasm for living and a playful, gently alluring, unmatched magnetism. Your idealistic, receptive, psychic, romantic, compassionate qualities are coupled with a great understanding of others. You can be a sucker for sad tales, gimmicks and fraud because of your naiveté and willingness to help, but you are a visionary who can be humane, artistic or political. These planets working together, especially in flowing aspect, bring out your aesthetic, ethereal and mystical traits. When the aspects are challenging, you may adopt a fearful approach to life, possessing low self-esteem and mood swings. You often act without a plan, can be purposely deceitful and lack reality.

You do best in careers that portray the world of make-believe, the helping professions of medicine, psychology, metaphysics, astrology and law. Music, art, writing and acting often attract you. Any aspect between the Sun and Neptune can depict the greatest "do-gooder" or the biggest flake who ever lived.

Neptune/Moon Aspects—"The Illumined One"

Idealism is highlighted here, just as with the Neptune/Sun aspects, but there is an inner restlessness that often leads to travel and scene changes. Difficult aspects suggest emotional instability and misunderstanding which often begin early in life. Neptune and the Moon have much in common; they are both restless and changing, emotional, receptive and caring. Your feelings can fluctuate between the ideal and darkest despair. The constant pull from one mood to the next can be erratic and hard for your associates to understand. Your standards are high and sometimes unrealistic, so just living on Earth is a challenge.

When you can direct this energy away from yourself and express it in the compassionate nurturing of others, there is no end to your ability to illuminate the space you occupy. Emotional nurturing returns to you through those you enlighten. Your inner vision and ability to see and feel along with your fertile imagination and perception can put you in a category with saints and gurus. Writers, teachers, nurses, mystics, artists, musicians, actors and actresses often have these planets in aspect.

Neptune/Mercury Aspects—"The Spiritual Seeker"

When used positively, you operate in a world rich in fantasy and can demonstrate an intuitive, psychic ability that may produce inspirational communication, clairvoyance, even trance ability. Much like having Mercury in Pisces, these aspects can give prophetic visions, vivid dreams that come true and utopian ideas. If Saturn is strong in your chart, you could have the ability to ground some important changes in your spiritual evolution. Witty and expressive, writing may be your forte.

If these aspects are used in a negative fashion, you may have problems putting your thoughts or ideas into words. Faulty thinking and self-deception may have to be dealt with, and you must determine what is right and what is wrong.

Sensitive and receptive to psychic phenomena, you

often know more than you are willing to tell, but you are very easy to communicate with since you pick up on subtle glances, body language and gestures. You need to keep your defenses up since you can be easily manipulated by the unscrupulous. Acting, writing (especially poetry and lyrics) and music come naturally to you. On another level, you may be able to channel energy from another dimension.

Neptune/Venus Aspects—"The Magic Touch"

This combination of planetary energies can symbolize true love. Your feelings are highly sensitized either on a one-to-one basis or on a universal level. Often you are moved by that which is out of this world, that which is beyond the mundane, that which cannot be expressed by mere words. Neptune represents what cannot be understood by the mind or spoken of in earthly terms. These aspects can depict a surrender of the heart to ethereal values. Your nature is affectionate, your feelings are tender and your touch is magic. You can dream of a world where everyone loves everyone else. If personal love is not satisfactory to you (which is often the case), you can surrender to a higher universal expression in religion or a collective movement that represents compassion.

Negative use of this combination often leads to attempts to avoid boredom and the mediocre through the use of drugs, alcohol, sex or by simply idling your life away. You may develop an erotic imagination, deviate from the accepted norm in sexual expression (particularly if Venus or Mars are retrograde) and experience sensations that are hard to ground. Artists, decorators, musicians and actors often throw themselves into their work because of feelings of discontent in their love lives.

Neptune/Mars Aspects—"The Devil May Care"

This aspect combination is connected with the giving and receiving of stimulation. Your energy is often directed in an unusual way, sometimes inwardly. It can be diffused by lack of initiative or vitality. Many of your dreams fall by the wayside because of an inability to follow your ideas through with definite action. You tend to focus your power and capabilities on unrealistic fields. You channel your drive into risky, thrill-seeking, bizarre areas that lead you into peculiar and hectic circumstances. You dream big, have a wild imagination and can get caught up in visions of grandeur. Yet, you have sex appeal and charisma and your devil-may-care attitude attracts others who are also seeking the "thrill of a lifetime."

The positive side of these aspects can give great creative talent on many levels—stage, screen, TV, the arts, dance, crafts and athletics. You enjoy travel, Nature, photography, the sea and professions connected with water. Curious, philosophical, psychic and investigative when you channel this energy properly, if you stay away from witchcraft, black magic and alchemy, you can charm the public and be very successful.

Neptune/Jupiter Aspects—"The Prophet"

These planets in combination seem to suggest mystic and prophetic abilities often expressed through metaphysics or religion. Enthusiastic, imaginative, even ecstatic in your self-expression, you exhibit a love for humanity on both individual and universal levels. You appreciate ritual and ceremony and may experience remarkable psychic dreams and visions when you make an effort to tune in. You tend to be in the right place at the right time and often benefit from fantastic luck. It is a simple matter for you to know how to guide and direct others from a spiritual standpoint when you demonstrate these aspects positively. You could experience a call to the ministry.

Negative use of Neptune/Jupiter may lead to wastefulness, bad judgment and unrealistic speculation. You have a need to be involved in big deals, and may be tempted to gamble on so-called "sure things" that are anything but sure. If the fantasy side of Neptune is too much in evidence, your beliefs and religious practices could border on the freaky and bizarre. Witchcraft, voodoo, possession and connection with ugly entities may attract you.

As with all Neptune aspects, you are attracted to music, the arts and acting, but Jupiter's influence adds an interest in sports, travel and the outdoors so that you may be drawn to a career in one of these fields.

Neptune/Saturn Aspects—"Dreams Take Root"

This planetary combination suggests a duality with a struggle between your higher and lower natures. Your need to dwell in the material world battles the need to express your highest ideals. Emotional inhibition, distrust of others, insecurity and dissatisfaction need to be overcome in order for you to find a way for your dreams (Neptune) to take root (Saturn).

Saturn tries to stabilize the lofty, ethereal qualities of Neptune. This planetary energy, when positively utilized, helps to focus your visions and to put your creative talents to practical use. You can bring long-term plans to fruition and work for years on a special project. It may take a lifetime to finalize what you really believe, but before you are through, you will manage to bring your dreams and beliefs into reality. You may be attracted to the arts and creative fields for a career, but your need is to apply your talents in a practical way through architecture, drafting, mathematics or music. You may be drawn to advanced studies of a spiritual or artistic nature. Often you are sympathetic and compassionate toward the elderly, so geriatrics could be your chosen field.

Negative expression leads to improper timing, lack of coordination, loss through mishandling of affairs, scandal and the accompanying discredit, and criticism from your peers and superiors.

Neptune/Uranus Aspects—"That Extra Something"

Your intuition and psychic awareness are well developed if you use the energy of this combination properly. Inner illumination, inspiration and enlightenment coupled with high idealism make it easy for you to utilize your subconscious as well as your superconscious.

The connection between these two transcendental planets can create an interest in the occult, metaphysics, astrology, mental health, healing and any practice that requires a keen mind and clear perception. Curiosity is a well-marked characteristic; your hunches are "right on," and you have a keen understanding of your fellow person. You love the unusual, the unique, adventure, travel, any kind of experimentation or investigation. The unknown, secret undertakings, mysteries and research attract you, and you may encounter people, places and experiences that are difficult to explain. An "anything goes" attitude is prevalent in your willingness to chance each adventure.

A negative approach to this combination may result in a lack of mental control, emotional tension that can produce nervous conditions, incorrect intellectual outlook, psychic flashes that are misinterpreted, confused mental states and peculiar interests and tastes that could result in the loss of friends as well as possessions. Your mood swings and sudden attractions can lead to mental and emotional instability.

Neptune/Pluto Aspects—"The Rainbow Bridge"

Self-knowledge comes through inner revelations with this planetary combination. Intensified instincts and feelings are common as is a compulsion to understand about life and death and unusual or unexplained events. You may attract larger than life problems to solve, and though this can be very enlightening, you may also have to deal with impulsive urges to act. Sometimes you are involved with "till death do us part" connections, foolish enterprises, haziness and disturbing influences that linger for a long time. You may be an advanced soul who discovers a cure for a disease that can help the masses.

You may experience a lack of vitality, an unwillingness to live life to the fullest or even a death wish if you use these planetary energies incorrectly. You could mix truth with the mystical and fantasy, being pulled into mass hysteria, poisoning, epidemics, earthquakes or other natural disasters. This combination is often associated with secret cults and groups that practice human sacrifice and bizarre activities unknown to most modern societies.

TRANSITS OF NEPTUNE

Neptune transits about one-half of the horoscope in the average lifetime of 80 to 85 years, conjuncting or opposing all your natal planets if you live a long life. Neptune transits bring higher awareness and the ability to see into the future, to be in tune with the cosmos and to understand esoteric teachings through perception, feeling and emotion. It concerns itself with growth of the subjective side of life . . . inner peace, love, joy in a subtle form, connections with other dimensions. Neptune's values are spiritual, not material. It represents what religion started out to be—the spiritual connection between man and God. When Neptune awakens you, you can quietly resonate with the universal Aum energy; you and your soul become one with God.

People born with Neptune prominent in their horoscopes are able to express many Neptunian vibrations. Those who do not have Neptune in high focus can learn to express these vibrations with each connection that transiting Neptune makes. Atonement, ruled by Neptune, is a necessary part of our evolutionary process. It makes living on this planet easier, but once atonement is reached, you may not have to return to planet Earth. From that time on, your sojourns may be to places much more to your liking.

Each time transiting Neptune contacts a natal planet, an opportunity for spiritual growth takes place. An initiation into a higher dimension is encouraged; a richer, more fulfilling soul-life opens up. Creative energy is unleashed that can open new doors and bring out facets of your personality that have lain dormant. Transiting Neptune brings a deep receptiveness to all conditions described by the planets, signs and houses involved in the aspect. Your eyes are opened to new possibilities often encompassing the mystical or strange; you are able to see and feel on new levels. Often it is a romantic, inspiring, emotional time. You may become interested in astrology when this transit is activating your chart. With a Neptune transit, you are of the Earth but at least a foot above it. If you desire to go beyond the mundane, scientific and material, opportunities for spiritual upliftment surround you. The choice is yours; it is a time for "letting go and letting God," for inner reflection, solitude and connecting with the more subjective side of life. It is a time to study Nature, music, art, creative writing, romance and the softer, lighter side of your being.

Caution and discrimination must be called into play because Neptune always veils, hides, fools and disguises. A more relaxed period is indicated if you can let go and flow with Neptune's energy. The challenge comes when you demand so much from yourself that you have a difficult time adjusting to Neptune's less exacting expectations. This change of pace can result in a lack of clarity and a sense of confusion. You should be willing to follow your inner promptings, to get in touch with your voice within and "To thine own self be true." This is not easy if you have not learned to listen to your inner self and "thine own self" is buried so deep within that you don't know yourself. Naturally, if the demands made upon you are to take it easy and you are involved with playing "beat the clock" on a daily basis, then Neptune can really shatter your routine, your efficiency, even your concentration.

Neptune's aspects teach or attempt to teach us that there is more to life than the success that is equated to ambition, goals and material gain. Many people do not understand the importance of taking time for simple rest, recreation and the aesthetic side of living.

One of the best ways to live life is to break each day into thirds. One third should be devoted to Saturnian discipline which includes order, form, perfection, concentration, duty, goals and ambition. One third of the day should be devoted to pleasure and doing what you enjoy (a Venus expression), different from the Saturn work which you may also enjoy in that it is of a creative and psychic nature, rather than concrete and directed. The last third should be spent in rest. Neptune has a difficult time breaking into the Saturn third but is often involved in the Venus portion. It enters readily into the sleep/rest period, your dreams and where your consciousness travels when you are asleep. When your life is lived in thirds, there is no problem with Neptune transits because you welcome its spirit and heavenly flow.

Neptune often prompts a need to be alone, giving you the chance to refuel, to get in touch with your identity, and to make decisions for your betterment rather than just living to please others, giving your soul a chance to get its message through to you. Long periods of introspection or deep sleep offers soul upliftment, which can also be gained during Neptune transits by selfless serving, giving with no expectation of return and subverting your ego. Neptune by transit magnetizes, allures, romanticizes, coaxes and urges you to take advantage of every scheme available to go beyond the veil and experience life in other dimensions. When you fight these promptings, chaos, confusion, despair or poor judgment can be the outcome. If you can let go and follow the promptings, neither fearing nor feeling guilty, a whole world of beauty, light, love and peace will encompass you, and your life on Earth will be more meaningful.

Often the use of drugs and alcohol or a total evasion of living participation in life is noted when transiting Neptune is active in a chart. Fetishes, neuroses, abnormal behavior or a peculiar mode of expression often accompany Neptune energy. Unfounded fears and anxieties are present, and events take place that have no explanation, contain an aura of mystery, or are disguised as Neptune masquerades and conceals its purpose.

The most important transits of Neptune are over the angles of your chart. Since it rarely contacts more than two angles in your lifetime, these transits usually mark a dramatic change in your values. As stated earlier, Neptune is considered the higher octave of Venus and goes beyond your Venus value system. Venus represents love, peace, beauty and romance. Neptune has an affinity with these things, but its expression is esoteric, aesthetic, ethereal and intrinsic. It reaches beyond the mundane to let you touch a dimension of what can be heavenly. Neptune detects, discovers, denounces . . . it does away with complicated procedures, sophistication, the laborious. Its whole purpose is to naturalize, initiate, and evolve. It enables you to submit yourself to the sublime.

Neptune Transiting the Midheaven

Since Neptune depicts the opposite form of energy than Saturn, the natural ruler of the 10th House, Neptune's passage here usually brings a time of business uncertainty, the feeling of the need to change careers and a time to set new goals that are more ethereal. Neptune often brings inspired ideas that are difficult to center in on and make happen. This transit may be accompanied by confusion, insecurity, even fear. A lack of drive and the dissolution of your ego needs are often evident. Perfection efforts, pride, ambition and the need to achieve may be dissolved by Neptune's spiritual energy. Modesty, simplicity, daydreams, and visualization replace many Saturnian aspirations. Lack of direction, disorganization and less self-confidence all creep in and confuse routine affairs. Your push and drive ebb; natural, more tranquil qualities emerge.

From Saturn's point of view, nothing is being established and carried out; business and efficiency are falling apart; things are going nowhere. Values associated with your goals and ambition do not seem so important at the time of this transit. You can become involved with unrealistic, senseless, fanciful schemes that you haphazardly try to get off the ground, going off on tangents that lead right back to your starting place. It is very easy to allow yourself to be swindled when Neptune transits your Midheaven. The goals you have always taken pride in do not mean much to you at this time.

As Neptune passes through the business quadrant from the Midheaven to the Ascendant, a major change in consciousness takes place. It is a form of initiation that offers you a new mode of expression from that of realist to dreamer. You may find yourself playing a make-believe role. It begins with a nebulous restlessness, and you are confronted with strange notions about your career, profession or business, where you are headed in life and where you want to go from here. Your attitude about success and the value of your time, energy, love and money change; the material world seems less important. You wrestle with your soul, maybe even experience desperation as you consider the possibility of surrender. For many, a "dark night of the soul" takes place before you are able to let go of material goals and begin to listen to the inner dictates of your heart. When and if this happens, you have won, for you have been allowed to glimpse another dimension. If you cannot or will not go with your heart, muddled, confused issues will remain.

As Neptune continues its transit into the 11th House, it can spiritualize your attitude toward friends, desires, and your life circumstances. You begin to see the less desirable characteristics of your associates. You might join a metaphysical, artistic, musical or literary group. This transit can attract you to some odd or peculiar folks. It is easy to be taken; it is a time to be cautious in associations and friendships due to the Neptunian ability to fool and defraud. Bonds that transcend time and space are often made when Neptune transits this segment of the natal chart. Friends are not chosen because they offer material position or value but because of kinship of the soul.

Neptune continues into the 12th House where it is at home . . . it is comfortable here. Its pervasive energy, quiet approach and secret detecting work are utilized without strain. Your psychic and perceptive energies are easily channeled. You find research and investigation simpler to carry out on many levels. You have better understanding of occult studies, and your deep feeling for the helpless and needy may take you into work (possibly volunteer) connected with large institutions such as hospitals, prisons, halfway houses, etc. Negative use of this transit can bring danger through secret enemies, psychic sources, fraud, your own subconscious thoughts or lack of good health that can hospitalize you. Meditation, prayer and quiet solitude are positive practices that can prove helpful during this period.

Neptune Transiting the Ascendant

As Neptune passes over your Ascendant, you become very susceptible to your environment; you are acutely self-aware; your intuitive energy and detecting abilities are enhanced. Thinking processes that normally operate below your conscious level (12th House) surface, and the ordinary, mundane and normal are replaced with an altered state of consciousness or a line of energy that seems to come from another dimension. There is a keenness to your perceptions that provides information on a psychic level, and you may tend to take on a mediumistic quality, whether or not you are aware of it. Very susceptible to those with whom you come in contact, your feelings, thoughts and mannerisms can be picked up from your associates. A lack of clarity or sudden burst of emotion can disturb your equilibrium, but you are capable of becoming a channel to express the purest and most refined energy. Much depends on your natal Neptune, as transits always do. If you have not yet come to terms with reality and your obligations, this can seem to be an unreasonable, senseless time.

Evasive or escapist mechanisms can come into play when Neptune transits the Ascendant and 1st House. You may be confused as to who you are and have a desire to exceed all limitations. Drugs and alcohol may be used to get out of the body, "space out" or evade uncomfortable demands—to escape into dreamed of dimensions. These same areas and feelings can be reached through meditation, but this takes patience, discipline and practice. You are not interested in these qualities under a Neptune transit. It takes Neptune about 42 years to transit a quadrant of the chart, so its transits are long lasting because of its slow movement. It takes time to recognize the changes Neptune brings. Its motion is never abrupt; it has a subtle method of softening, calming and spiritualizing.

The first quadrant of the chart (from Ascendant to the

IC) is very personal; any changes that take place in this sector relate to the personality, the physical body, the way you see things (1st House) and the value you place on time, energy, love, money, your talents, earning power and possessions (2nd House). As Neptune transits the 1st House, your personality and outlook may change. When it is in the 2nd House, your values may change or become confused. This is a time to be cautious in spending, to benefit from the time you spend on projects and other people and to invest your energies in the necessities of living rather than useless forms of love. (Since Neptune does not recognize any form of love as useless, it may only be as Neptune moves on that you become aware of ridiculous behavior in this area.) Your income may be uncertain; you could even be cheated financially if you allow Neptune's nebulous energy to affect you adversely. You must be conscientious, not lax, if you are to make the most of this transit.

As Neptune transits the 3rd and last House in the personal quadrant, your thinking is influenced by mystical, romantic, idealistic and sympathetic qualities. Your conscious mind becomes less conscious as unconscious or subconscious thoughts are intertwined with your normal thought processes. This enhances your ability to imagine, understand on higher levels, act more compassionately and show more sensitivity in your thinking, communicating in a more gentle way. Negatively, you can be muddled, confused, absent-minded and dream-like, lacking clarity in your ability to communicate or write. This may be a good time for receiving channeled messages, but if Neptune has challenging aspects, it is probably not an advantageous time to sign contracts or other significant papers. There may be mistakes in what you think the agreement states. Siblings or other family members can be a source of concern or may benefit you, depending, of course, on Neptune's natal placement and its aspects, both natal and by transit.

Neptune Transiting the Imum Coeli

Neptune has an affinity with the 4th House cusp because of its similarity to the 4th House sign of Cancer. Both the planet and sign evidence qualities of devotion, caring, helping, protecting, hiding, retreating, feeling and sensing. The Cancerian easily relates to the selfless love of Neptune: love that is unsophisticated and easily bestowed; the love of a mother for her child; the understanding love given to family; the unquestioned love of church or community. Neptune usually functions well in its transit through this house.

You may feel the need to withdraw into the privacy of your home during this passage. There may be a change of residence to a place that is peaceful where you can be in touch with Nature and live less pretentiously. Negative expressions of Neptune may find you dealing with peculiar home circumstances that may be difficult to cope with because of confusion and illusion. Sensitive, you may find yourself longing for the ideals you embraced as a child.

The 4th House represents the foundation of life, the roots of your beginning here on this planet. With Neptune transiting this area, there may be a longing for faraway places that is hard to figure out. Neptune's message may be unclear and hard to decipher; it is sensed and felt as a symbolic vagueness. Your dreams of and desires for new surroundings bring feelings of uncertainty that affect the other members of your family. They may not be too sympathetic to your longing for privacy. If you are fortunate enough to have a quiet mountain cabin, a summer home, yacht or other possible hideaway, you may find it easy to escape into serenity. If not, perhaps gardening, artistic endeavors, crafts or redecorating your home can create the same feeling. Unfounded fears and anxieties may intensify during Neptune's transit of the 4th House, and it is important to surround yourself with spiritual, enlightening and metaphysical people so that you can reach beyond the negative need for retreat and shutting out the world.

The principle at work is a refining of your soul-life. This principle is best activated in a private retreat or in the company of those already initiated into a higher dimension and who have an understanding of the process of evolution. As Neptune moves toward the 7th House cusp, what you learn at this time can be expressed publicly.

As Neptune begins to transit the 5th House, your feelings of affection come to life, and you may tend to look at love through rose-colored glasses. You show an interest in music, movies, theater, art, astrology, mysticism and deeply moving experiences on a soul level. You may become involved in fascinating, secret love affairs that perplex you. Seduction and misplaced passion may play a part in your fantasy world of romance and love. Enthusiasm, fun and games, and lighthearted relaxations can put you on top of the world, at least until Neptune moves on. Your feelings need to be expressed, and you anticipate a soul mate relationship with each encounter. Only highly idealized love can bring any sense of satisfaction at this time; so-called flings and far-out love experiences may not last.

This is a time for caution in investments, and speculative ventures should be avoided at all costs. Neptune here can attract schemes and fraud. Whenever Neptune transits any of the financial houses (2nd, 5th, 8th, 11th), *caution* should be your watchword.

As Neptune continues its journey through the second quadrant, it enters the 6th House. If you have grasped the opportunity for a richer soul-life (4th) and a higher expression of love (5th), the habitual mind (6th) automatically remembers the obligations you have to serve others, and you will avail yourself of the opportunity to serve humanity impersonally with compassion and spiritual strength. If you ignored the lessons of Neptune transiting the 4th and 5th Houses, you may experience some health or unbalanced conditions. You may have to care for someone who is helpless or in need, and you will have the opportunity to demonstrate faithfulness, devotion, patience and compassion.

Neptune's transit of the 6th House may bring confusion and vague job conditions in your daily routine or with coworkers or fellow employees. It may also aid in moving you into some sort of job that has to do with decorating, singing, writing, volunteer work, working in places having to do with alcohol, drugs, the sea, or liquids, or helping people less fortunate than yourself.

Neptune Transiting the Descendant

The transit of Neptune over the Descendant into the 7th House brings a great need to share the etheric side of life with others. Art, music, beauty, Nature and spiritual values all take on a more social expression. You take a deeper, more compassionate view of others and find ways to help awaken the public to spiritual views and a higher expression of energy. If other factors in your chart indicate a good relationship, this transit may bring opportunities to attract a more spiritual or higher representation of Venus. On a negative level, you may experience serious problems in an existing relationship relating to neurosis, drugs, alcohol, etc. Caution in all relationship matters is strongly recommended, especially as Neptune crosses the Descendant.

Since the 7th House represents other places, this transit can coincide with a change of residence, often to a faraway place, in the country or near water. The change can call forth new cycles of public relationships. Just as often, you may prefer to remain in the privacy of your new home, writing, composing, even instructing others, while keeping your environment secluded. In addition to partners, the 7th House shows peace, war and open enemies. Neptune's transit brings the opportunity to make peace with any enemies, avoiding the confusion that results by radiating universal love and light. Demonstrating this higher quality of love (Neptune) is far more significant than finding the perfect partner (Venus).

Neptune transiting through the 7th House makes it very easy for you to demonstrate an attitude of selflessness, but you must be cautious in trying to carry another's load or save a soul; it is only your own you have the right to save. Giving with no thought of return is the best way to deal with this transit.

As Neptune moves into your 8th House, your involvement with others' resources, such as time, energy, love and money, become significant issues. You must be careful of fearful acquiescence when called upon for financial support, time and energy for another's projects. It is difficult to play the role of the ideal for a partner; a peaceful, passive attitude may indicate to them your permission to take over your life. You will find it very easy to place your power in someone else's hands any time Neptune is in the third quadrant (7th to 10th) because you feel the need to have trust, faith and devotion to and from others. Find a trusted adviser to help with investments at this time. Inheritances or money coming to you through others may have strings attached, so getting help from someone else who is clear-sighted at this time is wise.

As Neptune moves into your 9th House, higher mind activities are accented. Neptune can broaden your mental channels by sowing the seeds of doubt about your own and other people's thinking, ethics and morals as well as the laws of the land. It may be a good time to investigate religion,

philosophy, metaphysics and other forms of advanced thinking. This broadening of consciousness may take you to
other lands and bring you in touch with different people
and their thoughts and ideas. You may be attracted to the
highest ideals that would have muddled or confused you at
another time. You begin to understand others' views without
making judgments.

If you can tune in to this delicate, mystical, etheric
energy, an initiation into a higher dimension takes place. If
you fight it, worry over it or simply ignore its purpose, confused thinking, disillusionment, daydreaming and absent-
mindedness take place. Since the 9th is the house of legality,
you must proceed cautiously in this area to prevent being
duped or pulled into bizarre situations as far as the law
is concerned.

At this time, transiting Neptune is in Capricorn, where
it has been since 1984 and where it will remain until 1998
when it enters Aquarius. We have been seeing large groups
band together (often entertainers) to raise funds for the
hungry, poor and needy. We are also becoming aware of a
trend toward world government that is trying to protect the
rights of all people. The massive Capricorn conjunction in
1990 will emphasize the need for upheaval in the world in
order for these events to occur. The trigger may well be
Jupiter in Cancer opposing Saturn, Uranus and Neptune.
Those in leadership positions may attain a higher awareness, and as Neptune enters Aquarius in 1998 just before
the turn of the century, a true sense and appreciation of
brotherhood will begin. Always at the beginning of each
new century, the visionaries see the needs of mankind and
are ready to spread the word. By the time Neptune enters
Pisces, the sign it rules, we could live in a world of peace,

compassion and all-knowing wisdom . . . the ideal of life on Earth.

Joan Negus

Joan Negus is a teacher, lecturer, consultant and writer in the field of astrology. She has a B.A. in Sociology with a minor in Psychology from Douglass College and uses her social science background in her astrology.

She is Director of Education for the National Council of Geocosmic Research and Scribe of the Faculty for the Astrological Society of Princeton, NJ, Inc.

Her books include: *Basic Astrology: A Guide for Teachers and Students; Basic Astrology: A Workbook for Students; Cosmic Combinations: A Book of Astrological Exercises;* and *Astro-Alchemy: Making the Most of Your Transits.* She has also written a pamphlet on interpreting composite and relationship charts, a computer text called *Contact Astro Report* and numerous articles.

PLUTO

It is amazing that Pluto, such a small planet so far from Earth, could have such profound astrological implications for life on Earth.

Considered a transpersonal planet, some astrologers feel that it has little to tell us about the individual. Granted, if you follow the path of Pluto in the sky, you can relate it to certain historic trends and events, but Pluto is relevant for the person as well.

Once any planet is placed in your horoscope, it becomes as personally yours as your Sun or Moon. It falls into a sign and house and forms aspects with the other planets and points in your chart. Therefore, you can expand your understanding of Pluto by examining both world events and the personal possibilities of the planet.

But first, let's look at the mythology of Pluto to gain insight into the meaning of the planet. Although astrologers do not name the planets (and the astronomers who do will tell you that astrology is bunk), it is strange that names selected are always appropriate for the astrological definitions ascribed to these planets. By looking at the description of the god chosen and his or her legends, you can learn much about the meaning of the planet in our lives.

MYTHOLOGY OF PLUTO

Pluto was the god of the underworld. This immediately elicits the idea of dredging things up from the depths. There is something dark and sinister connected with this god not only because he was the lord of the underworld but also because he was the warden of the dead. "But this pitiless guardian of the dead was simply strict and rigorous; he was not any kind of devil, and his realm, except for some places where notorious offenders were punished, was not a hell, but the common destination of mankind."[1] So the planet Pluto is associated with death, but some of the dread is removed when one considers the above statement. It negates the idea of a demonic figure tormenting us in the fires of hell—a concept that is familiar to us through the Christian-Judaic tradition.

The description of Pluto as "pitiless," "strict" and "rigorous" is illustrated not only in his dealings with the dead but also in his treatment of Persephone. He was coldly possessive. He was insensitive to her feelings and used any means at his disposal to keep her with him. He tricked her into eating the pomegranate seeds. This story points up his mercilessness and also the potential obsessiveness and subtle manipulation that we connect with the planet Pluto.

So mythology can give us insights into the meaning of Pluto, but we can learn even more by looking at the period during which the planet was discovered. The modern planets (Uranus, Neptune and Pluto) were all sighted at appropriate times. The world events that were occurring around the time of the discovery of each illustrate the principles that have become part of the planets' astrological definitions.

Pluto was discovered in January of 1930. In that year the world was experiencing the Great Depression, and Pluto can represent great deprivation. But Pluto can signify wealth as well. In fact, the word Pluto comes in part from the Greek word *ploutos* which means "wealth."[2] What we have with Pluto are *extremes*. Enormous wealth falls under

Pluto, but so does abject poverty.

It is not inevitable that we experience these extremes of Pluto. Deprivation usually occurs when you are not paying attention to the warnings of Pluto. Periodically, you have to get *back to basics* as Pluto demands, especially if you have been moving in the wrong direction. If you do not do it on your own, the outer world will probably push you into a change. There are those who believe that the 1930s depression could have been avoided if influential people had paid attention to what was happening and taken certain steps to correct the situation. In fact, safeguards were built into the system after the stock market crash.

An important Pluto theme is to mercilessly *bring to the surface and eliminate* anything that stands in the way of positive development. If you deal with Plutonian issues as they arise, you may never experience the kind of devastation that the Great Depression symbolized. Most people, however, tend to resist deep self-examination, and it is not until some great eruption occurs that they are forced to honestly look into their situation. Sometimes you have to have everything stripped away before you are willing to consider change. Conditions may have to deteriorate to the extent that you feel they can't get any worse. But even when you think you are ready to make a move, it may be difficult to get started. You may have constructed defenses in your subconscious that make it hard for you to take action. Sometimes you need help in unlocking the barriers. This is one reason why it is not uncommon for people to go into psychotherapy during Pluto transits.

This facet of Pluto is supported mythologically by the realm of Pluto being below the surface. It is further corroborated by the fact that at the time of Pluto's discovery psychotherapy was coming into the foreground in our society. You no longer had to be a raving lunatic to seek psychological help. Society was beginning to know the names

Sigmund Freud and Carl Gustav Jung, as well as their theories and their methods of psychiatry.

Another Plutonian concept is **power.** In mythology, Pluto was a powerful god. In 1930, the Plutonian power principle was also epitomized by gangsters who were an important part of the scene in America. They were coincidentally called *The Underworld.* This powerful group was a law unto itself. The life style of these people is an excellent example of Plutonian symbolism.

We could find specific gangsters who represented Plutonian energies, but we need only look at the overview of the group to grasp what raw Plutonian power is all about. There was tremendous emphasis on the issue of power— who was in charge. If one mob tried to invade the territory of another, violence usually ensued. There seemed to be no thought given to what was right or wrong in taking action. The emphasis was on letting the world know who was boss.

There were also more subtle power plays within gangs. An underling desiring the good graces of the boss might subtly try to undermine another gang member. This might be done by exerting more power or showing greater loyalty than a coworker. Or he might try to convince the boss that the other person either wanted to take over or had shifted allegiance to another gang. The end result was usually the quiet ousting and/or disappearance of one or the other. This is just as frequent a scenario in stories about this period as is the open gang wars. And this, too, is a Plutonian motif. So Plutonian power can be expressed in overt, drastic ways or through quiet undercurrents. There is an unrelenting quality that accompanies either expression of Pluto, and action doesn't cease until the threat to power is eliminated.

Atomic energy is also considered Plutonian. In 1932, the neutron was discovered, only two years after Pluto was sighted. The thought of the atom bomb can make you realize what tremendous power Pluto represents. The mobsters show in a small way the *lack of conscience* in Plutonian power, and the atom bomb demonstrates it in a greater way. As the bomb was dropped on Hiroshima, it didn't say "I will kill only the fighting men and spare the women and children."

Adolf Hitler also depicted this facet of Pluto. Although he started the Nazi movement in 1923 and did not come into power until 1933, the worldwide depression of 1930 helped him gain momentum. The consciencelessness of his total regime is definitely indicative of negative Plutonian energies. Both Hitler and the Chicago underworld are excellent illustrations of the lack of compassion and the thirst for power that Pluto signifies.

Pluto's position in your chart indicates where you might behave in this manner or attract those who act in this way. This is not inevitable, however. There are always choices. The better you understand the various possibilities, the more likely you will select the more desirable ones.

A number of years ago, a client with Pluto in the 1st House opposite Mars in the 7th House came in for a reading. Her most burning question was "Do I always have to be involved with men who beat me?" As a child her father beat her, and at the time of this reading she had just left her husband for the second time because he also beat her. My answer was no. She just had to learn to assert her own power and not give it away to others. This did not mean that she had to beat her husband, but Pluto in the 1st House states that she should be and can be in charge of her life. She divorced her husband, slowly began to take charge of herself and since that time has not been beaten by anyone.

But before we get more deeply into the natal chart, there is one more step that should be taken. We become accustomed to our own Pluto placements. Our unique Plutonian energies become such a natural part of our *modus operandi* that we are almost mechanical in their expression. We can even assume that everyone else views Pluto and deals with it in the same manner we do. I have a friend who has Pluto on the Ascendant, and on more than one occasion she has said to me that everyone is on a power trip. When she is dealing with others, she is always concerned with how they are trying to control or manipulate her. When I told her that not everyone feels this way, she looked at me as though I were very naive.

When Pluto enters your life in transit, you can become more conscious of its implications than when you consider the planet natally. This is because it usually focuses on you in a way that is different from its ordinary operation in your life. In fact, any planet in transit aspecting planets and points in the horoscope may activate a combination of energies with which you are unfamiliar.

True, a natal placement is an integral part of your total development. We interpret it in terms of its sign and house and its interrelationship with the other planets and points in your horoscope. You have choices as to how to use the energies, but you can become so accustomed to expressing them in the same manner that you take them for granted. You tend to get into a rut in terms of the planet and resist any change. Sometimes this may not be in your best interest. To use a simple example, if you have Pluto in the 12th House, you might find it difficult to overtly express your power, and you may establish a pattern of backing off when you are challenged. But this placement has other possibilities, such as taking charge behind-the-scenes. Retreat may become the easy way out, and if nothing ever pushes you out of your complacency, you might go on eternally reacting in this way.

Life *is* dynamic, however, and you can get shoved into action. Perhaps transiting Uranus comes along and squares natal Pluto, informing you that this is time to change (Uranus) the way in which you utilize power (Pluto). This could start as an internal dissatisfaction with your past performance, or someone might make you feel that you must change in terms of Plutonian symbolism. In other words, planets in transit indicate energies that are available to us at particular times, and the planets and points being aspected by the transiting planet define what we should be working on within ourselves.

Whether or not there is an aspect between planets in the natal chart, much can be learned as they are combined by one planet in transit aspecting the natal position of the other. If you have an aspect between these planets natally, issues that are often in the foreground in your life are highlighted. If you do not have an aspect between them, you will undoubtedly learn a lot about the combination before the transiting planet leaves the scene, especially if the transiting planet is a slow-moving one.

Planets represent functions whether they are in the birth chart or in transit. Transiting planets describe temporary conditions. You can see in the ephemeris when a transiting planet is about to activate a point in your natal chart so that you can be prepared for it and even possibly make plans to use it. If you are aware of what the basic functions of a planet are, you can begin to apply its principles, and as you start to do this, you will find that your understanding of the planet will deepen. You may even discover that there are qualities connected with it that you didn't know existed.

Transiting planets should not be used as excuses. You should not avoid taking action because some planet or other is aspecting a point in your chart. For instance, I have heard people say something like "I have Saturn aspects and I am going to be frustrated in anything I try to do. Therefore, I won't do anything." That is a cop out! There is always some way to apply the principles of the planet.

Some possibilities with transiting Pluto are being *assertive*, perhaps even aggressive, and *facing* and *analyzing* situations. It is also possible to be *subtle* and *manipulative* with Pluto aspects, but you should not attempt to ignore them. This can lead to manipulation by others, your power being usurped and even volcanic eruptions, internally or externally.

You will know rather quickly if you are not making positive use of the transiting planets. You could have a concrete experience or certain psychological or physical feelings.

Each planet can be associated with particular feelings, and appropriate feelings frequently emerge when a transiting planet is about to arrive on the scene. These should alert you as to what will be available to you. If you pay attention and try to make use of what is on the scene, the feelings may go away. If you do not heed the warning or if you are not moving in the right direction, the physical or psychological symptoms may persist or worsen. When you are ignoring or misusing the energies, you will undoubtedly experience the negative side of the planet. When you make good use of them, your life will become richer.

In the process of learning about each planet, you will undoubtedly experience both sides and various levels of the orb. I found that I learned a great deal about Pluto through living with a series of Pluto transits which lasted about 13 years. Transiting Pluto activated a Grand Cross in my chart and then went on to aspect several other points. By the time it moved out of range (for a little time at least), I had discovered many different sides of Pluto.

I also firmly believe that I could have avoided some of the devastation I experienced if from the beginning of the transit I had had a better grasp of Pluto. The astrology books to which I had access had both positive and negative definitions of the planets, but no instructions were given on how to accentuate the positive and eliminate the negative.

When I saw that Pluto was about to square my Saturn (the lowest degree of my Grand Cross), I read what the astrology books had to say about the planets. Although there were some key words that sounded great, such as "power" and "transformation" for Pluto and "clarification" and "security" for Saturn, my mind kept focusing on "disruption" and "devastation" for Pluto and "frustration" and "limitation" for Saturn. I felt helpless and extremely anxious. I just sat and waited to see what would happen.

That first pass of Pluto arrived on schedule and was just as miserable as I had expected it would be. As a matter of survival, I began to consciously take action to try to evoke the positive side of the planets. I overtly faced issues I had previously tried to ignore in hopes that they would go away. I asserted myself in situations in which I had previously retreated. At first, I was satisfied that I no longer felt helpless. Then I realized that my situation had improved. Finally, I noticed that my life had turned in a new and wonderful direction. I would like to have avoided the unpleasantness of that time, but it made me change my approach to astrology and confirmed the idea that we can make astrology *work for us*.

I do not believe that we have limitless free will. Our horoscopes set our parameters, but there is a great deal of latitude within those parameters. I also believe that the better we understand our limitations and our choices, the more likely we will be able to avoid the pitfalls and make our lives more fulfilling.

Since the feelings connected with the planets are usually our first indications that a planet is entering the scene, we should discuss these before we examine ways to bring out the best of Pluto. There are a number of physical and psychological feelings that are possible. These feelings do not all occur simultaneously, and certain feelings may never be experienced by some people.

The most common feeling seems to be a physical rumbling within the body. Perhaps it is easy to describe because it is similar to what happens when you haven't eaten in a while. What makes them different from the standard "empty stomach" rumblings is that they are usually followed or accompanied by the idea that something big and important is about to happen.

The reaction to this can be excited anticipation or fear, depending on your situation. One thing to keep in mind that might relieve anxiety is to know that you do not have to give up everything in your life and that the changes that should take place do not have to transpire immediately. In fact, you seem to know that changes once made will be hard to reverse. Therefore, you should examine your alternatives deeply and thoroughly before you take action.

Clients at this stage of Pluto transits usually heave a sigh of relief when they hear this, especially when they have the rumblings but do not know the direction they should take. It is at this point that I suggest they clean out closets, cellars and drawers. As strange as this suggestion seems, it works. *Elimination* is one of the key words for Pluto, and somehow literally eliminating anything that is not functional in your life makes room for the new. This includes getting rid of old clothes, old letters and even the daily garbage that begins to accumulate. If you do this, you could find that answers you have been searching for begin to appear.

If you have an idea of what you want to do or where you want to go, this is a good time to investigate these matters thoroughly. As you examine alternatives, it quickly becomes clear whether or not you are taking the right path. As facts are unearthed, they seem to fall immediately in the "pro" or "con" column. There isn't any "maybe" column. If what you are considering is wrong, the rumblings continue or increase. There can be a feeling of uneasiness as well. If you do not pay attention to these warnings, dramatic events can take place.

A client contemplating a move during a Pluto transit was offered a job in another city. He had mixed feelings about going, but decided that he should look into the situation (which he certainly should have done with Pluto on the scene). He had the rumblings mentioned above, and they didn't go away when he visited the city in question and had an interview. He felt uncomfortable in the interview. He looked at housing in the area and that left something to be desired. He knew astrology and was aware that Pluto could indicate that he needed to undergo transformation, especially since he was unhappy in his present job. Therefore, he told his prospective employer that he would think about it and give an answer on a particular day. (He selected the day on which the Pluto aspect was exact.) On the morning of the day, he still had not made up his mind. During that afternoon he fell and broke his ankle. That made him decide not to take the job. It didn't make the broken ankle go away, but the rumblings stopped. This points up the uncompromising quality connected with Pluto. Conditions are either right or wrong.

Instead of taking the new position, he analyzed the one he already had. As he determined the parts of his job that he did not like, he painstakingly began to take steps to improve his position. As he did this, his actions took on momentum. Ultimately, he stayed in his job and wondered why he had ever thought about leaving it. The main point here is that it isn't necessary with Pluto to eliminate everything in your life and start totally anew. You can change unsatisfactory conditions and build on what is left. A secondary point is that when you are moving in the wrong direction Pluto can be like a bulldozer and knock you right off your feet, literally.

A feeling associated with transiting Pluto is dull aches and pains. Some clients have described them by saying that they feel as though a bulldozer has run over their bodies. These feelings usually disappear when you begin to take action.

Another physical manifestation of Pluto worth discussing is the periodic fading out of voices. You may be trying to pay attention to what is being said, but sometimes you will stop listening in the middle of a sentence. Not everyone with Pluto experiences this, but it occurs often enough to merit mentioning, especially since it is usually of great concern with those who are dealing with it. People sometimes think they are losing their hearing or their powers of concentration. To me, this is usually indicative of a need to look deeply within. Something that has been locked in the subconscious needs to be brought to the surface. As you uncover what is buried within you, you will probably find that your attention span miraculously lengthens and your hearing improves.

A remark that usually accompanies the fading out of voices is "It makes me feel that I am all alone in the world." But loneliness can often be felt during Pluto transits, whether you think you have lost your hearing or not. You can believe that no one else has ever been so lonely and no one can possibly understand what you are going through. Strangely enough, this feeling can lead you into therapy. I guess you have to find out if what you are thinking is really true. But whatever the reason, psychoanalysis can sometimes be helpful in unlocking what is buried deeply in your subconscious.

The feelings mentioned are most common when transiting Pluto is activating a planet or point in your natal chart, but you might also experience them when your natal Pluto is being aspected by another transiting planet.

In the Plutonian symbolism described earlier, three of

the major functions of this planet are clearly: (1) power, (2) deep probing analysis and (3) transformation. These should be kept in mind as transiting Pluto is activating a particular planet in your horoscope.

When Pluto aspects your **Sun**, you are undoubtedly being advised that it is time to deeply examine your ego needs. If you do not heed the early rumblings, someone might wound your pride, try to undermine you or in some other way challenge your power. So if you do not examine this segment of your character, you could be prodded by someone else to do so.

Sometimes when Pluto is in range, there is the urge to eliminate everything in your life, especially if you are made aware of Pluto through some devastating experience. You want to get rid of anything that hurts or reminds you of a hurt. This isn't necessary. If you try to remove everything in your life and start totally anew, you could feel disoriented. Transiting Pluto is suggesting that you get back to basics, not start completely over again.

One reason you may need to transform is because you have been misusing the planetary principles. In another case, you may have developed some facet of your character as much as possible in a particular way, and it is time to express this part of yourself differently. Whether you have moved too far in the wrong direction or need to find a new way to express Pluto, it always takes time. You don't have to make drastic changes instantaneously. As you develop, you create patterns of behavior that become habitual. When Pluto is either activating your chart in transit or being activated natally, you are supposed to deeply analyze and evaluate these patterns. As Plutonian issues arise, you should investigate them thoroughly and one at a time in terms of your natal Pluto or the planet being aspected by transiting Pluto. Then you can decide what should be eliminated and what should be retained.

PLUTO IN THE HOUSES

The more prominent your Pluto, the more likely power will be an issue in your life. What is meant by prominent is an angular or heavily aspected Pluto. When a power motif comes to the surface, regardless of the prominence of Pluto, it will probably permeate more of your life than just the area in which Pluto is posited natally. If Pluto is not prominent, however, power issues will not be so continuously prevalent.

Ordinarily, people with angular Plutos make their presence felt. Even if they choose to let others express their power, they rarely seem weak. It's hard to believe that some of these people can ever be victims because they give the impression of being strong and very much in control. But if Plutonian people give away their power (or have it taken away), eventually they can become disenchanted with this arrangement. Some people may just complain about being controlled and do nothing visible to get their power back, but it is a subject that will probably be very popular with these individuals.

Aside from power, it should be remembered that wherever Pluto is posited is where you can be transformed. So if you are dissatisfied with what is happening in the area represented by Pluto's house position, analyze and change what you don't like about that compartment of your life.

Pluto in the First House

If you have a 1st House Pluto, you will probably claim that you want to be in charge of your own life, and this is undoubtedly true. The emphasis here is on wanting to be in control of yourself, but there can be concern about someone taking away your power. Both examples of this position already given illustrate that other people enter into the power picture. One woman felt that all people were into power plays and she had to be on guard against this. The other woman wanted to know if she always had to be a victim of beatings. This last one was a little more complex because Mars in the 7th House opposed Pluto. But this attitude is common in 1st House Pluto people, no matter what the aspects.

If you have Pluto in this position and you are involved with what you consider a power struggle, you may not always take the direct approach. Although it is possible to have confrontations, you might choose to be subtle. If the other person seems too strong to combat or other factors in your chart make you want to avoid battles, you could do a little manipulating. Manipulating, however, is not always bad, especially if you keep the peace and still get what you want.

There is also a strong psychological orientation to this placement. Individuals with Pluto in the 1st House seem to spend a lot of time analyzing their own and other people's motivations. They do not always accept what is happening at face value and tend to try to figure out the real meaning behind an action, a gesture or a statement.

Another potential manifestation is one of personal transformation. This can range from merely contemplating how to transform yourself to taking action and visibly changing. The transformation may be done consciously or unconsciously. You could consciously decide to dress differently, try a new hairdo or even change your life style. Or you might find that you are unconsciously drawn in a new direction. The transformation will probably not be so total that no one will recognize you.

Pluto in the Second House
With a 2nd House Pluto, there could be a connection between power and money in either wanting money for the power it brings or using money to attain power. As stated earlier, Pluto can represent both deprivation and great

wealth, although neither is necessarily guaranteed with this placement. One scenario might be a rags to riches story. Perhaps the ability to spend large sums of money in order to earn large sums might become apparent. This could, of course, backfire. You could overextend yourself financially and not reap the rewards you had expected.

Whatever route you choose, one thing is certain—you do not want someone else to be in control of your money. I had a client with Pluto in the 2nd House who was about to be married for a second time and came in for a relationship reading. Because her future husband was close to her in age, his Pluto also fell in her 2nd House. Since Pluto moves so slowly, this would be true of anyone who was born within a few years of her birth year. I told her that she needed to be in control of her own finances and she might feel more comfortable if she kept her money in a personal account.

They each owned a house, which they sold. They bought a house together and shared the cost equally. They did this with all of their expenses as well, and what was left of their individual salaries they kept for themselves. This was not a major issue in his chart, but it was important enough for her to work out this elaborate plan, since her first husband had financially used her. Thus far, the arrangement seems to be working out just fine.

Since the 2nd House can also describe how one earns a living, with Pluto here you might choose to be a psychologist, an undertaker or an entrepreneur. There are, of course, many other possibilities, and the 2nd House is only a small part of the career picture. You should look to the 10th and 6th Houses as well. But whatever career you follow, if you have Pluto in any of these three houses, you will not want dictatorial bosses. Yet you will probably have to deal at some time or other with a job situation in which power is an issue.

Pluto in the Third House

With a 3rd House Pluto, it will not be easy for you to whisper. Somehow whatever you say is heard, whether you want it to be or not. A child who has a 3rd House Pluto had just started school, and the mother called me in distress because the child's teacher thought the child was deaf. She didn't listen well in class and she spoke very loudly—both of which can be manifestations of a 3rd House Pluto.

Common sense should have told the teacher that if the child couldn't hear she wouldn't speak as well as she does. She is very clear and articulate. The reason this problem never arose at home was that the little girl was an only child and her mother always listened to what she had to say. In a classroom situation, when she couldn't monopolize the conversation, she just spoke louder and louder until everyone had to pay attention. The solution was that the little girl was periodically given an opportunity to speak up with the understanding that she had to listen just as intently when others were talking.

What also was evident in this situation was the power issue between the child and the teacher. The 3rd House is, of course, elementary education as well as communications. The child seemed to be asserting herself as much as she could to see just how far she could go.

An individual with Pluto in the 3rd House does not usually want to be in control of the world, unless it is through writing or verbal communication. Even then, it is to influence people, not to rule them. But with this placement, you could find yourself being put in charge of a neighborhood group, whether or not you wish to do this. Power could be an issue with siblings. You might have a brother or sister who tries to dominate you or who looks to you as a power figure.

Pluto in the Fourth House

Pluto in the 4th House is an angular Pluto, but for some reason this position does not quite have the intensity of the other angular houses. There can be power struggles with a parent (since the 4th is a parental house) that can be discussed overtly, but there doesn't seem to be the outward concern over others usurping power. If Pluto is in the 1st, 7th or 10th House of a chart, one of the basic issues in the life is power and other people challenging personal power. With a 4th House Pluto, you certainly do not want anyone to control you in the home area, but with the people I know who have Pluto here, this doesn't seem to be an issue.

My son does not give the impression of wanting to control other people. In fact, he does not seem to be on any kind of power trip at all. Yet his brother and sister used to ask why he always got his way and they did not. The reason was that they always asked for permission and he didn't. One illustration of this was the time he redecorated his room. We were away for the weekend, and when we returned, his room was transformed. The color scheme was yellow and brown with orange woodwork. We are still recovering from it 14 years later! When we suggested that perhaps he should have consulted us, his answer was that he didn't think we'd mind. It was his room, and he had used his money. It was not done defiantly, just matter-of-factly. And that is a Pluto in the 4th House attitude. You want to be in charge in the home, or at least allowed to do your own thing without interference.

If someone tries to control you, there could be explosions, but there is also a subtle way in which the aggressor can be handled—agreement. You agree to whatever is suggested and then quietly do as you please. I have seen this occur a number of times with this placement. It is a very simple way to keep peace and get what you want.

Another possibility with Pluto in the 4th House is to

transform your home at sometime in your life. With the extremes of Pluto, you could live in a hovel at some point and in a mansion at another. It is not essential to experience these extremes. Whatever your circumstances, wanting a large home and possibly achieving this goal is certainly in keeping with Pluto in the 4th House. Another alternative is that your taste in homes or decorating the home might noticeably change.

Pluto in the Fifth House
Pluto in the 5th House can indicate that power motifs are part of your relationship with your children. You could feel that they are always challenging your authority or that you just periodically need to put them in their place. If a parent with this placement comes to me and complains that a child is either manipulative or openly defiant, I suggest that it is a good idea to bring such behavior out into the open and analyze it together. If you just seethe and do not face power issues, this could lead to serious problems between the two of you. If you try to work it out together, the whole relationship could change for the better.

Another possibility concerning children is that you think about and analyze whether or not you want or should have children. A student of astrology told me that she interpreted her Pluto in the 5th House as fear of having children. She said that she had thought long and hard about whether or not she wanted children and had discussed the matter at length with her husband before they decided to have a child. I do not think of fear in relation to Pluto and asked some questions about the thoughts and feelings she could remember. We finally came to the conclusion that one of the issues in the foreground was the adjustment she would have to make if she had children. She is a professional person and was concerned with a child taking over her life. In other words, she might be giving her power to her child.

She and her husband worked out a way in which she could manage to have both a career and a child, and they proceeded to start a family. After the baby was born, her life was different—transformed by a child—but much more fulfilling as well.

Children, however, may not be the issue with Pluto in the 5th House. This is also the area of creativity, so it can be descriptive of a talent you have. You could have the ability to get to the bottom of matters or creatively take charge. This position of Pluto could be indicative of someone who is a risk taker. This manifestation is a strong probability since this house is one of gambling or speculation.

Another definition of the 5th House is romance or love affairs. With Pluto in the 5th, you could be attracted to strong lovers or ones who challenge your power. On this subject, most people I know with Pluto here say that they like to "call the shots" in romance, but they also admit that they are not interested in weak people.

Pluto in the Sixth House

With Pluto in the 6th House, you can give the impression that you are in charge in the work situation, whether you officially are or not. If there is a task to accomplish, you may not wait to be told what to do, and you not only start working yourself but begin delegating tasks to others as well. If you are not in charge and begin ordering other people around, your coworkers might resent you, and the real boss could be even more upset. Power could then become a problem. Since one does not usually start at the top in any career, you will probably have at least one job in which you have a strong boss with whom you have to cope. Later on, you might even consciously use this person as a model, either positively or negatively, in trying to behave in the same manner or by saying that you don't want to be like your former boss. Chances are that the things you believe you liked least about this person are what you will tend to manifest yourself.

If you find that you are continuously being placed in unsatisfactory work situations, here are a few options that may help. Remind yourself that you would probably not respect a weak boss and might not stay in a job without a power challenge. Bring problems into the open and analyze the situation with the possibility of making your position more satisfactory. Dramatically change your circumstances. Tell yourself that this placement of Pluto is excellent for ultimately being in a position of power on a daily basis, giving yourself the incentive to work hard to attain that status.

Pluto in the Seventh House

Pluto in the 7th House has a great deal in common with Pluto in the 1st House—power can be a prime issue in relationships. One difference is that with Pluto in the 1st House you can view everyone as being power-hungry. It may even be the first thing you think about when you meet anyone. With a 7th House Pluto, you usually are not concerned with power issues until you get close to another person. With this placement, you may not get close to many people, so power may not be as burning an issue as it is with Pluto in the 1st House.

One reason that you are not intimate with a large number of people when you have Pluto in the 7th House is that there is an intensity connected with close one-to-one relationships. You do not take relationships lightly and place a great deal of effort into partnerships. You can exhibit devotion and loyalty but also jealousy and manipulation. It may take you awhile to get deeply involved, but it takes you awhile to extricate yourself as well. You could stay in some relationships much longer than you should.

Since the 7th House is both what you have to give and what you need from partners, you want devotion and loyalty returned. You are attracted to strong, powerful types and may possibly complain that you're being dominated. A client with a 7th House Pluto married a real "macho" man. At first, it was marvelous. She admired his decisiveness and the way he took charge. But after awhile, she began to feel that he was running her whole life. According to her, he told her precisely what to do and when and where she could do it. He kept track of where she was every minute and was extremely possessive. Initially, she was flattered that he cared so much, but before long she began to feel oppressed. A few years later, the relationship ended in divorce.

She swore she would never get involved with someone like this again. Her next close involvement was with a man who let her run the relationship. But soon she lost interest in him because he would not stand up to her and she could not respect him. It is very common to swing from one extreme to another, especially with a 7th House planet.

I explained that sharing the power in the relationship was by far the best way to go. Each could be in control of certain segments of the partnership, and power could be shared in others. I have seen this approach work many times. I also remind people with this placement that if you face and analyze problems together you might not only avoid manipulation and/or confrontations but also transform anything that is unsatisfactory in the relationship. It is when you ignore difficulties in hopes that they will go away that explosions can occur.

Pluto in the Eighth House

We may still be dealing with others as we look at Pluto in the 8th House. It could mean a powerful sex urge or power issues arising in sexual matters. You would certainly not want another person to be in control of your sex life.

With Pluto here, you might be concerned with the possibility of becoming a sex object, or you could use sex to assert your power. I have a client who frankly admits using sex to get what she wants.

Since this area is also associated with other people's and joint resources, this placement of Pluto has other possible meanings evidenced in the lives of two corporate treasurers. For them, it means that their power comes from administering large amounts of money which belong to others. Also along financial lines, Princess Diana has Pluto in the 8th and she, of course, has a partner who has vast resources. Jackie Onassis also has Pluto here. I have, however, seen some people with Pluto in the 8th House try to avoid taking money from others. They don't want to owe anyone anything because seeming generosity can be connected with giving others control over their lives.

Aside from sex and finances, the 8th is also considered a psychological house and those with Pluto here are frequently psychologically motivated. They want to get to the bottom of matters and often use psychology to help them or others transform. Although the 8th House is supposed to be the house of death, to me, the kind of death associated with this area is connected more with transformation than literal death. We are given many opportunities in a lifetime to regenerate and be reborn, and it is through the 8th House that we can best view these opportunities.

Pluto in the Ninth House

With Pluto in the 9th you might do what Grace Kelly did with her 9th House Pluto and become a ruler of a foreign country. Unfortunately, there are not many openings available for this type of position. However, I do have several examples of people born in foreign countries who came here to find their power. I remember one man in particular who is vice president of a large company. He was born in Ireland but came here for his higher education (9th House). He stayed on because he felt that it would be easier for him to attain a position of power here than in his native country. It worked; he is in a very powerful position.

Another example of Pluto in the 9th House that presents a different possibility concerns a young man who was a junior in college. The student said that his professor "had it in for him." The professor found fault with everything the young man said or wrote and was constantly criticizing him and giving him poor grades. "He says I'm arrogant," the young man complained, "but what he is trying to do is control my thinking." It seems to be difficult for people with Pluto in the 9th House to understand that you might have to serve an apprenticeship in order to become the power figure. The way I explained it to the student was that the 9th House is higher knowledge, and with Pluto here he should research deeply some subject connected with his major. Then he could be on equal footing with his professor and perhaps even be more knowledgeable because Pluto indicates persistence and thoroughness. He said he liked the idea, but he also seemed to get satisfaction from the power skirmishes with his professor. I am not sure which path he selected, but at least he left the session knowing that he had a choice.

The 9th House is also the area of philosophy and religion. I recently had a client who exemplified a positive use of Pluto in the 9th in regard to religion. She said her religion was very important to her, but she resented some of the dogma of the church. She could have been a dissident, but she chose instead to become actively involved in church matters and use her influence internally to make changes. With a 9th House Pluto, it did not take much effort to be elected to office in a women's group at the church. She may not have a strong impact on the Pope, but she is satisfied with the local effect she is having. What she is most delighted about is her subtlety. She is able to do Plutonian manipulating without anyone but herself being aware of it. The fact that she is a Scorpio may partially explain why she finds the less obvious approach most satisfying.

Pluto in the Tenth House

As we move Pluto into the 10th House, it is not so easy to use subtlety. If you have Pluto in the 10th, you usually come across as being strong and powerful, even if you think of yourself as a mild mannered individual. You probably know that you do not want to be controlled in your career or in any role you play in the world. But you might not be aware of the impression you make on others. Many of the people I know with this placement eventually go into business for themselves, frequently after they have had at least one experience with a forceful boss.

It is not, however, absolutely necessary to have your own business just because Pluto is in the 10th House. You can be happy working for someone else if you have a position of authority and are allowed to operate without supervision. You are most content when you are in charge. But even if you are not in charge, you may tend to try to run the show anyway, especially if the boss is doing a poor job. This could be extremely annoying to whomever is supposed to be the authority figure. There are certain similarities between Pluto in the 10th House and Pluto in the 6th. The principle difference is that the 10th House Pluto is usually more evident and potentially more overtly combative.

You may feel that you are accused of being arrogant and overly aggressive when you believe that you are minding your own business. Several people with Pluto in the 10th have noted such accusations in their lives and seem honest when stating that they were totally innocent. One woman comes to mind immediately. In the ten years or so that I have known her, she has had three different jobs and in each position experienced a power struggle with some person of a higher rank. Her feeling is that she is just trying to do her job and others attack her for no reason. Whether or not she is the culprit is really irrelevant. She is miserable with her circumstances and undoubtedly not using Plutonian energies to work toward her best potential. As we discussed her behavior in the office, she said that she has always backed away from confrontations. I suggested that since she was unhappy with her situation she might try another approach. Perhaps Pluto was advising her to stand up for her rights rather than retreating. Now she is starting to defend herself, and it seems to be working.

Pluto in the Eleventh House

Pluto in the 11th House is also a placement that is usually highly visible. Since the 11th involves peers and large organizations, you could be quite influential in groups. You do not have to be emperor of the world, but you might discover that you are not ignored when you are involved with groups, even if you think you've been very unobtrusive.

With this Pluto placement and with Pluto in the 3rd House as well, I frequently think of the television commercial where once the broker speaks, everyone stops and listens. With Pluto in either of these houses, you should be careful of what you verbalize because it will be heard, even if you are just whispering to your neighbor.

I have talked about the possibility of being unconscious of your being noticed in groups, but if enough people tell you they saw or heard you, you must eventually believe them. When you get involved in groups, you will probably find yourself in a position of authority and/or being challenged by power figures. Sometimes this can cause you to avoid groups either because you've been misquoted too often or because you don't want to hassle with group involvement. Periods of retreat may be all right, but you should express your Pluto in the 11th House in some way. Analyzing and planning in advance what you want to say, perhaps even documenting it, may help with the communications. If you investigate and choose a group or cause that you think is worthwhile, you might even enjoy being a power figure there.

Pluto in the Twelfth House

Pluto in the 12th House is an excellent placement for delving deeply into the subconscious and unconscious mind. Like the 8th House Pluto, Pluto in the 12th is interested in psychology. You always want to get to the bottom of things and know the real meaning of your actions as well as the motivations of others.

Although Pluto in the 12th theoretically should be an excellent placement for an individual in charge of a large institution (12th House), this is not necessarily the case. Most people I know with this placement tend to avoid taking positions of authority. This does not mean that they are powerless. They just prefer to exercise control from behind-the-scenes. Whoever coined the phrase "power behind the throne" probably was thinking of Pluto in the 12th House.

This does not mean that you are destined always to lurk in the shadows. You simply need to get in touch with your own power and understand it in order to use it overtly. Then you have a choice. When your confidence is built-up, you can then decide if you want to be the authority figure or merely advise the person in charge. The amount of time it takes to build up your confidence will vary, possibly depending on your treatment in childhood.

In interpreting the charts of babies and small children, I tell the parents that planets in the 12th House can become buried and create problems if they are not brought out in childhood. If a child with Pluto in the 12th is given power by the parent or supported when seeking power, it will not need so many years to build up confidence in taking charge.

We can more specifically define the function of Pluto in our lives by looking at the sign in which Pluto is posited and the aspects formed between it and other planets and points in our charts.

The sign in which we find Pluto is less individualistic than the aspects because it is in a sign from 12 to 32 years. Therefore, we share our general concept of power with our contemporaries. For example, even though Pluto is "strict" and "rigorous," those with Pluto in Cancer might be more compassionate in their expression of power than those with it in Leo or Virgo. But this will be modified or supported by the aspects to Pluto.

The connection of Pluto to planets and points in your chart, besides modifying or supporting the message of the sign and the house in which it is placed, will also describe specific personal needs generally prevalent in the life in regard to power, analysis and transformation.

If we were to start with the holistic view of the native in terms of elements, modes and signs emphasized, we could get an idea of how the individual generally operates. Then we can investigate and more clearly define the Pluto principle in the chart (or the principle of any planet) within the parameters of the horoscope.

I have used the basic, simple approach of looking at Pluto through the houses to show you that there are a number of choices as to how you might apply Plutonian principles in your life. You can use, misuse or try to ignore the qualities involved with any planet. There may be times when you would like to have Pluto removed from your horoscope, but to feel complete, you must live your entire birth chart. And, as I have attempted to point out, there are always positive ways to use the energies.

It is usually fear of the unknown that keeps you from making the most of your assets, and each part of your horoscope can be an asset. The more you are aware of your alternatives, the more likely you will be to make the most positive choices.

You could already be making the most of the Plutonian principles in your life. Therefore, what is written here might merely reinforce what you already know about the planet. But if any of the information is new to you—if Pluto is now less of an enigma—and if you are not content with the way you have been expressing Pluto, perhaps you should re-examine your horoscope, willing to transform the unsatisfactory.

Footnotes

1. *Man, Myth & Magic: The Illustrated Encyclopedia of Mythology, Religion & the Unknown,* Vol. 16. Ed. Richard Cavendish. Marshall Cavendish Corporation, 1970, p. 2209.

2. *Ibid.*

STAY IN TOUCH

On the following pages you will find listed, with their current prices, some of the books and tapes now available on related subjects. Your book dealer stocks most of these, and will stock new titles in the Llewellyn series as they become available. We urge your patronage.

However, to obtain our full catalog, to keep informed of new titles as they are released and to benefit from informative articles and helpful news, you are invited to write for our bi-monthly news magazine/catalog. A sample copy is free, and it will continue coming to you at no cost as long as you are an active mail customer. Or you may keep it coming for a full year with a donation of just $2.00 in U.S.A. ($7.00 for Canada & Mexico, $20.00 overseas, first class mail). Many bookstores also have *The Llewellyn New Times* available to their customers. Ask for it.

Stay in touch! In *The Llewellyn New Times'* pages you will find news and reviews of new books, tapes and services, announcements of meetings and seminars, articles helpful to our readers, news of authors, advertising of products and services, special money-making opportunities, and much more.

The Llewellyn New Times
P.O. Box 64383-Dept. 381, St. Paul, MN 55164-0383, U.S.A.

• • •

TO ORDER BOOKS AND TAPES

If your book dealer does not have the books and tapes described on the following pages readily available, you may order them direct from the publisher by sending full price in U.S. funds, plus $2.00 for postage and handling for orders of $10 and under. Orders over $10 will require $3.50 postage and handling. There are no postage and handling charges for orders over $100. UPS Delivery: We ship UPS whenever possible. Delivery guaranteed. Provide your street address as UPS does not deliver to P.O. Boxes. UPS to Canada requires a $50 minimum order. Allow 4-6 weeks for delivery. Orders outside the U.S.A. and Canada: Airmail—add $5 per book; add $3 for each non-book item (tapes, etc.); add $1 per item for surface mail.

FOR GROUP STUDY AND PURCHASE

Our Special Quantity Price for a minimum order of five copies of *Planets* is $38.85 Cash-With-Order. This price includes postage and handling within the United States. Minnesota residents must add 6% sales tax. For additional quantities, please order in multiples of five. For Canadian and foreign orders, add postage and handling charges as above. Credit Card (VISA, Master Card, American Express) Orders are accepted. Charge Card Orders only may be phoned free ($15.00 minimum order) within the U.S.A. by dialing 1-800-THE MOON (in Canada call: 1-800-FOR-SELF). Customer Service calls dial 1-612-291-1970. Mail Orders to:

LLEWELLYN PUBLICATIONS
P.O. Box 64383-Dept. 381 / St. Paul, MN 55164-0383, U.S.A.

SPIRITUAL, METAPHYSICAL & NEW TRENDS IN MODERN ASTROLOGY
Edited by Joan McEvers

This is the first book in a new series offered by Llewellyn called the *New World Astrology Series*. Edited by well-known astrologer, lecturer and writer Joan McEvers, this book pulls together the latest thoughts by the best astrologers in the field of Spiritual Astrology.

She has put together this outstanding group with these informative and exciting topics.
- Gray Keen: Perspective: The Ethereal Conclusion.
- Marion D. March: Some Insights Into Esoteric Astrology.
- Kimberly McSherry: The Feminine Element of Astrology: Reframing the Darkness.
- Kathleen Burt: The Spiritual Rulers and Their Practical Role in the Transformation.
- Shirley Lyons Meier: The Secrets Behind Carl Payne Tobey's Secondary Chart.
- Jeff Jawer: Astrodrama.
- Donna Van Toen: Alice Bailey Revisited.
- Philip Sedgwick: Galactic Studies.
- Myrna Lofthus: The Spiritual Programming Within a Natal Chart.
- Angel Thompson: Transformational Astrology.

0-87542-380-9, 288 pages, 5¼ x 8, softcover   **$9.95**

PLUTO: The Evolutionary Journey of the Soul
by Jeff Green

If you have ever asked "Why am I here?" or "What are my lessons?," then this book will help you to objectively learn the answers from an astrological point of view. Green shows you how the planet Pluto relates to the evolutionary and karmic lessons in this life and how past lives can be understood through the position of Pluto in your chart.

Beyond presenting key principles and ideas about the nature of the evolutionary journey of the Soul, this book supplies practical, concise and specific astrological methods and techniques that pinpoint the answers to the above questions. If you are a professional counselor or astrologer, this book is indispensible to your practice. The reader who studies this material carefully and applies it to his or her own chart will discover an objective vehicle to uncover the essence of his or her own state of being. The understanding that this promotes can help you cooperate with, instead of resist, the evolutionary and karmic lessons in your life.

Green describes the position of Pluto through all of the signs and houses, explains the aspects and transits of Pluto, discusses Pluto in aspect to the Moon's Nodes, and gives sample charts and readings. It is the most complete look at this "new" planet ever.

0-87542-296-9, 6 x 9, 360 pages, softcover.   **$12.95**

TRANSITS IN REVERSE
by Edna Copeland Ryneveld

Have you ever wondered whether you should take that trip or ask for that raise? How about knowing in advance the times when you will be the most creative and dazzling?

This book is different from all others published on transits (those planets that are actually moving around in the heavens making aspects to our natal planets). It gives the subject area first—such as creativity, relationships, health, etc., —and then tells you what transits to look for. The introductory chapters are so thorough that you will be able to use this book with only an ephemeris or astrological calendar to tell you where the planets are. The author explains what transits are, how they affect your daily life, how to track them, how to make decisions based on transits and much more.

With the information in each section, you can combine as many factors as you like to get positive results. If you are going on a business trip, you can look at the accidents section to avoid any trouble, the travel section to find out the best date, the relationship section to see how you will get along with the other person, the business section to see if it is a good time to do business, the communication section to see if things will flow smoothly, and more. In this way, you can choose the absolute best date for just about anything! Electional astrology has been used for centuries, but now is being given in the most easily understood and practical format yet.

0-87542-574-3, 320 pages, 6 X 9, illus., softcover   **$12.95**

URANUS: Freedom From the Known
by Jeff Green

This book deals primarily with the archetypal correlations of the planet Uranus to human psychology and behavior to anatomy/physiology and the chakra system, and to metaphysical and cosmic laws. Uranus' relationship to Saturn, from an individual and collective point of view, is also discussed.

The text of this book comes intact in style and tone from an intensive workshop held in Toronto. You will feel as if you are a part of that workshop.

In reading *Uranus* you will discover how to naturally liberate yourself from all of your conditioning patterns, patterns that were determined by the "internal" and "external" environment. Every person has a natural way to actualize this liberation. This natural way is examined by use of the natal chart and from a developmental point of view.

The 48-year sociopolitical cycle of Uranus and Saturn is discussed extensively, as is the relationship between Uranus, Saturn and Neptune.

0-87542-297-7, 192 pages, 5¼ x 8, softcover   **$7.95**

THE ASTRO*CARTO*GRAPHY BOOK OF MAPS
by Jim Lewis & Ariel Guttman

Everyone believes there is a special person, job and *place* for him or her. This book explores those special places in the lives of 136 celebrities and famous figures.

The maps, based on the time of birth, graphically reveal lines of planetary influence at various geographic locations. A planet affecting a certain area is correlated with a person's success, failure or activities there. Astro*Carto*Graphy can also be used to bring about the stronger influence of a certain planet by showing its angular positions. Angular positions involve the Ascendant, the IC, the Descendant and the Midheaven. The maps show where planets would have been had you been born at different locations than at your birthplace.

Charts and maps of personalities in the entertainment field, such as Joan Crawford, Marilyn Monroe, Grace Kelly, James Dean, John Lennon and David Bowie, are included in this compilation. Activists like Martin Luther King, Jr. and Lech Walesa, spiritual pioneers like Freud, Jung and Yogananda and events in the lives of painters, musicians and sports figures are explored as well as the successes, problems and tendencies of such politicians as FDR, Harry Truman, JFK, Richard Nixon, Ronald Reagan, George Bush, and Margaret Thatcher.

0-87542-434-1, 300 pgs., 8½ × 11, charts, softcover $15.95

THE AZTEC CIRCLE OF DESTINY
Bruce Scofield & Angela Cordova

The ancient Mesoamerican calendar and divination system known as the *Tonalpouhalli* has been revived for the third Llewellyn New Worlds Kit by authors Bruce Scofield and Angela Cordova, using both historical research and a fascinating variety of psychic techniques.

The 260-day calendar of the Aztec and Maya civilizations had been buried for centuries through neglect and repression by conquistadores and missionaries. Dream programming, automatic writing, trance work and dowsing all played an important role in the authors' reconstruction of associations for each of the 20 day names. The result is a diverse yet complete collection of astrological associations that offers contemporary readers a detailed and entertaining system of divination.

The beautiful images created by Bruce Scofield for the 20-day card set are done in the bold colors of ancient Mesoamerican art. Images of the gods adorn the book's pages, which also contain sample card layouts, readings and a complete list of associations for the calendar days. Also included are 13 wooden number chips, a cloth bag and the 20 four-color cards.

0-87542-715-4, 256 pg. book, 13 wooden number chips, 20 cards, cloth bag, colorful box. $24.95

THE WISDOM OF SOLOMON THE KING
72 Spirits Card Deck for Divination and Ritual
as interpreted by Priscilla Schwei
Now you can learn to use the deepest secrets of Solomon the King in this new kit. It includes a 72-card deck and a 208-page book. Together the deck and book allow you to work with the famous 72 *Spirits of Solomon*. The cards each have the name and seal of one of the spirits, as well as astrological, timing, and other information. The book includes clear, easy-to-understand instructions for doing several types of magic, including candle magic, divination, ceremonial magic and the use of talismans. Learn to make use of this powerful system of divination and magic.
0-87542-701-4, 208-page book, 72 cards **$14.95**

ARCHETYPES OF THE ZODIAC
by Kathleen Burt
The horoscope is probably the most unique tool for personal growth you can ever have. This book is intended to help you understand how the energies within your horoscope manifest. Once you are aware of how your chart operates on an instinctual level, you can then work consciously with it to remove any obstacles to your growth.

The technique offered in this book is based upon the incorporation of the esoteric rulers of the signs and the integration of their polar opposites. This technique has been very successful in helping the client or reader modify existing negative energies in a horoscope so as to improve the quality of his or her life and the understanding of his or her psyche.

There is special focus in this huge comprehensive volume on the myths for each sign. Some signs may have as many as *four different myths* coming from all parts of the world. All are discussed by the author. There is also emphasis on the Jungian Archetypes involved with each sign.

This book has a depth often surprising to the readers of popular astrology books. It has a clarity of expression seldom found in books of the esoteric tradition. It is very easy to understand, even if you know nothing of Jungian philosophy or of mythology. It is intriguing, exciting and very helpful for all levels of astrologers.
0-87542-08805, 592 pgs., 6 x 9, illus., softcover **$12.95**

CHIRON
by Barbara Hand Clow

This new astrology book is about the most recently discovered planet, Chiron. This little-known planet was first sighted in 1977. It has an eccentric orbit on a 50-51-year cycle between Saturn and Uranus. It brought farsightedness into astrology because Chiron is the *bridge to the outer planets*, Neptune and Pluto, from the inner ones.

The small but influential planet of Chiron reveals *how* the New Age Initiation will affect each one of us. Chiron is an Initiator, an Alchemist, a Healer, and a Spiritual Guide. For those who are astrologers, *Chiron* has more information than any other book about this planet.

Learn *why* Chiron rules Virgo and the Sixth House. Have the necessary information about Chiron in each house, in each sign, and how the aspects affect each person's chart.

Chiron is sure to become a best-selling, albeit controversial, book in the astrological world. The influences of Chiron are an important new factor in understanding capabilities and potentials which we all have. Chiron rules: Healing with the hands, Healing with crystals, Initiation and Alchemy and Alteration of the body by Mind and Spirit. Chiron also rules Cartomancy and the Tarot reader. As such it is an especially vital resource for everyone who uses the Tarot.

0-87542-094-X, 320 pgs., 6 x 9, charts,softcover   **$9.95**

OPTIMUM CHILD
by Gloria Star

This is a brand new approach to the subject of astrology as applied to children. Not much has been written on developmental astrology, and this book fills a gap that has needed filling for years. There is enough basic material for the novice astrologer to easily determine the needs of his or her child (or children). All it takes is the natal chart. A brief table of where the planets were when your child was born is included in the book so that even if you don't have a chart on your child, you can find out enough to fully develop his or her potentials.

In *Optimum Child* you will find a thorough look at the planets, houses, rising signs, aspects and transits. Each section includes physical, mental and emotional activities and needs that this child would best respond to. It is the most comprehensive book yet on child astrology. This one is definitely not for children only. Every parent and professional astrologer should read it thoroughly. You should use it and help your child develop those talents and potentials inherent in what is shown within the natal chart.

0-87542-740-5, 360 pgs., 6 x 9, softcover   **$9.95**

PLANETS IN LOCALITY
by Steve Cozzi

DIRECTION . . . it's what we all need, what we all seek. Is there a method that is clear, simple, concise and logical that will bring this needed direction to our lives? Yes. It's called Locational Astrology, a comprehensive system on the cutting edge of contemporary astrological thought and practice. Steve Cozzi, an expert in locality charts, computers, and the creator of this system of Locational Astrology, has put together a book that will show the average student of astrology as well as the professional how to use this innovative system to help not only themselves, but also their clients.

This is not only a historical analysis of Local Space Astrology—it is also a practical guide for the individual reader, applicable to most aspects of everyday activities. Did you know that your route to work each day could actually shape the way you perform or how others perceive you? That where your home is located in your town could affect your state of mind? That where you decide to relocate could change your whole sense of self or your ability to create what you desire? This is all proven fact. Cozzi shows you how to determine your own planetary lines and how to best use them to further your ideals. *Planets in Locality* has over 50 figures and maps, geomantic compasses and other illustrations to help you find and plot planetary lines within your home, town, region and on out to the country and the world. It is an essential astrological volume.

0-87542-098-2, 320 pgs., 6 × 9, illus., softcover   **$12.95**

THE NEW A TO Z HOROSCOPE MAKER AND DELINEATOR
by Llewellyn George

This is a new and totally revised edition of the text used by more American astrologers than any other—135,000 copies sold. Every detail of: How to Cast the Birth Chart—time changes, calculations, aspects & orbs, signs & planetary rulers, parts of fortune, etc.; The Progressed Chart—all the techniques and the major delineations; Transits—how to use them in prediction, also lunations and solar days. Rectification. Locality Charts, a comprehensive Astrological Dictionary and a complete index for easy use. It's an encyclopedia, a textbook, a self-study course and and a dictionary all-in-one!

0-87542-264-0, 600 pgs., 6 x 9, softcover   **$12.95**

PLANETARY MAGICK
by Denning and Phillips
This is the latest book from Denning and Phillips, and may be their best one yet! It is a complete ceremonial system and makes available a vast range of previously unpublished magickal techniques and workings. Through the use of this book, level after level of the psyche will be safely opened, and its perceptions and powers will be balanced and strengthened. Your creative potential will be enhanced and directed to the achievement of magickal benefits for yourself and others.

This is an account of Planetary Magick with its cosmic, magico-religious and psychological bases, its methods and purposes and symbols. Included are extensive tables of correspondences and the *Times of Power*.

The style of this book is direct and easy to follow. It is intensely alive in the sense that you are introduced to powerful practical magick on the basis of sound understanding and a minimum of preliminaries.

- **Secrets of Planetary Magick published for the first time!**
- **A complete system of magick**
- **For groups and individuals**
- **Powerfully effective**
- **Easy to do**

Some of the topics in this book include:

- **Planet power**
- **Mirror magick**
- **Ancient knot magick**
- **Raising and sending planetary forces**
- **Invocations of the Olympic Planetary Spirits**

This book is for all people who practice magick, whether Qabalistic, Pagan or general, whether individual or group-oriented. *Planetary Magick* expands the parameters of practical magick for everyone.
0-87542-193-8, 512 pgs., 6 × 9, color plates   **$19.95**

THE HOUSES: POWER PLACES OF THE HOROSCOPE
Edited by Joan McEvers

This volume combines the talents of 11 renowned astrologers in the fourth book of Llewellyn's anthology series. Besides compiling all this information into a unified whole, well-respected Joan McEvers also contributes her viewpoint and knowledge to the delineation of the 12th House.

Each house, an area of activity within the horoscope, is explained with clarity and depth by the following authors:
- Peter Damian: The 1st House and the Rising Sign and Planets
- Ken Negus: The 7th House of Partnership
- Noel Tyl: The 2nd House of Self-Worth and the 8th House of Values and Others
- Spencer Grendahl: The 3rd House of Exploration and Communication
- Dona Shaw: The 9th House of Truth and Abstract Thinking
- Gloria Star: The 4th House of the Subconscious Matrix
- Marwayne Leipzig: The 10th House of the Life's Imprint
- Lina Accurso: The 5th House of Love
- Sara Corbin Looms: The 11th House of Tomorrow
- Michael Munkasey: The 6th House of Attitude and Service
- Joan McEvers: The 12th House of Strength, Peace, Tranquillity

0-87542-383-3, 400 pgs., 5¼ x 8, charts, softcover   **$12.95**

EARTH MOTHER ASTROLOGY
by Marcia Starck

Now, for the first time, a book that combines the science of astrology with current New Age interest in crystals, herbs, aromas, and holistic health. With this book and a copy of your astrological birth chart (readily available from sources listed in the book) you can use your horoscope to benefit your total being—body, mind and spirit. Learn, for example, what special nutrients you need during specific planetary cycles, or what sounds or colors will help you transform emotional states during certain times of the year.

This is a compendium of information for the New Age astrologer and healer. For the beginner, it explains all the astrological signs, planets and houses in a simple and yet new way, physiologically as well as symbolically.

This is a book of modern alchemy, showing the reader how to work with earth energies to achieve healing and transformation, thereby creating a sense of the cosmic unity of all Earth's elements.

0-87542-741-3, 288 pp., 5¼ × 8, illus.   **$12.95**

THE LLEWELLYN ANNUALS

Llewellyn's MOON SIGN BOOK: Approximately 400 pages of valuable information on gardening, fishing, weather, stock market forecasts, personal horoscopes, good planting dates, and general instructions for finding the best date to do just about anything! Articles by prominent forecasters and writers in the fields of gardening, astrology, politics, economics and cycles. This special almanac, different from any other, has been published annually since 1906. It's fun, informative and has been a great help to millions in their daily planning. **State year $3.95**

Llewellyn's SUN SIGN BOOK: Your personal horoscope for the entire year! All 12 signs are included in one handy book. Also included are forecasts, special feature articles, and an action guide for each sign. Monthly horoscopes are written by Gloria Star, author of *Optimum Child,* for your personal Sun Sign. Articles on a variety of subjects written by well-known astrologers from around the country. Much more than just a horoscope guide! Entertaining and fun the year round. **State year $3.95**

Llewellyn's DAILY PLANETARY GUIDE and ASTROLOGER'S DATE-BOOK: Includes all of the major daily aspects plus their exact times in Eastern and Pacific time zones, lunar phases, signs and voids plus their times, planetary motion, a monthly ephemeris, sunrise and sunset tables, special articles on the planets, signs, aspects, a business guide, planetary hours, rulerships, and much more. Large 5¼ × 8 format for more writing space, spiral bound to lay flat, address and phone listings, time zone conversion chart and blank horoscope chart. **State year $6.95**

Llewellyn's ASTROLOGICAL CALENDAR: Large wall calendar of 52 pages. Beautiful full color cover and color inside. Includes special feature articles by famous astrologers, introductory information on astrology, Lunar Gardening Guide, celestial phenomena for the year, a blank horoscope chart for your own chart data, and monthly date pages which include aspects, lunar information, planetary motion, ephemeris, personal forecasts, lucky dates, planting and fishing dates, and more. 10 x 13 size. Set in Central time, with conversion table for other time zones worldwide. **State year $7.95**

Llewellyn's MAGICKAL ALMANAC
Edited by Ray Buckland
The Magickal Almanac examines some of the many forms that Magick can take. The almanac pages for each month provide information important in the many aspects of working magick: sunrise and sunset, phases of the moon, and festival dates, as well as the tarot card, herb, incense, mineral, color, and name of power (god/goddess/entity) associated with the particular day. **State year $9.95**